# REAL QUEER AMERICA

# REAL QUEER AMERICA

LGBT Stories from Red States

## SAMANTHA ALLEN

Little, Brown and Company

*New York  Boston  London*

Little, Brown and Company
Hachette Book Group
1290 Avenue of the Americas, New York, NY 10104
littlebrown.com

First Edition: March 2019

Little, Brown and Company is a division of Hachette Book Group, Inc. The Little, Brown name and logo are trademarks of Hachette Book Group, Inc.

The Hachette Speakers Bureau provides a wide range of authors for speaking events. To find out more, go to hachettespeakersbureau.com or call (866) 376-6591.

Portions of the introduction appeared in the *Daily Beast* in 2017. Used with permission of The Daily Beast Company LLC.

ISBN 978-0-316-51603-7
LCCN 2018949002

10 9 8 7 6 5 4 3 2 1

LSC-C

Printed in the United States of America

# CONTENTS

*For my parents, Nina and Gil, and my passenger, Corey*

Harry, I have no idea where this will lead us, but I have a definite feeling it will be a place both wonderful and strange.

—Federal Bureau of Investigation
Special Agent Dale Cooper

# REAL QUEER AMERICA

# Introduction

# QUEER IN TRUMP'S AMERICA

I was reborn in a car.

It was a silver 2005 Honda Accord SE with seat warmers, a six-CD stereo, and delightfully slippery black leather seats. When driven by a jobless college student like me in the year 2007, it practically screamed, "This belongs to my dad!" — and it did. But that year, it was mine.

By appearances, I was one of thousands of young men studying at Brigham Young University, school of choice for the Mormon faithful. But most nights found me cruising around the eerily neat grid of Provo, Utah, in that hand-me-down sedan, searching the city's plentiful parking lots for isolated corners where I could apply makeup and change into women's clothing unseen.

My nocturnal transformations weren't pretty. I

Portions of this introduction previously appeared in the *Daily Beast* in the article "I'm Proud to Be Queer in Trump's America" (January 21, 2017).

smeared my eyeliner. I confused tube tops for skirts and vice versa. But the awkward, liminal creature I saw in the visor mirror was me—or at least a shadow of me, a precursor of the woman I would one day become.

That possibility was still unimaginable to me in 2007. Coming out as a transgender woman didn't feel like a real option then; my enrollment at BYU and my full-ride scholarship both depended on my obedience to the school's strict anti-LGBT honor code, which forbade "cross-dressing" and "homosexual conduct." Mom and Dad, I safely presumed, would not be thrilled if the "son" they financially supported dropped out of college to become their daughter. But the veneer of male heterosexuality that I was putting on for BYU—and for my Mormon girlfriend at the time—was growing less convincing every day.

I tried to tell myself that I was happy being just a "cross-dresser"—that transition was not my eventual goal—but even *I* didn't believe me.

I was honest with myself only in that car. Shielded from the conservative college town by just a few inches of glass and steel, I felt like I could reach out and brush my fingers against the barest outline of a female future. Two thousand miles of Route 80 lay between my devout Mormon parents and myself. My clean-cut roommates either had no idea where I went after midnight with an overstuffed backpack slung over my shoulder, or they didn't care.

So I changed. And I drove.

I drove north past the Mormon Temple that looks like a gleaming white birthday cake with a single candle, past the mall on U.S. Route 189 where I saw my first R-rated movie in a theater, and then up the canyon highway where there were no more stoplights to slow me down. I hurtled up that canyon road until the lights of the valley were below me and the stars stood out against the jagged swath of night sky between silhouetted peaks on either side. When morning came I would be back in khakis, bowing my head in prayer at the start of my first class. The dreary Mormon ruse would begin anew. But as long as my foot stayed on that pedal, I felt alive. That's how I started the messy process of becoming Samantha—and that's how I fell in love with the road.

The reassuring hum of an engine, the thrill of a blurry world whooshing past your windshield—these are seductive enough forces in their own right. When they provide the only momentum in a life that feels stalled, they become irresistible.

I'm still driving today—now with a passenger. Years of hormones and surgeries later, the outline of that once-impossible future has been filled in, the "M" on my birth certificate erased and replaced with a reaffirming "F." I officially resigned from the Mormon Church in 2008, dealt with the resulting familial drama, and came out as a transgender woman four years later. Most important, I got married to another woman in 2016—a woman named Corey who not only accepted me but who guided

5

me through the early stages of gender transition. With her help, I can finally—kind of—do my eyeliner.

Much of my painful past is now in the rearview mirror, and my car long ago stopped being the only place where I felt free, but I have never stopped roaming. That need to feel the asphalt under my wheels, to count the mile markers as they whiz by, to track down the best-lit gas station on a dark highway at 2 a.m.—that hasn't gone away. Cars, for me, are still places of refuge, portals to distant possibilities.

I have crisscrossed the United States half a dozen times and counting. I came out as transgender in Atlanta, Georgia; fell in love in Bloomington, Indiana; and found my ride-or-die friends in East Tennessee. This is what I've learned on my travels: America is a deeply queer country—not just the liberal bastions and enclaves, but the so-called real America sandwiched between the coasts. I was once terrified to be transgender in Utah and queer in Georgia. Not anymore. I love this damn country too much to write off the majority of its surface area.

That's why I wrote this book. *Real Queer America* is the product of a six-week-long cross-country road trip through LGBT communities in red states. It is, for me, a direct continuation of those late-night drives up Provo Canyon. Call it a spiritual successor. I will take you along with me on a trans-America trek: a journey stretching all the way from Provo, Utah, to the Rio Grande Valley, from the Midwest to the Deep South, meeting and interviewing extraordinary LGBT people along the way.

When I told friends and family I was writing this book, their immediate response was usually one of concern: "Be careful." I get it. This might seem like a frightening time to be queer in the U.S.A., let alone for a transgender reporter to cross its most conservative regions by car. Many of the states on my itinerary had draconian anti-LGBT laws on the books at the time of my trip—and many still do. Some had even more pernicious bills waiting in the wings.

With President Donald Trump in the White House, too, the federal government was stacked with figures who posed an unprecedented threat to LGBT rights: our right to work, our right to marry, even our right to use the bathroom—and there's no way to get from coast to coast without having to pee in half a dozen different states.

But in my experience, too many folks in liberal enclaves are under the misconception that the anti-LGBT bigots who backed Trump wield uncontested control over conservative parts of the country. Some still think that red states are irredeemable cesspools of hatred, to be avoided at all costs. "Flyover country" they call it, dangerously assured of their own relative safety and moral superiority. Never mind reports of anti-transgender violence in places such as Bushwick, Brooklyn,[1] or Capitol

---

1 "AVP Learns of an Anti-Transgender Attack in Bushwick, Brooklyn," https://avp.org/avp-learns-anti-transgender-attack-bushwick-brooklyn/

Hill, Seattle[2]—both neighborhoods where no one would ever warn me to "be careful."

*Real Queer America* is an attempt to document what's *actually* happening in the "real America" that more and more LGBT people are calling home—to capture some of the progressive cultural shifts that people on the coasts don't read enough about in a media environment that focuses mostly on a handful of horrific incidents and regressive laws.

It's not that red states don't have problems; they do. As an LGBT journalist, I spend much of my time reporting on anti-transgender "bathroom bills" and other red-state attacks on my rights. But places are so much more than their laws. And the only way for people on the coasts to understand how states such as Mississippi, Texas, and Tennessee are evolving is to stop flying over them and start going *to* them. Nothing could be queerer than getting out of your comfort zone.

"The word 'queer' itself," literary theorist Eve Kosofsky Sedgwick famously wrote in her explanation of the term's etymology, "means *across*."

"Queer is a continuing moment, movement, motive," she wrote, "recurrent, eddying, *troublant*."[3]

Queerness crosses sexual boundaries, gendered expec-

---

2 "Anti-Trans Attack in Capitol Hill Restaurant Not Caught on Tape," https://seattle.eater.com/2017/9/22/16352266/transphobic violence-attack-rancho-bravo-capitol-hill

3 Eve Kosofky, *Tendencies* (Durham, NC: Duke University Press, 1993), xii.

tations, and political borders. It is always in motion because to stop moving would be to surrender to the bigots who want to box us in—who want to check our birth certificates at bathroom doors or determine whom we sleep with before they bake us a cake. That is the beauty of queerness: it is irrepressible, like a spring rushing up to fill cracks in the earth. Queerness shows up uninvited. It doesn't check your voting history or your religious affiliation before knocking on your door. It didn't quiz Dick Cheney about his politics before delivering a lesbian daughter to his doorstep, and it certainly didn't ask my Mormon parents whether they wanted a transgender child before all ten pounds and fifteen ounces of me made my Long Beach, California, debut.

We LGBT people are already everywhere. We are born at the same unstoppable pace in every state—North, South, red, blue—and to every household, religious or not. According to the Public Religion Research Institute, 7 percent of millennials—and as a thirty-something, I fall in the upper end of that age bracket—now identify as LGBT.[4] And not every LGBT person born into a conservative part of America wants to get out.

As Monica Roberts, a longtime transgender blogger and my activist hero in Houston, wryly told me when I shared my plans to write this book, "We live here, too,

---

4 "Millennials Are the Gayest Generation," http://www.thedailybeast.com/millennials-are-the-gayest-generation

and we get tired of being told to move to California or whatever."

Monica is still noticing lots of "[LGBT] people leaving rural areas in red states" like Texas, but she says they are going to "oasis cities like Houston, Dallas, Austin, San Antonio, El Paso" because "they don't need to go all the way to San Francisco or Los Angeles or New York."

The data back her up: if you think all the queer youngsters are still migrating to New York or the Bay Area, think again. A 2016 ConsumerAffairs.com analysis looked at U.S. census and Gallup polling data and found that costly, queer-friendly cities are starting to lose some of their luster among LGBT people, whereas cities such as Louisville, Norfolk, and Indianapolis are rising in stature. Blue-state LGBT hot spots like New York and Seattle still saw increases in the percent of the population that identifies as LGBT, but many red-state cities saw much larger increases.

A ConsumerAffairs.com representative told me that the trend "lines up with people—especially young people—choosing less to live in huge, expensive cities, which were traditionally friendlier toward LGBTQ individuals, and choosing instead to make lives for themselves in small and mid-tier cities in the middle and southern states."[5]

---

5 "Why LGBT People Are Moving to Red States," http://www.thedailybeast.com/why-lgbt-people-are-moving-to-red-states

The fact that many of these smaller and mid-tier cities have been passing nondiscrimination protections for LGBT people makes it easier to live there, even if there is no legal recourse to be found at the state level. According to the Movement Advancement Project, which ranks states on their LGBT policies on a scale from "negative" to "high," 47 percent of the LGBT population now lives in states ranked "low" or below.[6] That means almost half of queer people in this country are spread across the South and the Midwest, Texas and the Dakotas, and other red regions.

If the dominant LGBT narrative of the twentieth century was a gay boy in the country buying a one-way bus ticket to the Big Apple, the untold story of the twenty-first is the queer girl in Tennessee who stays put.

*Real Queer America* is a testament to the simple fact that LGBT people exist in red states—that our identity is not contingent on our geography. It is proof that the "real America" has been and will always be a queer country. It is a rough and admittedly incomplete sketch of the next chapter in our country's LGBT history: a collection of stories about the people who are staying.

But it's also something more: a celebration of queer life and activism under the challenging circumstances that come with more conservative surroundings. My new

---

6 "Equality Maps," http://www.lgbtmap.org/equality-maps

friend Adam Sims, a volunteer at a Provo LGBT center called Encircle, put it best when he told me, "Oppression and opposition can build the most beautiful connections."

There is a vitality to queerness where you least expect it. A refusal to be complacent. A warmth in being bonded together by the omnipresent atmospheric pressure of bigoted policies and legislative threats. Because we are still climbing up from the bottom, we still need each other.

"Often in red states, we have the enemy in our face every day," Monica Roberts told me. "We know who the enemy is, so we are still fighting and clawing and scratching just to get the stuff that people take for granted in New York, California, and the West Coast—and even when we do pass stuff, we have to fight tooth and nail just to keep it."

And we fight together. Near the end of my five years living in Atlanta in my twenties, when I was working on my PhD at Emory University, the state of Georgia was one stroke of the pen away from legalizing anti-LGBT discrimination in the name of "religious freedom."[7] But we stopped that bill from happening and went right back to living in a city where you can go to a queer dance party at midnight and eat a sausage sandwich with Krispy Kreme doughnuts for buns two hours later at Delia's.

---

7 "Nathan Deal Vetoes Georgia's 'Religious Liberty' Bill," http:// politics.blog.ajc.com/2016/03/28/breaking-nathan-deal-will-veto -georgias-religious-liberty-bill/

Atlanta is still the best place in the country to be gay or bi or trans, and I'd gladly split a Publix sub with anyone who wants to debate me.

It is in states like Georgia that LGBT people intuitively understand critical theorist José Esteban Muñoz's description of queerness as a "longing that propels us onward," as a "rejection of the here and now and an insistence on potentiality." We work hard because we have to, and we play hard because we want to—and through both work and play we build spaces where we can be ourselves and love each other. In Muñoz's words, we are "always dream[ing] and enact[ing] new and better pleasures, other ways of being in the world," because the world we have before us is so obviously lacking.

Because we know queerness, as Muñoz beautifully wrote, is "not yet here."[8]

That's why I feel lucky to have lived all my queer adult life up to now in red states: we dream big and we don't take progress for granted.

Since my 2007 rebirth, I have found homes and second homes in states that all went red in 2016: Utah, Montana, · Georgia, Indiana, Tennessee, and, most recently, Florida.

My love story, too, takes place against a largely red-state backdrop. I met my wife, Corey, in Bloomington, Indiana, in the summer of 2013 and she moved to Atlanta

---

8 José Esteban Muñoz, *Cruising Utopia: The Then and There of Queer Futurity* (New York: New York University Press, 2000), 1.

to be with me the following year. When I think about my life with her, my mind is flooded with moments we've shared in the states that helped elect Trump, like kayaking the pristine Weeki Wachee River in Hernando County, Florida, which broke 63 to 34 for Trump, or slamming down an enormous plate of bacon cheese fries at an East Tennessee diner with my bisexual best friend—and paying only seven dollars for the privilege. I think about Corey and me cramming our butts into the same creaky Cracker Barrel rocking chair, or sipping coffee together while the Chattahoochee crawls past our favorite bench.

And to be honest, I try to block out most of our memories of New York, which I not so lovingly call Garbage Island in an homage to my favorite episode of *Broad City*.[9] I try to forget about our weekend in San Francisco, where a plate of chicken fingers at a downtown diner once ran me an appalling twenty dollars. These might be vaunted LGBT hot spots, but they are also exhausting and brutal places to visit, let alone live. The queer communities there can be cliquey, too, because people are spoiled for choice; in red-state oases, I've felt so much more adhesiveness between the L and the G and the B and the T.

So not only am I not afraid to be queer in red states, red states are where I prefer to be queer.

Even with an attorney general like Jeff Sessions whis-

---

9 The episode, called "Pu$$y Weed," aired Jan. 29, 2014.

pering in the president's ear, I would much rather be queer in Alabama than queer in the Castro District. I'm happier in Florida, where I can drive down to No Name Key on a whim as lightning shreds a stormy summer sky, than I would be in Brooklyn, where I could, I guess, take a train out to Montauk? And at a moment when some progressives are weighing the option of abandoning red states or even fleeing the country altogether, I think it's important for people with the privileges that I have—like financial security and whiteness—to do exactly the opposite: to dive deeper into the heart of this country and prove that it can't possibly be unqueered.

Over the next few years, laws will come and laws will go. And over the coming decades, presidents with different opinions on LGBT people will move in and out of the White House. Things might get very bad indeed for queer folks before they start to get better.

But we will always be here and we will always be queer—whether people get used to it or not.

Queerness itself is forever. It is everywhere. And it is irrefutably American. If you want to learn that for yourself, all you have to do is get in the car and drive. Take this book with you.

# Chapter 1

# SEEING RED

If you stick your head in the sand, problems don't
just go away.

—*Michael Hardwick,*
*after losing* Bowers v. Hardwick, *1986*[1]

The first color in the LGBT Pride flag isn't blue; it's red.

Red like 2,600 U.S. counties were in the 2016 presidential
election. Red like Donald Trump's neckties. And red like
my anxiety-flooded face the day after he won, when my
wife, Corey, raised the possibility of leaving the country.

Just four months earlier, she and I were taking selfies
with our freshly minted marriage certificate in the parking
lot of the Coral Gables, Florida, city hall. We laughed about
our officiant, Mario, who accidentally referred to Corey as
my "husband" when he recited the heterosexual ceremony
script out of habit. The next day, on our impromptu honey-
moon, we drove down the Overseas Highway to Marathon

---

1 "The Unintended Battle of Michael Hardwick," https://www
.washingtonpost.com/archive/lifestyle/1986/08/21/the-unintended
-battle-of-michael-hardwick/73fb94db-2b0f-4bf8-8220-aa5070e996
c6/?utm_term=.729f05e7e065

and walked to the end of the Old Seven Mile Bridge, an eroding railroad turned walking trail stretching out over the warm waters of the Florida Strait, so we could watch the sun drop down behind Pigeon Key.

Corey's statement-piece Adidas were bright red against the neglected pavement. When we reached the fence at the abrupt end of the path, it felt like our love was the pink in the sky.

We didn't know then that, come November, Florida would turn the same color as Corey's shoes, as would most swing states—or that the Keys, which Obama won by fewer than two hundred votes in 2012, would pivot decisively in Trump's direction this time around.

Watching that sunset, we had no idea that we would soon be contemplating taking our four-month-old marriage out of the country—or at least out of a state that helped elect a president who wraps anti-LGBT policymakers around him like a security blanket. But that's precisely the question we asked ourselves on November 9: To stay or not to stay?

I found my answer at the top of the Pride flag. There's no way, of course, that the color of its first stripe was intended as a commentary on our geographically divided political climate. Red didn't mean "Republican" or blue "Democrat" until the year 2000 anyway.[2] Red is simply

---

2 "When Republicans Were Blue and Democrats Were Red," https://www.smithsonianmag.com/history/when-republicans-were-blue-and

the first color in the rainbow, not a sign from the cosmos meant for me personally.

But back when Gilbert Baker designed that now-ubiquitous emblem of LGBT rights in 1978, he *did* want that red stripe to signify "life."[3] And shortly after the election, I realized that I owe my life to someone who decided to stay in red-state America nineteen years ago.

In 1999 a young man from Indiana named Michael Shutt moved to Washington, D.C., for an internship at a prestigious HIV/AIDS advocacy organization. At the time, our nation's capital was one of the best places in the country to be gay—at least on paper: anti-gay discrimination in private employment had been banned since 1977, and same-sex couples had been able to register as domestic partners since 1992.[4]

Fresh out of a master's program and swooning over his then-boyfriend (and now-husband), Brian, Michael pictured a future full of cherry blossoms and brick houses and queer activism.

There was just one problem: he hated it there.

"I very quickly learned that I would rather eat glass

-democrats-were-red-104176297/
3 "Meet Gilbert Baker, the Man Who Invented the Gay Pride Rainbow Flag," http://newsfeed.time.com/2012/06/26/meet-gilbert-baker -the-man-who-invented-the-gay-pride-rainbow-flag/
4 https://doh.dc.gov/service/domestic-partnership

with a Tabasco chaser than live in Washington, D.C.," he tells me over the phone shortly after the election.

Two things happened to disabuse Michael of the notion that the District of Columbia would be his forever home: First, he was robbed the same day his internship began. Second, he realized that many of his new coworkers at the HIV/AIDS advocacy organization were more interested in climbing ladders than they were in saving lives.

"I was very excited to work with them," he recalls. "And within days I saw that no one cared about the work—they cared about who you knew and what their next job was going to be."

The worst side of Washington was the same then as it is today: a bubble of money, privilege, and power in which jockeying for position too often takes precedence over the task at hand. Veteran newscaster David Brinkley once called D.C. "a city filled with people who believe they are important." LGBT people are not immune to that belief, as Michael learned firsthand. When his internship ended three months later, he rushed down to Roswell, Georgia, with Brian in tow, taking up residence in his sister's spare room with no job prospects in sight.

He was just happy to be out of D.C.

Instead of trying to make a name for himself in our nation's capital, Michael ended up becoming a queer pioneer in the South. Five years and a few job descriptions after he left Washington, he founded Georgia's first public-university LGBT student center at the University of Georgia in the Atlanta exurb of Athens.[5] (Michael "didn't know what a damn Bulldog was" when he first started working at UGA, he admits to me, but that changed fast.) And after his pathbreaking time at UGA, he took a job as director of the Office of LGBT Life at Emory University in Atlanta proper.

It was there in 2012 that I found myself sitting across a desk from him, trembling as I made an admission that felt foreign and familiar all at once: "I'm transgender."

I didn't look the part, certainly. From the outside I was a scruffy male graduate student with unkempt hair, an execrable wardrobe, and anxious, deer-in-the-headlights eyes. But when it comes to being transgender, there is no type. Some of us carry this secret with us our whole lives, hiding it, whether out of shame or fear, from almost everyone we know: Patricia Davies, a British World War II veteran, finally came out as transgender at age ninety even though she had known that she was different as early as three years old—and had told her wife the news all the way back in 1987.[6, 7] Others, especially these days, find the courage and

5 The LGBT Resource Center, https://lgbtcenter.uga.edu/content-page/about-us-content-page
6 "World War II Veteran Comes Out as Transgender at 90 Years Old," http://people.com/bodies/90-year-old-world-war-ii-veteran-comes-out-as-transgender/
7 "90-Year-Old WWII Veteran Comes Transgender," http://www.washingtonblade.com/2017/03/30/90-year-old-wwii-veteran-comes-transgender/

support to come out at a young age: TLC reality star Jazz Jennings socially transitioned when she was just five years old.[8]

All things considered, I feel lucky that only twenty years of my life went by before my own identity began coming into focus at BYU in 2007. Even then, it took me five more years to say the word *transgender* out loud—first to myself, then to a friend, and then, crucially, to Michael.

No one comes out as transgender because they are having a great day. We come out because we can't stop running anymore. We come out because we have been driving away from the storm cloud that is gender dysphoria for so long that we run out of fuel, get stuck on the side of the road, and end up having to walk all the way back to the nearest service station in the rain.

When you come out as "transgender," people tell you that you're "brave." I didn't feel brave. I felt like a coward. I had been hiding for so long.

By the time I dragged myself into Michael's office in 2012, I had spent twenty-five years trying to outmaneuver the insistent voice in my brain telling me that something had gone deeply wrong when the doctor declared me a boy at birth. That profound and unsilenceable bodily

---

8 "Jazz Jennings: The Transgender Teen and Wannabe Mermaid the Internet Needs," https://www.cosmopolitan.com/entertainment/tv/a40068/jazz-jennings-internets-most-fascinating/

knowledge was—for me—coextensive with being alive: my earliest memories are of raiding my sister's dresser for clothes and daydreaming a little too ardently when my mom joked that she was hoping for another girl but had me instead. Little did she know...

The only way to lower the volume of that voice even halfway, and never entirely, was with a life-consuming distraction: from seventeen to twenty, that distraction was my family's religion, Mormonism, which maintains that "gender is an essential characteristic of individual premortal, mortal, and eternal identity and purpose."[9] (In other words, it can't be changed. You have to live forever with the hand you were dealt.) And from twenty to twenty-four, after I had renounced my Mormon faith, it was a series of relationships that failed spectacularly, because it's hard to give yourself over to someone when you don't know who you are yet.

After that, the voice started shouting. My old diversions were useless. There was nothing left to do but ponder a past that felt wasted and a future drained of hope. I was alone, scared out of my mind, envisioning a lifetime of discrimination, violence, and rejection if I ever transitioned from male to female. And I was in Georgia—Atlanta, sure, but still Georgia.

At that point, I still mistakenly believed that people like

---

9 https://www.lds.org/topics/family-proclamation?lang=eng&old=true

me would be hated down here. Wasn't the South supposed to be a hotbed of prejudice?

But I didn't have the luxury of waiting for a different time or a different state. I had been telling myself for years that transition would somehow just happen. Perhaps I would wake up one day and just *be* a woman, inside and out. Maybe, I thought at my most desperate, I would lose a certain offending part of my body in a freak car accident and I could tell the EMTs, "Don't try to fix me. Let's lean into this! Bring me some estrogen."

But it didn't just happen, of course. Professor Harold Hill's "Think System" couldn't teach the children of Gary, Indiana, how to play Beethoven's Minuet in G, and it wouldn't change my gender, either.

So, before I ended up spending the latter two-thirds of my life resenting myself for ignoring the increasingly obvious fact of my womanhood, I stopped in my tracks. I turned around. And I walked all the way back in the rain.

I know now that Michael once had a similar moment of reckoning. As a nineteen-year-old freshman at Michigan State in the mid-1990s—back when the Clintons were anti-gay, too—he did his best to assure his peers that he was a typical straight dude from Indiana, playing the part so convincingly that he got a girlfriend that spring. But then a certain hunky man returned from a study-abroad program and moved back into his old room in Michael's dorm.

"He was Dreamy McDreamboat," Michael remembers now, with more than a hint of wistfulness in his voice. "He was pretty. He was smart. He was one of those people that I just wanted to be around."

Michael followed him all over the floor of the dorm like a little gay shoofly, harboring what he calls an "unhealthy" crush that was totally apparent to the—alas!—heterosexual man. All the while that he was trailing in McDreamboat's wake, Michael's straight relationship was getting more and more serious. Wedding bells were ringing in the distance, however faintly. Finally, with heterosexuality closing in around him, Michael found the courage to come out to McDreamboat, telling him privately one day, "I've got this problem: I think I'm gay."

Dreamy's unforgettable response: "Why don't you tell me what the problem is?"

No, that didn't lead to a night of unbridled passion. The man really, truly was straight—although Michael still has his wishful suspicions. But that exchange helped Michael embrace his identity. And just as I later realized that I would kick myself for decades if I never transitioned, Michael had a disturbing vision of his own possible future: "I was having the moment of 'I don't want to be on *Oprah* in ten years with kids, having to tell my wife that I'm gay.'"

So he came out to his girlfriend, who told her mother, who, on the couple's visit home the following weekend, loudly summoned him upstairs: "Michael!"

"I pretty much thought I was going to die at that moment," Michael remembers.

Instead, his girlfriend's mom hugged him. She told him she was proud.

Looking back, Michael should have anticipated the positive reaction: his girlfriend's mom was an enthusiastic ally who donated clothes to gay male friends for their drag personae. But college-age Michael was still worried that she would resent him for breaking her daughter's heart.

To the contrary, Mom essentially told her daughter to "move on."

Although his girlfriend did eventually marry a straight man and have kids, Michael still feels bad that his jilted sweetheart didn't get the care she needed at the time.

"It was a challenging time for me," he recalls. "I was still facing major coming-out struggles myself, I was being celebrated while I entered a new phase in life, *and* I wanted to be the most supportive person I could be to someone I had hurt. It was hard doing all of these things."

I had made a similar mistake moving in with my own serious girlfriend, Michelle, before coming out. She and I were students together at Rutgers in New Brunswick, New Jersey—where I transferred after I left BYU—when I found out I had been accepted into a PhD program at Emory University. With nothing keeping her in the Northeast after graduation, Michelle decided to make the move south with me in the fall of 2010. We, too, were a daytime TV story in the making—whether or not she suspected it, and whether or not I was willing to admit it to myself.

Looking back now, as the portion of my life that I have lived as my authentic self eclipses the previous chapters, it seems absurd that I ever thought I could be happy in this world as a heterosexual man—and cruel that I ever asked anyone, especially someone as kind as Michelle, to believe in that premise long enough to move to another state with me.

But I did it for the same reason that Michael kept dating his own sophomore sweetheart: I was certain there was no other way forward. If only I could stay on the well-worn track of heteronormative social expectations long enough, I told myself, perhaps I'd find some satisfaction in them. And maybe that insistent voice in my head would finally shut up.

That was the delusion under which I was operating when Michelle and I loaded up our cars and started rolling down I-81, past the Pennsylvania shopping malls into the mild Virginia hills. To say I wasn't really in love with her would be too easy. I *was* in love with her. The problem was the instability of that "I"—the indeterminacy that led me to selfishly cling to any relationship I was in like a reassuring buoy.

*If I'm in love,* I thought, *I don't need to transition.* But that premise was deeply flawed.

Two years later, the side effects of my secret broke

us up: the anxiety, the depression, and the restlessness that welled up in me as I felt the routines of a cisgender heterosexual world wrapping around me like a python, closing off more avenues of escape the longer it held me in its grasp. I grew distant, I cheated, it ended.

After I came out, Michelle was hurt but ultimately wanted me to be happy, even helping me come out to my family. We understand each other now as women.

Years later, I have many regrets about that relationship. But when you have a life as filled with pain, turbulence, and second chances as mine has been, you have to take the good with the bad. You have to find the subtle logic behind the things that hurt you and—as much as you'll never forgive yourself for them—the times you hurt other people. Michelle and I left each other brokenhearted. But we also learned the sorts of lessons that come only from sharing space with someone who sees the world differently than you do. And I will always be grateful to Michelle for teaching me the joys of the South.

I was a prissy product of Los Angeles and the New York City suburbs when Michelle and I first met in college. The piece of nature I saw most frequently as a child was the L.A. "River," a paved flood-control channel I rode alongside on my bike to get strawberry ice cream at Thrifty's. But in school Michelle started tugging me back down to earth, taking me out to the cranberry bogs in central New Jersey and to her family's little place near the lake in Browns Mills.

I had always appreciated a walk through the woods, but Michelle showed me that there was a whole way of life that revolved around car rides and creature comforts, winding mountain trails and steaming mugs of hot tea. She showed me the faded beauty of Southern pines and the glow of fireflies on mild summer nights.

And as surprising as it may sound, I couldn't have asked for a better place than the South to finally tell the truth about myself and begin my transition.

That fateful day in Michael's office, after I stammered out my confession that I was transgender, I had no idea how he would react. He didn't blink. He didn't ask any of the invasive questions that I've been asked a million times since. Instead, with a healthy dose of Midwestern compassion that I have grown to love, he began dispensing helpful information.

Had I heard about the weekly discussion group for transgender students? Was I aware that Faughn Adams over at the student counseling center specialized in such issues? Did I know that Emory's endocrinology division employed a world-renowned expert in transgender medical care named Vin Tangpricha—and that our student health insurance plan was trans-inclusive as of two years ago? The answer to all of these questions was no. I had stumbled into his office that day with nothing but fear in my heart and a confession on my lips.

But in a matter of minutes—perhaps without even realizing the significance of what he was doing—Michael

Shutt illuminated a path forward out of a life that felt unlivable.

I didn't know then that Michael had spent the five years leading up to our fateful meeting laying the groundwork for students like me.

In 2009 — almost a decade after Emory's Office of LGB Life officially became the Office of LGBT Life — Michael helped launch the first discussion group for transgender people at the university.[10]

By the time I came out there was a core group of attendees who welcomed me right away, scooping me off rock bottom on a weekly basis. They held my hand through those first harrowing steps of a gender transition, when I was still walking out into the world with a wig on my head and stubble on my face. We drove each other to doctor's appointments and shared tips for surviving holidays back home. We vented about being misgendered by classmates and celebrated each other's transition milestones: hormone prescriptions, surgery dates, name changes. All that was possible because Michael made space for it.

In 2010 — Michael's second year on the job — he spearheaded the institutional fight to secure hormone therapy and mental health counseling coverage for transgender students under Emory's health insurance plan. Thanks to that instance of advocacy, I could walk out of our

---

10 Campus Life, "History," http://www.lgbt.emory.edu/about/history .html

2012 meeting in his office and make an appointment with Faughn Adams—who, in turn, helped me get a prescription for those miraculous little green estrogen pills a few months later.

Back then, some nagging part of me still felt uncertain about going through with transition, even though all of my symptoms were textbook gender dysphoria.

*What if I'm making a huge mistake?* I thought.

Said the sage Faughn one day from her office armchair, "If it doesn't feel right, just stop."

I never worried again after that. The hurricane raging in my head calmed as I took those pills. Eventually they would reshape my body as well. And because of the work Michael had done, I never paid a dime to absorb Faughn's wisdom—and my monthly bottle of estrogen cost less than a chicken sandwich with waffle fries.

In 2011—the year before I appeared in Michael's office—he and a small group of transgender advocates on campus had finally succeeded in getting surgical benefits included in the student health insurance plan. His tactics, he later told me, included subtly "guilting and shaming" the university president during a series of closed-door meetings.

Three years later I drove across the country with Corey to undergo sex-reassignment surgery in San Francisco. If my insurance had not covered most of the cost of the procedure, I would still be paying off loans for it today—or, worse, I might not even have a vagina yet. That wouldn't just be an inconvenience, either: the American Medical Association has recognized the potential "medical necessity" of surgery in the treatment of gender dysphoria for people like me who couldn't imagine living with the wrong anatomy much longer.[11]

Forty percent of respondents to the 2015 U.S. Transgender Survey said they had made a suicide attempt in their lifetime. Although I'm lucky not to be in that camp, I am one of the 82 percent who have soberly considered it.[12] What kept me from acting on those suicidal thoughts was how quickly I was able to access the medical treatments, such as surgery, that I needed. My experience is backed up by data: a mountain of peer-reviewed literature has found that transition-related health care improves mental health.[13]

I have tried to tell Michael many times that he saved my life—that there are plenty of people in student affairs who, if placed in his position, wouldn't have gone on a crusade for transgender inclusion just as their career was taking off. But he won't hear it.

"In Georgia, you know that the work needs to get done," he tells me, with no false modesty in his voice—

---

11 "Professional Organization Statements Supporting Transgender People in Health Care," http://www.lambdalegal.org/publications/fs_professional-org-statements-supporting-trans-health

12 http://www.ustranssurvey.org/reports

13 "Analysis Finds Strong Consensus on Effectiveness of Gender Transition Treatment," http://news.cornell.edu/stories/2018/04/analysis-finds-strong-consensus-effectiveness-gender-transition-treatment

just old-fashioned Midwestern determination inflected with Southern frankness.

Michael was just doing his job.

Georgia isn't a queer paradise—but it's a little closer because people like Michael are in it. Are there still people in red-state America who are more interested in their job title than they are in helping LGBT people? Absolutely. Power is appealing no matter your race, gender, or sexual orientation. But in Michael's experience, at least, queer advocates in Georgia prioritize taking care of business over their next promotion.

That's how Michael got a university in the American South to cover sex-reassignment surgery a year before Harvard, that bastion of American liberalism, agreed to foot the bill.[14] That's why a school like Emory had a fully inclusive transgender health insurance plan before Princeton and MIT could say the same.[15]

Michael once watched a colleague from his UGA days leave for a brand-new job in California, only to report back a month later that "everyone out here is apathetic." It's a process he has witnessed repeatedly as his former

---

14 "Health Plans to Cover Lower Surgery for Gender Reassignment," http://www.thecrimson.com/article/2011/11/17/Health-Lower -Surgery/

15 "Colleges and Universities That Cover Transition-Related Medical Expenses Under Student Health Insurance," https://www.campuspride .org/tpc/student-health-insurance/

coworkers assume that, just because a state has more progressive laws on the books, it will be a more energizing place to do LGBT-related work.

The entire country witnessed the effects of blue-state apathy firsthand in 2008 when California—yes, the godless liberal Golden State—made same-sex marriage illegal by a margin of six hundred thousand votes. Complacent even in the face of one of the most ruthlessly efficient and well-funded armies of homophobes the United States has ever seen, too many progressive California voters stayed home on election night instead of showing up to vote down Proposition 8.[16]

In a postmortem for the "No on 8" movement published on the LGBT website *The Advocate* that November, some of the leaders responsible for defending same-sex marriage rights suggested that low turnout in San Francisco and Los Angeles could be attributed to the fact that "voters may not have bothered trudging to their polling places once it was clear that Obama had won."[17]

LGBT blogger Joshua Meadows pointed to the increasingly desperate tone of the "No on 8" Twitter account as it pleaded with people to leave their freaking houses and get to a polling place: "LOW voter turnout in Hollywood, West Hollywood, and Silverlake. CALL YOUR

---

16 "Mormons Tipped Scale in Ban on Gay Marriage," https://www.nytimes.com/2008/11/15/us/politics/15marriage.html

17 "Anatomy of a Failed Campaign," https://www.advocate.com/news/2008/11/19/anatomy-failed-campaign

FRIENDS AND GET THEM OUT NOW! One Hour Left."[18]

The result shocked the coastal media: How could enlightened California ban same-sex marriage? To Michael and other LGBT people living in red states, however, the answer was obvious: homophobia, racism, and transphobia are like toxic gases. Left unchecked, they fill whatever space they're given to fill. Assuming safety only leaves you vulnerable.

"California thought that their shit didn't stink and guess what? Surprise!" Michael says, still animated about the issue today. "And everybody was so upset about it. It was sort of like Trump's election."

Even within red-state liberal oases such as Atlanta, that same complacency can be observed on a smaller scale, as Michael can personally attest.

LGBT people and other progressives in Atlanta often refer to I-285, a sixty-mile-long highway looping the city, as the dividing line between the area "inside the perimeter," where everything is safe and liberal and happy, and "outside the perimeter," where hungry homophobic hillbillies will supposedly eat your brains as soon as you stop for gas. Inside the perimeter is where brunch happens. Outside the perimeter is what you

---

18 "Proposition 8 and Why the Gay Community Failed to Protect Its Own Rights," http://ctrlclick.com/2012/05/proposition-8-and-why-the-gay-community-failed-to-protect-its-own-rights/

must endure to get to Savannah for the weekend. It's a distinction that Michael rightly calls "absurd." There are plenty of LGBT safe havens on the other side of that arbitrary dividing line—among them the Appalachian town of Blue Ridge in northern Georgia—and plenty of bigotry inside it.

In 2004, when Georgia unsurprisingly passed a constitutional amendment banning same-sex marriage by a landslide, none of the counties inside the perimeter could lay claim to being the statistical leader of the pro-LGBT resistance: in Atlanta proper, both DeKalb and Fulton counties voted against the discriminatory measure by a still-impressive-for-the-time 40 percent.

But drive sixty miles outside the supposedly protective perimeter of I-285, all the way to Clarke County— where Michael was then working at UGA—and an even more substantial 48 percent of voters stood up for same-sex marriage. That was nowhere near enough to tip the overall state result, of course, but it sent an important message.[19]

"It was sort of a middle finger to people inside the perimeter," says Michael, who has since moved inside the perimeter—but only just—and who, like me, avoids the trendy gay-friendly Midtown area in the city center as if it were radioactive. (When a new neighbor

---

19 http://www.cnn.com/ELECTION/2004//pages/results/states/ GA/I/01/county.001.html

pointed out how far he has to drive to "go out" at night, Michael thought, "What the fuck do you think I do? When I go out, I find the closest Mexican restaurant.")

Georgia is proof that LGBT people in red states know that we can't let our guard down. We don't have a lot of pretenses about how progressive we are. The odds are against us—and they unify us. We often feel disconnected from the mainstream of LGBT activism, not just culturally but financially. A 2016 study from Funders for LGBTQ Issues found that the South receives only about 8 percent of annual domestic LGBT funding even though roughly 30 percent of LGBT adults live there.[20] But we work miracles with what we have.

Indeed, if queer people in red-state America manage to reach certain milestones before our blue-state friends—or simply seem to fight harder with fewer resources against the same prejudice—it might be because we know how bad things can get if we don't try every day to make them better.

Michael had seen the worst of it as a child in Angola, Indiana. He remembers hearing children throw the word *faggot* around in a cruel playground rhyme as early as the

---

20 Funders for LGBTQ Issues—Special Report, Part 3: The Opportunities, "Out in the South," https://www.lgbtfunders.org/wp-content/uploads/2018/04/Out_in_the_South_Part_Three_-Opportunities-_for_Funding_LGBT_Communities_in_the_U.S._South.pdf

first grade. His T-top Camaro-driving dad, Michael says, saw him as a "wuss" and a "pussy." By the time he entered high school, he was "starting to get read as gay" and classmates hurled slurs in his direction.

The resulting social isolation drove Michael, at age twelve, to take on a time-consuming job at the Lake James Country Club, right on the shore of the Lower Basin. He eventually saved up enough money for a car and, although he wasn't exactly rich by the time he graduated from high school, he developed a reputation for being two things: probably gay and remarkably self-sufficient.

In his senior yearbook, he was voted "Most Likely to Be Donald Trump"—a comparison that now horrifies and amuses him in equal parts.

I ask Michael today if he would rather have grown up outside rural Indiana, perhaps in a state where he would have experienced less bullying—although it would have been hard to avoid such torment in the Reagan eighties—and judging from data collected by GLSEN, an organization working to end anti-LGBT bullying, it's still alarmingly prevalent for queer kids today no matter where they live.[21] But Michael wouldn't choose a childhood anywhere else.

Not only did he love life in the country—he spent his

---

21 "Has It Really 'Gotten Better' for Gay Kids?" http://www.thedaily beast.com/has-it-really-gotten-better-for-gay-kids

childhood on the water and in the woods as the "quintessential eighties latchkey kid," never at home, always exploring—he knows those bad experiences at school shaped him.

"I don't know what I would be like if I didn't have the challenges that I had," he tells me.

The truth of that statement haunts me if I think about it too long. Without experiencing ridicule in grade school, Michael might not be the kind of determined LGBT advocate who would land a cushy job at a private university and spend all his capital pushing for controversial new policies that would help only a sliver of the student body just because it was the right thing to do.

Without the after-school job at the Lake James Country Club, he might not have developed the kind of drive it takes to open an LGBT student center at a public university in Georgia—especially at a time when his higher-education mentors were warning him that he would never make Dean of Students if he chose to wear his sexual orientation on his sleeve.

And who knows? If it weren't for Indiana, he might never have become the Michael who hated D.C. and moved to Roswell, Georgia, all those years ago.

In some alternate version of the year 2012, Michael is a Washington bureaucrat and I walk into an office at Emory occupied by someone who didn't hit the ground running on transgender issues as soon as they arrived. Then, perhaps, I don't transition for years. My mental health deteriorates. I miss the opportunity to meet my future wife in Indiana the following year. And that possibility is so shattering I can't even continue.

Do I owe the course of my entire life to 1980s schoolyard bullies in Angola? It's quite possible I do. But I also owe it to the fireflies—to Faughn, Michelle, and the sprawling lakes of northeast Indiana. I owe it to every little thing that shaped us into who we were: the hikes, the afternoons on the lake, even the robbery in D.C. Above all, I owe it to hard and unpretentious labor in the face of encroaching anti-LGBT sentiment.

I owe it to Michael, to Red America, and to Georgia.

On November 9, 2016, Michael didn't post a long doomsday message to Facebook.

He didn't think about leaving.

Instead, he shared an article about Sam Park, a first-generation Korean-American who—on the same night Trump won—became the first openly gay man to be elected to the Georgia General Assembly.

"The good news of the day," wrote Michael in the caption, and he left it at that, ever the optimist.

Park himself was aware of the meaning behind his victory, telling NBC News that "to hear from so many people, not just in Georgia but throughout the world, that we gave people some hope—a silver lining—that, to me, was really humbling."[22]

There were other queer wins in red-state America, too. Pat McCrory, the governor who signed North Carolina's cruel anti-transgender bathroom bill into law, got the boot. Florida, like North Carolina, voted for Trump but got another openly LGBT legislator sent up to the statehouse.[23]

But not every victory happened at the ballot box. The same day that liberals were dreaming about leaving conservative parts of America—and even America in general—overloading the Canadian immigration website with anxious clicks,[24] queer red-staters like Michael woke up and did exactly what they have been doing for decades: they dug in their heels instead of cutting out. Talking to Michael, hearing him take Trump in stride, made me want to be more like him—to buckle down and just see this thing through. I wanted to be a part of that red-state resistance. I wanted to stay in the "real" America—and so did Corey, once the initial shock wore off.

---

22 "Meet Sam Park, First Openly Gay Man Elected to Georgia's General Assembly," https://www.nbcnews.com/news/asian-america/meet-sam-park-georgia-s-first-openly-gay-state-legislator-n689211

23 "Florida Increases LGBTQ Representation in State Legislature; Victories for David Richardson and Carlos Guillermo Smith," https://victoryfund.org/news/florida-increases-lgbt-representation-state-legislature-victories-david-richardson-carlos-guillermo-smith/

24 "Canada's Immigration Website Crashes as Donald Trump's US Election Lead Grows," https://www.theguardian.com/world/2016/nov/09/canadas-immigration-website-crashes-as-donald-trumps-us-election-lead-grows

And soon after talking to Michael, I felt something even more powerful: a desire to revisit the red states that have shaped me into who I am today. I wanted to get away from my keyboard and tell new stories about the old places I love. To deepen the ties that have kept me alive.

I couldn't abandon Tennessee, because my queer family there would never abandon me. I wanted to check in on Georgia, where I lived for five fast but formative years. I even wanted to return to Provo, to hear the stories of the LGBT Mormons who stayed when I left in a hurry.

So, as Michael did in 1999 when he left D.C. for Roswell, Georgia, I got in the car and I went somewhere redder.

# Chapter 2

## PRODIGAL DAUGHTER

How beautiful on the mountains are the feet of
those who bring good news...

—*Isaiah 52:7*

The unofficial nickname for Provo, Utah—a Mormon
college town nestled against a stunning subset of the
Wasatch Mountain range—is "Happy Valley." When you
live there and you are closeted and angsty and miserable,
it's the sort of moniker you laugh about ruefully, especially on days when it seems like the smog is sticking to
the ground only to underscore your sadness. But even
during my most difficult times at Brigham Young University, I would catch sight of those mountains in the
morning and utter an involuntary, unironic "Wow."

And I would smile—not wide, but enough.

I decided to make Provo the first stop on my *Real Queer
America* road trip because it is the place I least want to
revisit. I do not have many fond memories of my time
here. This is the city where I first felt the strange sensa-

tion of being certain that I was going to hell: a sinking feeling that starts in your heart, slips uneasily past your solar plexus, and slouches into your gut. I felt it every time I wore women's clothing after dark and tearfully prayed to Heavenly Father for forgiveness the next morning. When I finally apostatized—and predictably lost my believing girlfriend in the process—depression filled the empty hours of my newly solitary life.

There were whole weeks during the summer of 2007 when I didn't talk to anyone at all—unless you count laconic 2 a.m. transactions at the Del Taco drive-through window.

"Two grilled chicken tacos.... That's it.... Thanks."

And then it was back to my apartment, where I was still hiding my defection from my roommates, my school, my bishop, my parents—everyone.

At least I had tacos.

In 2007, it seemed impossible to be openly transgender in Provo. It was *Provo,* the capital of the country for Mormon youth, a literal breeding ground for God's army of heterosexual foot soldiers. On weekends, BYU students were everywhere—*dating.* Identical-looking straight couples held hands while walking around campus, eating frozen yogurt, and spectating Ultimate Frisbee games. One of their favorite activities was hiking up a nearby mountain to the "Y," a gigantic capital letter first painted in the early 1900s that is visible from the entire valley below.

I never climbed the Y. I avoided daytime Provo, that

city-size playground for chaste college sweethearts, and lived instead in its literal shadows, eating midnight meals at the 24/7 Denny's or going to the dollar theater alone to watch virtually empty showings of R-rated movies such as *Pan's Labyrinth*—because PG-13 is as risqué as most Mormons are willing to get.

I wanted nothing but out—and get out I did, leaving the Church the following year and landing at Rutgers shortly thereafter. So it is unnerving now to be back of my own volition, my thirty-year-old mind a sponge all too ready to be saturated with memory.

I roll into Provo on the afternoon of July 10, 2017, and these streets feel eerily real again under the sanitizing ninety-degree sun. Any turn I take in my rented Subaru recalls another scene from my past: my parents in early 2006 dropping me off at the Missionary Training Center, a fenced-in compound where I would be sequestered for six weeks to learn Mandarin so I could go proselytize to Chinese-Americans in San Diego; me spending sleepless nights after my mission in the Foreign Language Student Residence—or the "Flisser," as we called it—grappling with my faith, and losing; my girlfriend and me watching *Eternal Sunshine of the Spotless Mind* on an empty soccer field late at night when the sprinkler system spurts to life, sending us scrambling to cover up her laptop with a blanket and flee through the spray.

If I linger on them long enough, these memories still have the power to pierce me. This is a place filled with the sort of pain that can only be confronted, not avoided. But it is also the city where I started to find myself—indeed, where I took my first cautious steps *as* myself into Provo Canyon parks, in the twilight hours when it would take a discerning eye to spot my cheap wig and awkward gait. And even as I contemplate my own history on this quick tour of the town, I know that many queer people in red states feel this exact same ambivalence: the places that haunt us the longest are also the places that shaped us the most indelibly.

Places like Provo are crucibles, inhospitable but formative.

"How are you doing?" my friend Billy, who has kindly agreed to come along on the *Real Queer America* journey, asks me from the passenger seat.

"I'm doing okay," I half lie.

Any road trip worth its salt needs a sidekick. I am lucky to have one like Billy, a skinny transgender guy from a Sicilian family on Long Island, who has a short, scruffy beard threatening to overtake his whole face and a whimsical shock of curly reddish-brown hair on his head. In fact, Billy's whole body is a veritable blanket of fur—a genetic inheritance he discovered only *after* he started taking testosterone—so my only complaint about traveling with him is that the bottom of the bathtub looks like a bearskin rug by the time he's done showering.

Billy is five years my junior but we both started transitioning in 2012, when he was in his sophomore year of college. After spending his early years as a "tomboy"—and his middle-school years awkwardly presenting in a more feminine fashion—he finally admitted to himself that he was a "lesbian" in eleventh grade, after developing an unhealthy obsession with a female contestant on the MTV dating show *A Shot at Love with Tila Tequila*. But he continued to live a double life, publicly dating a boy named Patrick while semi-secretly dating a girl named Corey (who would later become my wife). Finally, at college in New Paltz, New York, he met some other transgender guys and it clicked for him: he wasn't a tomboy or a lesbian, but a man.

Luckily for me, Billy and Corey broke up before he transitioned—for unrelated reasons—but the two have remained close; in fact, it was Corey's idea that he accompany me on this voyage.

Billy is quiet, often inward-looking. But he is also perceptive from his own closely guarded vantage point—and now that we're driving into Provo together, he can sense the effect this city has on me. It's true that I am not crushed by the mere atmosphere of this place the way I would have been a decade ago, but I am still shaken. I pull into the Baymont Inn and Suites by the Provo River, where I have blocked out a five-night stay.

There will be no leaving Provo early this time.

I grab my bag from Billy, look up at the mountains, and take a deep breath.

\*    \*    \*

The best cure for my nerves is a morning hike to Battle Creek Falls with Emmett Claren, one of the few openly transgender members of the Mormon Church.

Emmett rolls up to the trailhead in a red Hyundai SUV, jaunts out of the car while stashing his wallet and keys in the loose pockets of his summery shorts, and strides over to meet us with an alacrity that defies the earliness of the hour. He is a twenty-three-year-old explosion of charisma, the kind of guy who cheerily announces, "I'm a hugger" before you have a chance to notice that you are, in fact, receiving the best hug of your life.

Like me, Emmett was baptized into the Mormon Church at the customary age of eight—although unlike me, he converted to the religion rather than being born into it. Raised by a single father in California, Emmett was just three years old when two female missionaries—known as "sister missionaries" in Mormon parlance—knocked on their door and began teaching them the gospel. One year later, in 1998, Emmett's dad married one of the missionaries.

Emmett remained devoted to the Church through childhood moves to Wisconsin and Nebraska, completing all the Personal Progress requirements in the Young Women's program. And in 2013, when he turned nineteen, he followed the example set by his stepmother and went on a mission of his own—an eighteen- to twenty-four-month period of 24/7 evangelical work in an assigned location, during which communication with friends and family back home is forbidden, except for weekly letter writing. A still-closeted Emmett was assigned to be a sister missionary in Salt Lake City.

Emmett would have much rather worn a suit and tie than a floral-print dress. When he got home from his mission at age twenty-one and moved to Utah, he transitioned from female to male. Instead of leaving the Church and Utah, as I had, Emmett decided to stay in both—risking discipline and even excommunication in the process.

I was the first national reporter to interview Emmett about his predicament (for the *Daily Beast,* in 2016[1]), and I'm eager to talk to him again on the hike this morning. I am drawn to his story for admittedly personal reasons: I want to know how he can live in Utah when I felt such pressure to leave. I want him to tell me how he reconciles his transgender identity with his Mormon faith. But most of all, I want to know why he seems so happy—to find out what's behind that smile I see in the YouTube videos and Instagram posts through which he documents his transition.

I remember almost crying when Emmett told me that, whenever he fears retribution from the Church, he thinks about a line from his favorite Mormon hymn. It was once

---

1 "Why It's Not Easy Becoming an Ex-Mormon," http://www.thedailybeast.com/mormon-man-risks-excommunication-by-sharing-his-transition

one of my favorites, too: "I believe in Christ so come what may."

Those words form a sort of lyrical armor against the punishments Emmett could face for being an openly transgender Mormon. The Church of Jesus Christ of Latter-day Saints—as the Mormon Church is formally known—is not LGBT-inclusive, to put it mildly.

The Church currently allows cisgender gay and lesbian members to remain in good standing only if they do not act on their "same-sex attraction" at all—effectively requiring them to remain celibate or risk disfellowshipping and excommunication. This policy is relatively generous compared with the Church's past positions: in 1969, for example, Church leader Spencer W. Kimball wrote that homosexuality was "an ugly sin," arguing that it was "curable" and maintaining that "it can be overcome."[2]

In 1981 the Church published a now-out-of-print guidebook called *Homosexuality* that, as University of North Florida sociologist Richard Phillips noted, essentially endorsed Kimball's idea that homosexuality was a choice and advised gay Mormon men to keep dating women.[3] Additional guidebooks published in 1992 and 2007 backed away from that ill-advised recommendation, drawing a line between homosexual "thought" and

---

2 Spencer W. Kimball, *The Miracle of Forgiveness* (Salt Lake City: Bookcraft Publishing, 1969).

3 Rick Phillips, *Conservative Christian Identity and Same-Sex Orientation: The Case of Gay Mormons* (New York: Peter Lang Publishing, 2005).

homosexual "behaviors." The latter would be subject to church discipline; the former would not.

But after the Supreme Court legalized same-sex marriage nationwide in the 2015 *Obergefell v. Hodges* decision, the Church stopped softening its stance. That same year, the leadership pointedly reiterated that a same-sex wedding is considered an act of apostasy and an excommunicable offense.[4]

Current policy on transgender members such as Emmett is less clear but no less discouraging. The Church— as I mentioned earlier—teaches that gender is an "essential characteristic of individual premortal, mortal, and eternal identity and purpose," which doesn't exactly make it sound malleable. And although one top Church leader recently gave transgender members hope by saying "we have some unfinished business in teaching on that [issue],"[5] the handbook still gives leaders permission to discipline members who undergo sex-reassignment surgery.

Back when I first interviewed Emmett, I asked the Church's official spokesperson for clarity on the issue of transgender membership. He told me that "the Church

4 "New Policy on Gay Couples and Their Children Roils Mormon Church," https://www.nytimes.com/2015/11/14/us/mormons-set-to-quit-church-over-policy-on-gay-couples-and-their-children.html

5 "A Mormon Leader Signals New Openness on Transgender Issues. This Could Be Huge.," http://www.slate.com/blogs/outward/2015/02/13/mormons_and_transgender_elder_dallin_h_oaks_says_the_lds_church_is_open.html

does not baptize those who are planning transsexual operations, and those who choose to have a transsexual operation may place their membership at risk."[6]

Neither one of these policies has been publicly changed. That means Emmett—who at the time of my visit has just shown the scars from his chest-masculinization procedure to his new girlfriend for the first time—lives daily with the specter of excommunication.

But the only struggle that we discuss as we start our hike is my fight to keep pace with him on the gentle but persistent upward slope of the canyon trail to Battle Creek Falls. My slow speed isn't helped by the fact that I'm wearing a drapey long-sleeve cardigan instead of sunscreen—and dripping with sweat as a result.

"I love Utah," Emmett gushes, as I catch my breath. "I love the hikes. I love the mountains."

Looking at the verdant growth along the trail, I can't help loving how much *he* loves Utah. As hints of the cool air coming off the waterfall touch our skin on the last few bends of the trail, Emmett turns to me and grins as wide as a Disney prince. He looks the part: Emmett—who has Latino, Caucasian, and Native American ancestry—recently submitted an audition tape for the live-action version of *Aladdin*.

---

6 "Why It's Not Easy Becoming an Ex-Mormon," http://www
.thedailybeast.com/mormon-man-risks-excommunication-by-
sharing-his-transition

It's hard to picture this vivacious, lovestruck, curly-haired twentysomething ever wanting to die. Statistically speaking, though, I suppose it shouldn't be. Most transgender adults who report having made a suicide attempt tried to take their own lives before the age of twenty-five.[7] Emmett is one of them. He speaks matter-of-factly about it now.

After his mission ended in 2015, Emmett spent just a few months attending school at BYU–Idaho, a school that somehow manages to be more conservative than its larger and more popular Provo equivalent. In a near-constant state of agony, he spent hours on the phone with his gay uncle, the only person who even remotely understood what he was going through.

"I wanted to be myself," Emmett remembers. "I wanted to be the boy that I always felt that I was. But [I thought] if I do, I'm probably going to get kicked out of the Church and if I do, my parents will never speak to me again."

Those fears drove Emmett to the brink of suicide: "I was praying every single day because I knew what I was feeling and I knew it was real and I knew that if I didn't do it, I was going to die because I didn't want to live anymore."

Emmett came out to a school therapist, who promptly

---

7 The Trevor Project, "Facts About Suicide," http://www.thetrevorproject
.org/pages/facts-about-suicide

dropped him as a client without offering a referral to an LGBT-affirming provider. He figured that if she was going to give up on him, he might as well give up on himself. After taking a double dose of antidepressants, Emmett found himself in the middle of a manic episode, trying to jump off a balcony "because I thought I could fly" before his roommates stopped him. They rescued him from another attempt, too.

"Idaho was where I was going to die," he tells me. "I was not going to make it."

From childhood on, Emmett has always turned to nature for refuge. ("I could put my hair in my hat, some dirt on my face, and just *be* a boy when I was in nature," he recalls.) So after he transferred from BYU–Idaho to a school in Utah—thereby escaping an honor code even stricter than the one I was bound by in Provo—he became an avid hiker, spending most of his weekends outside, looking for new waterfalls and creeks to explore.

"The mountains were where I felt close to God," he remembers. "I felt like I could just be myself—like I didn't have eyes on me all the time and I could just be me."

One night, Emmett went for a solitary hike to the top of nearby Squaw Peak—a challenging and dangerous trek that he freely admits now he shouldn't have done alone. But he needed to know whether God would support his transition.

"I just sat there and listened to the wind moving through the valley and between the mountains," he recalls. "I could hear it and I could feel it and I just felt so much peace. I asked so many questions that I wanted answers to and I felt this calming release—like it's all going to be okay."

That was a pivotal moment for Emmett.

"Utah saved my life, being here," he says. "The mountains saved my life."

Which helps explain why hiking to the end of this trail with Emmett feels like a kind of religious experience.

"I can already feel it," he says over the sound of the gushing water, ushering us into the mist from the waterfall waiting around the last bend.

Turning the corner, we see the two-tongued waterfall, pouring in five-story-tall currents over a striated rock face, perpetually wet patches of stone shimmering in the sun. At the base of the waterfall the twin flows fan out across a shallow field of boulders. To the left, two hikers are rappelling down the rock face. And all around us a gaggle of Mormon kids play on the slippery rocks as their modestly dressed mothers supervise them from drier footing.

I am exhausted and in awe of these Mormon moms who carried their little ones up this trail; I barely managed to get here myself without fainting.

Emmett has the sort of untempered enthusiasm that can seem forced at first. But as we stand here amid these Mormon families, I see longing in his eyes and know that he means every word.

"I want this," he tells me, gesturing at it all—the babies, the big Mormon families, the morning hikes—and he hopes that his new girlfriend wants it, too.

When Emmett started transitioning at the age of twenty-one, he had no family of his own in the state. But he assembled one. He found plenty of support from an unofficial group for LGBT Mormons known as Affirmation, from a local parenting group called Mama Dragons,[8] and, crucially, from the LGBT center Encircle right here in Provo.

The first local congregation he attended while transitioning, Emmett recalls, was "really kind" to him—even though he remembers looking "odd" when he "came to church in dress pants and a shirt and tie" long before he "passed" as a man. Still, it has been incredibly hard for him to find an active member of the Church who would be willing to date a transgender guy. He met his girlfriend at an Affirmation event a few months ago.

Emmett's devotion to Utah makes sense; it wasn't just the mountains in this state that saved his life but the people as well. But I still can't get my head around how he can remain so devoted to a religion that refuses to fully embrace him.

He approaches being both Mormon and transgender with an assuredness that should probably give the Church

---

8 "Mama Dragons Lead the Fight for Their Gay Mormon Kids," http://archive.sltrib.com/article.php?id=2438383&itype=CMSID

pause—and that sometimes baffles me. He has no intention of leaving the faith unless he gets kicked out. For Emmett, the matter is simple: his "spirit is male" but he was "born in a female body," which he has since changed with hormones and surgery.

But for leaders of local congregations, Emmett presents a complex doctrinal challenge: should he be disciplined for seeking out what transgender men call "top surgery" to remove his breasts? Can he attend all-male priesthood meetings? Should he even be allowed to stay on the membership rolls? His status in the faith is in a perpetual state of limbo.

I found leaving the Church to be a simple decision: Mormonism forbade me from being who I was, so why would I stay? But I also lost my faith for a variety of personal, intellectual, and political reasons that went beyond my transgender identity. Emmett's faith, on the other hand, is still intact. I want to understand why.

"I tried to leave," he admits to me. "I tried not going to church. I tried to just change my life and be like, 'The heck with it! I'm done! I don't need to do this Mormon thing anymore.'"

But as his use of the swear-word substitute *heck* proves, Emmett is as unshakably Mormon as he is unshakably male.

"I didn't like who I was becoming," Emmett says of his attempted departure. "I didn't like the person I was. I felt like something was missing and so I started going back to church. I'm not Emmett without my faith. I'm not Emmett without going to church on Sunday."

Emmett tells me that some local Church leaders recently intimated that he might face discipline if he went through with his top surgery, even setting an ominous date for a "meeting" in which "[his] membership was going to be discussed." He braced himself for the worst—he had always known it was a "gamble" to seek the surgery—but he went through with the procedure and has not been kicked out yet.

There is only one scenario in which he would leave: "If the Church told me I had to detransition in order to be in the Church, I would absolutely say no," he tells me. "I would die. I would die before I thought to detransition."

I am all but certain that Emmett is on the Mormon Church's radar at a level higher than the local. A dozen national and international media outlets have now covered the broad strokes of his personal story. He is a known quantity, public about his transition for the sake of the youth who come after him. He has made peace with the price he may have to pay for that choice.

"I honestly just feel like it's all up to God," he says. "If the leaders pick up on my story and they're like, 'Mmm, you're too public, sorry, we're going to excommunicate you,' then so be it."

Come what may.

I embarked on this hike hoping Emmett would tell me how he reconciles his religion and his gender, but shouldn't Mormonism have to reconcile itself to *him*? He is standing, knocking at the door of the faith he loves, asking to be let in. The leaders of the Church are the ones who have some explaining to do, not this young man. So I don't ask Emmett any more questions. Instead, we snap a selfie and enjoy the easy downhill walk back to our cars.

I fall quiet and listen to Emmett and Billy do what any two transgender guys do in private: compare beard growth and share how long they've been on testosterone. Emmett, clean-faced, is jealous of Billy's ample scruff. Having lasered away my facial hair long ago at great expense, I have nothing to contribute to the bro-sesh.

But the topic soon shifts back to Disney via Demi Lovato—and more specifically to *Mulan:* how every transgender guy we know loves to sing "I'll Make a Man out of You" at karaoke nights and how every transgender girl inevitably picks "Reflection," with its perfect line about wanting the mirror to show you who you are inside. We talk about being in-group stereotypes—the kind of transgender people who would unironically belt out those anthems if given a stage and a microphone, fully aware of how cheesy we sounded.

I once felt like I couldn't come out in Provo.

And now, here we are, laughing in the full Utah sun, unashamed.

What do you think of when you hear the word *Utah*?

When I tell friends who have never been here that I went

to BYU, I can practically pinpoint the second that their minds make the jump to *Big Love* or *Sister Wives*. As soon as they start to ask, "Did you ever watch…" I know that I have my work cut out for me. Many Mormons share my frustration: the faith, now fourteen million members strong, formally abandoned plural marriage in 1890. And although some tiny offshoot sects still practice it throughout the American West, the official Church of Jesus Christ of Latter-day Saints excommunicates polygamists.

But other stereotypes about Utah are harder to combat because there's more truth to them.

It's true that Utah is a deeply conservative state—and that Mormonism has a lot to do with that. Apart from Lyndon B. Johnson's historic near-sweep of the country in 1964, the last time the state's electoral-college votes went to a Democratic presidential candidate was in 1948, to Harry S. Truman. And even though you wouldn't think Mormons would back a crass, thrice-divorced New Yorker, Utahans still voted for Trump over Clinton, 45.5 percent to 27.5 percent, with Mormon Independent alternative Evan McMullin just barely cracking the 20 percent mark.[9]

It's also true that the state can function as a de facto theocracy. In 2016, the *Salt Lake Tribune* tallied the various religions of the overwhelmingly Republican state legisla-

---

9 "In Conservative Utah, Trump Underperforms, but So Does McMullin," http://www.latimes.com/world/europe/la-na-trump-utah-20161109 -story.html

ture and found that 88 percent of them were Mormon, even though only 63 percent of the state's population belongs to the Church.[10] And although the Church of Jesus Christ of Latter-day Saints has a stated position of political neutrality, it does, according to its website, "[r]eserve the right as an institution to address, in a nonpartisan way, issues that it believes have significant community or moral consequences or that directly affect the interests of the Church."[11]

Outside Utah, the Mormon Church's aggressive involvement in California's Proposition 8 campaign remains the primary example of that disclaimer's power.[12] Inside the state, it means that any new laws on heated social issues effectively must get past the Church first.

As Democratic state senator Jim Dabakis, a gay former Mormon, told the *Tribune:* "On those touchstone issues, you're beating your head against the wall if you think you can change things without first sitting down with the Church and coming to an understanding."[13]

So how do I explain the fact that Salt Lake City has an openly lesbian mayor, a major downtown street called Harvey Milk Boulevard, and a bustling gay nightlife that

---

10 "With Utah Legislature's Mormon Supermajority, Is It Representative of the People?" http://archive.sltrib.com/article.php?id=4663941&itype=CMSID

11 http://www.mormonnewsroom.org/official-statement/political-neutrality

12 "Mormons Tipped Scale in Ban on Gay Marriage," http://www.nytimes.com/2008/11/15/us/politics/15marriage.html

13 http://www.mormonnewsroom.org/official-statement/political-neutrality

seems to stun reporters from coastal newspapers such as the *Boston Globe*?[14] What can account for Utah's being the only state at its longitude with a nondiscrimination law that covers both sexual orientation *and* gender identity—or for Utah's being one of only two states to successfully repeal a prior "no promo homo" law banning the discussion of homosexuality in public schools?[15]

I don't have the answers—but Troy Williams does. He's helped make it all happen.

Troy, the executive director of the LGBT advocacy organization Equality Utah and the unofficial "gay mayor"[16] of Salt Lake City, has piercing blue eyes that pull me in like tractor beams as he greets me one afternoon in his hip and airy downtown office—a space that someone with his scrappy activist background is still getting used to.

"I came up out of the working-class grassroots where I didn't have access to money," he says. "And now I'm in this new world where I put on the suit and tie and interact with millionaires."

Back in September 2014, when Troy got the top job here, the *Tribune* described him as "vocal" and "some-

14 "Welcome to Salt Lake City, America's Super Gay, Super Cool Hipster Haven," https://www.bostonglobe.com/lifestyle/travel/2017/07/13/welcome-salt-lake-city-america-super-gay-super-cool-hipster-haven/Z7c6gkIeTDLaDBYLXgCgeJ/story.html

15 Movement Advancement Project, "Non-Discrimination Laws," http://www.lgbtmap.org/equality-maps/non_discrimination_laws

16 "Controversial Activist Named Head of Equality Utah," http://archive.sltrib.com/article.php?id=58459325&itype=CMSID

times radical"—an activist and former radio host with a "brash style" and an "in-your-face" image, who would be a "controversial" pick for a role that required "build[ing] bridges with legislators." It didn't help Troy's image with the moneyed crowd that he was one of the Capitol 13, the nickname given to a group of activists who were arrested earlier that year for blocking entry to a committee hearing during a pro-LGBT protest at the Utah statehouse. How was this spiky-haired firebrand going to sit through polite meetings with Church leaders?

"They had to sort of corral me a little bit," Troy jokes, remembering the early days, "because I was a little bit more strident of an activist and a little bit more on the radical side of things."

But he proved to Equality Utah's board of directors that he could indeed put on his Sunday best and go be a "gay missionary" up at the State Capitol.

The following January—after Equality Utah had secured an ally in a Mormon Republican state senator named Steven Urquhart—top Church leaders made the surprise announcement that they would "support legislation where it is being sought to provide protections in housing, employment, and some other areas where LGBT people do not have protections," so long as "religious freedom was not compromised."[17]

---

17 "Mormon Leaders Call for Laws That Protect Religious Freedom," http://www.mormonnewsroom.org/article/church-news-

From my computer two thousand miles away, I was suspicious, seeing the announcement as a halfway step toward full equality. But Troy saw an opportunity to do something big.

In any other state, cutting a deal that leaves room for "religious freedom"—which is already protected by the Constitution—might be dangerous. That phrase is so often a dog whistle for outright bigots seeking a license to discriminate. But Troy, with his intimate understanding of both Mormonism and Utah, didn't think that was what the Church was after in this case.

"Mormons have never fallen on the sword of wedding-cake bakers and photographers—that's never been their concern," Troy explains, referring to the religious freedom debates that have cropped up in the aftermath of same-sex marriage.

Troy has a point: Mormons tend to fall somewhere between white evangelical Christians and mainline Protestants on LGBT issues.[18] They don't *always* meaningfully diverge from the fundamentalist organizations that seem hellbent on punishing queer people for simply existing, as the Church's involvement in California's Proposition 8 proves. But there is a reason Church leaders such as Apostle Dallin H. Oaks criticized Kentucky

---

conference-on-religious-freedom-and-nondiscrimination
18 "Attitudes on Same-Sex Marriage by Religious Affiliation and Denominational Family," https://www.prri.org/spotlight/attitudes-on-same-sex-marriage-by-religious-affiliation-and-denominational-family/

county clerk Kim Davis for refusing to grant marriage licenses to same-sex couples in 2015: members may have strong and often regressive opinions about LGBT people, but lately they aren't quite as mean-spirited about turning those views into law as some other religious groups seem to be.[19]

Even back in 2008, when top Mormon leaders were beating the drum on Proposition 8, a vocal contingent of members went public with their discomfort at watching the Church double down on this issue.[20] And today, 52 percent of Mormons oppose refusing service to gay people based on religious beliefs[21]—as compared to 42 percent of white evangelicals.[22]

"Don't get me wrong, there's bigotry and racism and sexism and patriarchy and all of these things, but Mormons in their hearts are kind people," Troy says. "I always felt like this culture war was something that they reluctantly took on here. Like, Mormons love musical theater and they love Les Misérables and they love ballroom dancing."

19 "Mormons Say Duty to Law on Same-Sex Marriage Trumps Faith," https://www.nytimes.com/2015/10/23/us/mormons-still-against-same-sex-unions-take-a-stand-against-kim-davis.html

20 "Mormons Divided on Same-Sex Marriage Issue," https://www.npr.org/templates/story/story.php?storyId=96405866

21 "Mormons Are Changing Their Tune on Same-Sex Marriage," https://religionnews.com/2017/06/27/mormons-are-changing-their-tune-on-same-sex-marriage/

22 "Most American Religious Groups Support Same-Sex Marriage, Oppose Religiously Based Service Refusals," https://www.prri.org/spotlight/religious-americans-same-sex-marriage-service-refusals/

But drafting a nondiscrimination law that would pass muster with the Mormons still wasn't easy—despite their endearing affinity for certain pillars of gay pop culture.

Troy describes the early-2015 negotiation process as the "most stressful forty-five days of my life"—a "big, epic compromise" that "could have fallen apart at any moment." Equality Utah was willing to make some concessions, such as exempting nonprofit organizations with religious affiliations from the bill,[23] in order to get vital LGBT protections passed, but they weren't willing to compromise on *who* within that acronym would be covered.

"We were very adamant that if we were going to move forward it was gay folks moving side by side with trans folks and there wasn't going to be a negotiation about that—that we are all in this together and we're crossing the finish line together," Troy tells me—an admirable stance considering how often the mainstream LGBT rights movement has left the T in the dust.

The Mormon Church, Troy recalls, also drew some uncrossable lines in the sand, among them exempting BYU student housing from the bill's prohibition on housing discrimination. But giving the Mormons a few thousand rental units in order to get hundreds of thousands of units covered statewide seemed like the right thing to do, Troy reasoned.

---

23 "Utah 'Compromise' to Protect LGBT Citizens from Discrimination Is No Model for the Nation," http://www.slate.com/blogs/outward /2015/03/18/gay_rights_the_utah_compromise_is_no_model_for _the_nation.html

Attorneys talked to attorneys ad nauseam. LGBT activists and state legislators worked their way through rounds of revisions. The first draft of the bill, Troy tells me, was "awful and we really had to fight over it," but by the end of the process, all parties agreed on a single piece of proposed legislation: Senate Bill 296. They called a press conference.

And then there was Troy Williams of the Capitol 13, the spunky ex-Mormon upstart everyone had doubted, shaking hands with two Mormon apostles—two of the twelve most powerful men in the religion standing shoulder to shoulder with an openly gay activist.

"This had never ever happened in the history of Mormonism *ever*," Troy says.

He keeps a photo of that encounter in his office, alongside a photo of the moment in March 2015 when Mormon Republican governor Gary Herbert signed SB 296. "Utah—yes, Utah—passes landmark LGBT rights bill" was the headline the *Washington Post* used, as if it should be a surprise that this happened[24]—and on paper, I suppose it was a bit of a shock.

But if you understand Utah like Troy Williams understands Utah, it makes perfect sense.

---

24 "Utah—Yes, Utah—Passes Landmark LBGT Rights Bill," https://
www.washingtonpost.com/news/morning-mix/wp/2015/03/12
/utah-legislature-passes-landmark-lgbt-anti-discrimination-bill
-backed-by-mormon-church/?utm_term=.2ed0e9103f9d

⋆　　⋆　　⋆

When I ask Jeannie what Encircle means to her, she says simply, "Home."

I meet the nineteen-year-old by chance, sitting around the wood-slat kitchen table in the Provo LGBT youth and family center, while I drink a Diet Coke. She has a fresh buzz cut, a long hot pink wig in her hands, and an angelically round face that breaks out into a goofy smile whenever she finds an excuse to talk about *Doctor Who*—and believe me, she *frequently* finds an excuse to talk about *Doctor Who*. I immediately want to be her friend.

*Home* is the right word for our setting. Encircle feels like home in part because it used to be one—a historic two-story Victorian house built around 1891 that has been lovingly redone.[25] The kitchen is stocked with sodas and snacks, every *Harry Potter* book ever published can be found on the shelves, and the rugs are so thick they practically compel you to take your shoes off, sit down, and play a board game. The second story has rooms for hanging out, private offices for low-cost therapy sessions, and a full bathroom for anyone who doesn't have access to a shower.

But one of the best parts of Encircle is its location:

---

25 "Encircle Home in Downtown Provo to Bring Services to LGBT Youth and Families," http://www.heraldextra.com/news/local/central/provo/encircle-home-in-downtown-provo-to-bring-services-to-lgbt/article_3735eedd-adca-5bb6-a2a1-260a9c0d90a7.html

looking out through the original windows, which are lined with stained glass in a pattern reminiscent of a rainbow, you can see the downtown Mormon Temple across the street. "No sides, only love" is the Encircle motto, meaning they open their doors to believers and nonbelievers alike.

"I don't know where I would be if this place didn't exist," Jeannie tells a newcomer to Encircle when we first meet. "I probably would have been on the streets."

Later, when Billy and I get the chance to catch up with her privately, we learn exactly how this place saved her. Jeannie tells us that she left home when her uncle—also her landlord—saw her Pride swag, called her a "gay freak," and told her to get out. She subsequently dropped out of high school and, for the time being, sleeps at a local homeless shelter for women and children. She has spent almost every day at Encircle since it opened in February 2017.

Like Jeannie, a disheartening 40 percent of homeless youth in Utah are LGBT, which places the state on the upper end of national estimates for that same figure.[26] And 60 percent of homeless youth in the state, like Jeannie, come from Mormon homes.[27] Jeannie identifies as lesbian and as bi-gender. "One half of me is female and the other is male," she explains to me. It hurts me to

---

26 "LGBTQ Youth," https://www.equalityutah.org/issues/lgbt-youth

27 "Program Aims to Stop Suicide, Homelessness in LBGT Mormon Youth," http://archive.sltrib.com/article.php?id=57682784&itype =CMSID

think that anyone ever looked at Jeannie and reduced the rich complexity of her identity to an ugly slur—and then made her a part of these crushing statistics.

Because anyone who sends Jeannie packing is missing out.

During one of several afternoons Billy and I spend at Encircle, we learn that Jeannie has two drag personae: one named Pixie Blush ("more girly and very pink," hence the wig) and the other named Golden ("more shimmery and Hollywood glam"). She has eclectic taste in music and wants to save enough money to buy a computer so she can start her own radio station, which would apparently alternate between playing the musical comedy group Ninja Sex Party and Canadian harpist Loreena McKennitt. She has made friends here—and hopefully ones who are more familiar with her favorite Tumblr rabbit holes and CW show fandoms than I am.

Many obstacles stand between Jeannie and ever getting out of Utah. She has no state ID, for one. And besides, she tells me, her "life is total crap at the moment." But even if she could get out, she's not sure she'd want to.

"I'd lose this place," she says. "And I don't want to lose this place."

Over the course of a week in Provo, Billy and I fall into a pattern, coming to Encircle at the start of every day to meet new people before going on an early-evening hike. But every time we show up to the LGBT center expecting to hang out for an hour or two, we end up staying for five.

The first afternoon I knock on the door of the center, I happen upon a program in the kitchen for parents of LGBT children called Lunch with Lisa, hosted by marriage and family therapist Lisa Hansen.[28] I want to sneak away and give the group their privacy but before I know it, I'm being invited to sit down, handed a rainbow bracelet, and offered a sub: "White or wheat?"

I listen as these parents talk about loving their kids even if they don't fully understand them, about remaining committed to both their faith *and* their families. I tell them that I wish there had been a group like this near my parents five years ago. Maybe my relationship with them would have healed faster than it did if we had all gone to Encircle.

As soon as the group meeting ends, a middle-aged Mormon man from the group pulls me aside.

"You're road tripping," he confirms.

"Yes."

"Do you need any money?" he asks, his face knotted in concern.

When I tell him that I'm all set, he tells me that he "just wanted to be sure you weren't shoestringing it." I am dumbfounded by how quickly he leaped to my aid.

I am starting to remember the fondness I had for Mormons—the fondness that Emmett and Troy still have

---

28 https://encircletogether.org/lunch-with-lisa/

for this religion in their own different ways. When Mormons are kind, they are extraordinarily kind, exhibiting the sort of Christlike generosity that stops you in your tracks.

This place was built on that same generosity. As the *Huffington Post* reported, Encircle has wealthy Mormon backers such as former San Francisco 49ers quarterback Steve Young; his philanthropist wife, Barb; and Skullcandy cofounder Holly Alden. Alden bought the house and rents it to Encircle executive director Stephanie Larsen, also a Mormon, for one dollar a month.[29] With lower overhead costs, more attention can be paid to the space itself. (I've been in LGBT centers that feel like a doctor's office waiting room; Encircle feels like the house of the friend who you always hoped would invite you over after school.)

Another day here, I spot a gaggle of queer and transgender teenagers with awesome undercuts—one of them wearing a vintage *Jurassic Park* T-shirt I wish I could have for myself—hanging out around the kitchen counter, listening to Bonnie Tyler's "Holding Out for a Hero," as if they could get any cooler. I'm too intimidated to approach them—I'd feel a bit like that famous Steve Buscemi "How do you do, fellow kids?" GIF—but one night Billy and I end up sitting in the exact spot on the carpet where a con-

---

29 "LGBT Center to Open Its Doors Across from Mormon Temple in Utah," http://www.huffingtonpost.com/entry/lgbt-center-to-open-its-doors -across-from-mormon-temple-in-utah_us_5845ddfee4b02f60b02476e1

tingent of teens decides to play the card game B.S., which non-Mormons may know by a more profane name.

They are so beautifully, effervescently happy, giddily asking each other their names and pronouns as a simple matter of course while Kyle, an older volunteer, deals the deck. Some of the kids have obvious tells when they bluff; others boldly claim that they're throwing down three jacks and stare me down, daring me to defy them. We sit on the shaggy rug, shedding cards, taunting each other and just being loud. They act like it's their house because it *is* their house.

A kid named Jay asks me how old I am, and when I admit I'm thirty, he yells, exasperated, "I am literally fifteen years old!"

Everyone cackles, but I'm not even a little bit mad at being made to feel ancient; I'm just glad they have found such joy and camaraderie so early in life. They are already using vocabulary I didn't learn until I was in my twenties: "asexual," "pansexual," "gender fluid"—the kind of terms that help people make sense of otherwise inchoate feelings and experiences. And because these kids have one another and this place, they will be spared the loneliness I felt here.

One day, they will probably *miss* Provo. Imagine that.

After cards that afternoon it is time for arts and crafts, because if there's anything people from Mormon backgrounds love, it's *activities*. An Encircle volunteer teaches us how to make carousel books using scissors, card stock, glue sticks, and, of course, our imaginations. As she circles the room, inspecting our work, she counsels us to make firm but gentle creases when folding: "Don't try to make the paper be something that it's not."

"Relatable," someone fires back.

And whenever I catch a glimpse of the Temple outside the window, I feel like Alice through the looking glass. I feel like I must have conjured up an unbelievable wish-fulfillment version of Provo—like I'm going to wake up and it will be 2007 and I will roll out of bed onto a pile of empty Del Taco bags and none of this will have been real. But Encircle is concretely *here*, built on sturdy century-old bones, as immovable as the mountains beyond the Temple's spire.

Encircle is here only because people care enough about Utah to stay—or to come back. Adam Sims, a twenty-five-year-old gay Utahan and natural-food-store worker who volunteers at Encircle in his spare time, tells me in the living room one day that he was born here and never wants to move.

"Almost anywhere can become a home," he says, "so why expend extreme amounts of energy trying to chase something that I can create here?"

Before he left the Mormon Church, Adam served a mission in New York City and still remembers the thrill of coming home by plane to Utah's more striking natural topography.

"After two years of not seeing these mountains, I looked down out of the window and was just blown away," he remembers. "It took my breath away to see something so huge, so massive."

He hikes every weekend with a group of friends of varying religions and political stances. Why would he bother moving to a more expensive and less beautiful place?

Encircle intern Jacob Cook, who becomes a fast friend to Billy and me after we meet him in the living room one afternoon, is an ex-Mormon from Chicago who thought he would never come back to Provo after leaving the Church. ("Oh, hell no" are his exact words when I ask if he ever pictured himself back here.) The last time he was in Utah, Jacob was training to be a missionary at the same center where I once memorized barely enough Mandarin for my own mission.

I came home on medical leave six months into my service, but Jacob wound up staying in the closet for ten excruciating months of proselytizing. The first person he came out to was his mission president—the rough equivalent of an army general for Mormon missionaries.

"Something hit me one day and I was like, I'm not even being honest to myself; how can I be honest to anyone for the rest of my life?" Jacob remembers.

The mission president ultimately decided to send him home so he could "work on things," which was the last thing a terrified and still-believing missionary wanted to do. ("At the time, I wasn't even comfortable with my sexuality so I was like, 'No, please let me stay!'" Jacob tells me.)

Jacob's attitude changed once he got back to Chicago. Removed from the regimented, almost militarized environment of the mission, Jacob quickly grew into the extroverted gay man he is today. The thought of him knocking on doors in a suit and tie seems far removed from the relaxed air with which he now carries himself. He feels the same discomfort that I feel being back in Provo—and then some.

"Being here and growing up Mormon, it feels like almost a triple edge: I'm ex-Mormon, I'm Hispanic, and I'm openly gay," he says. "And I cuss a lot and I like to drink and I drink coffee."

The lack of racial diversity here is indeed palpable. Provo is 84 percent white, only 15 percent Hispanic, and less than 1 percent black. Fred Bowers, a gay black Affirmation volunteer who describes himself as a "Christian in the Mormon tradition," had warned me over the phone that "most of our LGBT Mormon people of color" could be found "in D.C., in Atlanta, [or] in other places where the people of color diversity and population are greater than in Utah." *Ex*-Mormon LGBT people of color, I would imagine, clear out of Provo even quicker.

But of all the places Jacob could have spent the summer of 2017, he came here.

"I never thought I would be here in Utah as an openly gay man," he says. "But this is why I'm here: I heard about Encircle and I felt like if I could make some sort of difference, and be across from the Temple, and be in the middle of it all, and help some kids who are suffocating, then that is so life-changing and important."

Staci LaClure, a forty-seven-year-old intersex woman who was mistakenly raised male and spent twenty-five years in the Mormon Church before finally coming out as herself in 2013, tells me that she comes to Encircle for a similar reason: "After going through the things that I've gone through and having the experiences that I've had, I couldn't be authentic to myself if I couldn't help someone else."

Staci calls herself a "bonus mom" for the Encircle kids. Along with Jeannie, she is one of the staples of this place, here almost every time Billy and I show up. She tells us that being intersex is the "gray area of the Church's proclamation"—a reference to the 1995 document the Church published saying that gender was an "essential characteristic" of personhood and that "all human beings—male and female—are created in the image of God."

The Church still doesn't have any official public teachings on intersex people, and the only acknowledgment of the subject that I can locate in the remarks given by top leaders is an aside in this fiery 1974 condemnation of transgender people by former president Spencer W. Kimball: "With relatively few accidents of nature, we are born male or female. The Lord knew best. Certainly, men and women who would change their sex status will answer to their Maker."[30]

But Staci is no accident of nature. And if there is a Maker, I'm sure she's part of the plan.

As she puts it, "There's still a reason I'm here."

The leading cause of death for Utah youth is suicide.

That awful fact weighs on almost everyone I talk to during my week in Utah—whether it's Troy Williams telling me about all the queer kids who feel "cut off, exiled from their family, exiled from their religion, [and] bullied in school," or the supportive Mormon parents I meet at Encircle, many of whom say that their first reaction to finding out they had an LGBT child was to do everything in their power to keep their kid alive.

The high suicide rate is more than just a statistic—it is a stain on the state, a reminder that all the progress LGBT activists are making in Utah is worthless if the youth die before they can see it.

According to the Utah Department of Health, children ages ten to seventeen account for over 22 percent of all suicide attempts in the state, even though they constitute only 13 percent of the population. From 2012 to 2014, Utah had the eighth-highest youth-suicide rate in the

---

30 "God Will Not Be Mocked," https://www.lds.org/ensign/1974/11/god-will-not-be-mocked?lang=eng&clang=ase

country[31]—and that rate has *tripled* since 2007.[32] Since 2013, suicide has been the most common cause of death for that age group. But as of this writing, the Utah Department of Health website still makes no mention of how anti-LGBT discrimination might factor into this sudden and staggering rise.[33]

"Utah officials unsure why youth suicide rate has nearly tripled since 2007" was the Associated Press headline atop an article that did not seek any comment from local LGBT activist groups.[34] ("No, we know why" was Troy's immediate reaction to that report.) There may not be official data collection on the subject, but LGBT groups in the state have seen enough death over the past decade to realize what's happening: queer kids are killing themselves.

A seventeen-year-old transgender boy named Miles came dangerously close to doing the same.

Miles has just come out to his mother, Wendy, a few weeks before Billy and I find ourselves sitting across from them in a small furnished room off the foyer of their

---

31 Violence and Injury Prevention Program, "Suicide," http://www.health.utah.gov/vipp/teens/youth-suicide/

32 "Utah Officials Unsure Why Youth Suicide Rate Has Nearly Tripled Since 2007," http://archive.sltrib.com/article.php?id=4075258&itype=CMSID

33 "Utah Blames the Weather, Not Homophobia, for Teen Suicide Epidemic," http://www.thedailybeast.com/utah-blames-the-weather-not-homophobia-for-teen-suicide-epidemic

34 "Utah Officials Unsure Why Youth Suicide Rate Has Nearly Tripled Since 2007," http://archive.sltrib.com/article.php?id=4075258&itype=CMSID

mostly empty house in northern Utah Valley. They've just moved in—a lot of change happening all at once. The atmosphere isn't tense so much as it is raw in a way that Billy and I both recognize; we know all too well what it's like to be at this early stage with our own parents, when emotions run high and mistakes happen daily. Wendy is still getting used to talking about her transgender child, and she uses a name that Miles would later change because he thought it sounded too feminine.

"[Miles] just has so much bravery marching out into the world," she tells us, before slipping up: "She's very open—*he's* very open...I'm still getting the pronouns, so please—I'm sorry. He's been very patient with me."

Billy and I, who both came out later in life than Miles did, are floored by how quickly this Mormon mother corrects herself. Wendy, a playwright and adjunct professor at nearby Utah Valley University whom I had met a few days earlier at Lunch with Lisa, is an active member of the Church but calls herself a "pretty independent thinker for a Mormon." After Miles came out to her, Wendy went to see the leader of their local congregation and asked if he could attend Sunday classes with other young men. She was told that Miles wouldn't be able to receive the priesthood—an authority granted to young Mormon men at age twelve—but he could go to classes.

"I'm someone who pushes for change but I usually do it kind of quietly from the inside," Wendy explains. "There's two ways to make change, you know: revolution, you burn it to the ground and rebuild; or you work for change and it's slower—and you know it's going to be slower and more frustrating—but you work for change within the system."

Miles, wearing all black and a fitted baseball cap, seems shy but he clearly wants to ask Billy and me questions, mostly about how things went down with our parents: Do they use our pronouns?

"They do," I tell him. "It took them a little while to get used to it, though, for sure."

There is a magic moment early on in any transgender person's process when you can watch the burden of dysphoria being lifted off them in real time. You can see the newfound clarity in their eyes, a certain hesitance to use smile muscles that haven't been properly exercised in years. The imprint of their pain is still visible but it is fading, giving way to the delightful unfamiliarity of positive feeling. Miles is so transparently in that moment now and it feels almost sacred to be in the same room with him.

"I just feel so much happier," he tells us, slowly emerging from his shell. "Some people have been a little weird about it but most people have been really supportive and good. I just feel good about life. I want to live now."

"That's everything," adds Wendy.

When I was a depressed teenager and my parents had no idea what was wrong, my frustrated father used to tell stories about how outgoing I had been as a toddler. His go-to example: one Christmas Eve, while he was driving all four of us kids around Los Angeles to give my mom time to wrap presents, I asked him to take me to his coworkers' houses so I could sing carols—and that's exactly what I did, marching up and down the sidewalk belting out my best "Rudolph the Red-Nosed Reindeer" while my embarrassed siblings hid on the floor of the minivan.

After transitioning, that extroversion returned—and Wendy sees Miles returning to form, too.

"You're with this child your whole life and you see their unfiltered personality as a young child," she says. "So it's been really fun for me to see what I perceive as his natural personality starting to bubble back up to the surface. It's the confidence and kind of, like, *feistiness,* even. Thank goodness, you know, we all need to have some feistiness in us. I'm really happy to see it."

I've known Miles for all of an hour, but I can imagine the pain that came before; the ghosts of it still follow him into the room, even though they are losing their power.

After Miles found the courage to tell his mom that he is transgender, one of Wendy's first thoughts was, *Finally.* Finally there was an explanation for the self-harm. As Wendy herself puts it, "There was something that needed to come out." And once it did, she hoped that her unconditional love for her son would *finally* make a difference in his mental health.

"I hoped that it would be a shift and I didn't dare think or expect that it would be what it was," she tells us. "And then a month later, it's been this shift."

★    ★    ★

Trying to change Mormonism from within will probably be about as slow and frustrating as Wendy expects it to be. Ever since the Church endorsed Utah's March 2015 nondiscrimination legislation, LGBT Mormons and their allies have been on a roller-coaster ride of shifting stances.

In the fall of 2015—shortly after the landmark Supreme Court decision *Obergefell v. Hodges*—news broke that the Church would be implementing a strict new internal policy barring any child of a same-sex couple from being baptized unless that child moves out of the house and "specifically disavows the practice of same-gender cohabitation and marriage."[35] That policy—which the Church described on its website as "a firm line"[36] necessitated by the nationwide legalization of same-sex marriage—triggered what the *Guardian* described as a "wave of resignations" from the faith.[37]

Then, in 2016—as a disappointed Senator Urquhart put it—the Church "effectively snuffed out" a hate-crimes bill that would have covered religious and LGBT

35 "LDS Church Releases New Clarification About Children in Families with Same-Sex Parents," http://fox13now.com/2015/11/13/lds-church-clarifies-stance-on-children-in-families-with-same-sex-parents/

36 "Understanding the Handbook," http://www.mormonnewsroom.org/article/commentary-understanding-the-handbook

37 "Meet the Utah Lawyer Helping Thousands of Mormons Leave Their Church," https://www.theguardian.com/us-news/2015/nov/19/utah-lawyer-thousands-mormons-leave-lds-church-gay-marriage

people alike. In a statement, a Mormon spokesperson said that the Church didn't want to "alter [the] balance" established by the 2015 legislative compromise that Equality Utah had worked so hard to pass.[38] Combined with the previous year's regressive internal policy, that statement made it seem like the top brass wanted to pump the brakes on LGBT acceptance now that same-sex marriage was legal.

But then in 2017, a repeal of Utah's anti-gay "no promo homo" law easily cleared the Mormon-dominated legislature.[39] And in August, almost a month to the day after we sat down with Wendy and Miles, the Church issued a formal statement of support for the LoveLoud Festival for LGBT Youth, held in Orem—the town just north of Provo—and a staggering seventeen thousand people attended.[40] (Then, as if turning on a dime, Church leadership in September 2017 signed onto an amicus curiae brief supporting a Colorado bakery that refused to make a cake for a same-sex wedding on religious grounds[41]—

---

38 "Mormon Church Smites Hate-Crime Bill That Protects Faithful and LBGT People," http://www.thedailybeast.com/mormon-church-smites-hate-crime-bill-that-protects-faithful-and-lgbt-people

39 "Utah Says No to 'No Promo Homo' Law, but Other States Lag Behind," http://www.thedailybeast.com/utah-says-no-to-no-promo-homo-law-but-other-states-lag-behind

40 "LoveLoud Festival Draws 17,000 with Bands, Messages of Acceptance," https://www.deseretnews.com/article/865687601/LoveLoud-Festival-draws-17000-with-bands-messages-of-acceptance.html

41 "Mormon Church, Utah Senators Lend Their Support to Bakers Refusing to Make Cake for Gay Weddings," https://www.sltrib.com/news/2017/09/12/mormon-church-utah-senators-lend-their-

despite polling suggesting most members of the Church don't consider such a cause a priority.[42])

Although Church leadership is sending mixed signals, attitudes among the members are moving in the right direction, however slowly. According to the Public Religion Research Institute, 37 percent of Mormons support same-sex marriage[43]—up from 26 percent in 2015.[44]

If Miles hits a breaking point with the faith—if acceptance doesn't come fast enough for his liking—then "it is what it is," Wendy says. But so far, the mother-son pair have had positive experiences with neighbors and their congregation. And for her part, Wendy is determined to stay inside the system—in Mormonism, in Utah—and agitate in her own quiet but powerful way.

"There's going to be some things that might be tough," she admits. "But I feel like the Church and certain members are shifting and getting more educated. It's not going to be as fast or as full as we want, but it's changing."

Billy and I feel rejuvenated but also sobered by our conversation with Wendy and Miles—a window into an al-

support-to-bakers-refusing-to-make-cake-for-gay-weddings/
42 "Most Religious Americans Don't Support Protections in 'Religious Freedom' Executive Action," https://www.prri.org/spotlight/trump-religious-liberty-executive-order-lgbt-discrimination/
43 "Most American Religious Groups Support Same-Sex Marriage, Oppose Religiously Based Service Refusals," https://www.prri.org/spotlight/religious-americans-same-sex-marriage-service-refusals/
44 Ibid.

ternate past where we got the support we needed sooner than we did—so we head to a local bar called City Limits that is just barely on the right side of divey.

The crowd is a curious mix of townies, beautiful late-night weirdos, and Mormon college kids who are apparently feeling a little naughty this evening.

City Limits is one of only three bars in a town of over one hundred thousand people, so Provo's alcohol drinkers can't afford to be choosy about the company they keep. In the back of the space, beyond the requisite pool tables and the curved bar top, is a booth-lined dance floor that abruptly gives way to a small carpeted stage. The only backdrop is a glass block window straight out of 1986, with neon Budweiser and Heineken signs hanging overhead.

In other words, the perfect setting for a drag show.

A skinny young man wearing a crop top and suspenders circles the dance floor, collecting tips in a pitcher on behalf of the performers—who, we are told, cannot handle money directly under some puritanical statute that would consider them to be sex workers if they did. I would much rather hand my spare cash directly to Victor Vincent—a goateed drag king whose signature move is slinging his prop electric guitar over his shoulder and thrusting at the audience during performances of Def Leppard's "Pour Some Sugar on Me" and Maroon 5's "Sugar"—but I throw my spare bills in the pitcher anyway.

Mr. Vincent's lyrically linked song choices alone are enough to make him my favorite performer—second only to a drag queen named Jackie Ohh Starr, who brings up her partner for a bondage-themed number, spanked to the tune of Rihanna's "S&M." (By day, I later learn, Ms. Starr is James Bunker, a longtime Provo resident and president of Provo Pride.[45])

Jacob Cook shows up partway through the evening, gives us both hugs, asks when we're leaving Utah for the next state, and hugs us again when he finds out that the answer is "soon."

I once couldn't wait to get out of Provo, but now I am sad to leave. I wish I had found a place like Encircle or a friend like Jacob back in 2007. Maybe if I had looked harder—or maybe if I had figured myself out faster—I could have found a queer niche in Provo ten years earlier than I did. Who knows how many LGBT people watching this very drag show were also here back then, wandering this lonely valley in the dark?

The fear and self-hate that so many LGBT people experience while growing up keep us from finding our fellow travelers in queerdom precisely when we need them the most.

But on our way back to the hotel after midnight, I look over at Billy and realize how lucky I am to have finally

---

45 http://www.provopride.org/about-us-2/

found my lifelines. I turn into the drive-through of the same Del Taco that I practically lived on during my lowest low in Provo.

"Hungry?" I ask him.

I don't know what exactly prompts me to do it, but one evening at Encircle—instead of waiting around for the tempting batch of peanut butter cookies that just went into the oven—I ask Billy if we can leave. Then I plug Y Mountain into the GPS.

Back during my doldrum days at BYU, when I used to look up at the Wasatch Mountains for a reprieve from depression, that gigantic Y was a reminder that my life still revolved around the Church-owned school. It *watched* me—as paranoid as that sounds. The hillside letter was a sort of surveillance camera, a panopticon with a view of the whole valley, reminding me no matter where I stood that an unrepentant violation of the Honor Code could get me expelled.

So maybe I just want to step on the damn thing. Perhaps it's nothing more than a childish impulse to stamp my feet that prompts me to finally hike the Y.

But I could use the exercise anyway.

Billy and I consult the map at the trailhead, which promises a strenuous uphill climb with thirteen switchbacks and a thousand-foot elevation gain. Already panting by the time we reach switchback number one, we briefly consider going back to the hotel, but the promise of a sunset view propels us forward. Whoever maintains the trail must know that we need motivational assistance, too, because the signs posted at the switchbacks each bear a different encouraging message, reminding us to "keep calm" or that "you can do it!" (*Can we, though?* I wonder.)

The only thing to count besides the number of switchbacks are the young heterosexual Mormon couples who pass us by, their sweaty palms glued together, determined to hold hands for the entire hike. I admire their persistence and covet their fitness. But they don't make me feel out of place the way they used to; I feel I have just as much right to this path as anyone else.

As we lean into the trail, I think about how social change happens—about how LGBT people can reclaim a city like this, 88 percent Mormon as it is. There are no headline-making, Stonewall-level events I could cite as turning points for Provo on that front. Shortly before my visit, Encircle was pointedly disinvited from the Fourth of July parade at the last minute,[46] sparking justifiable outrage and attracting a bit of national media coverage.[47] That's the most noticeable recent incident on record. And

---

46 "LBGTQ Group Uninvited from Provo's Freedom Festival Parade," http://fox13now.com/2017/07/04/lgbtq-group-un-invited-from-provo-city-parade/

47 "LGBT Youth Center Booted from Provo, Utah, Independence Day Parade," https://www.advocate.com/youth/2017/7/04/lgbt-youth-center-booted-provo-independence-day-parade

yet I feel ten times more comfortable being openly queer in Provo than I would have ten years ago.

Social progress, I realize, happens not just through the sort of revolutionary actions that generate Oscar-baiting biopics but through the underestimated power of conversation—through small exchanges of generosity and goodwill, through questions asked in good faith, through love expressed with no preconditions or expectations of return. I have spent a week doing nothing but talk to people. But talking is far from nothing. Words are the literal stuff of change.

In Matthew, Jesus tells his disciples that words can alter geography, that "if ye have faith as a grain of mustard seed, ye shall say unto this mountain, Remove hence to yonder place; and it shall remove; and nothing shall be impossible unto you."

I wish I could stand here on this mountain overlooking Provo, shout, Whitmanesque, "Homophobia and trans-phobia, begone!" and instantly rid this place of prejudice. But almost every word uttered at the Encircle house, whether spoken in a support group or in a pickup game of B.S., chips away at that bigotry.

The truth is that you could scour a transcript of every-thing said between Wendy and Miles—or between my own Mormon parents and myself—and you probably wouldn't find any outstanding moments of reconciliation worthy of an indie melodrama. But you would almost certainly find a thousand inconsequential little talks that together add up to something more substantial, the same way a thousand footfalls up a mountain can suddenly make the ground seem far away.

The sky starts to drizzle, cooling Billy and me down by a couple of degrees—enough to make the remainder of the hike more tolerable. But still, when we reach switchback number ten and are faced with the choice between hiking to the bench at the bottom of the Y and taking another two uphill turns to the top of the giant insignia, we unanimously vote "bench."

Once there, I turn and look at the now-miniaturized city below, a tree-covered grid that begins where the browning grass at the base of the mountain ends. Beyond it, the sloping sun punctures the clouds with such force that it looks like it's lighting an oval patch of Utah Lake on fire.

I can see everything from here: the birthday-cake Temple, the Missionary Training Center, the library where I took my first trembling steps into a women's restroom, the parks where I walked with girlfriends of yesteryear, and all the lonely roads I drove at night, dysphoric and depressed. I can see it all—a staggering mise-en-scène of emotional trauma and compounded life history that seems to be happening simultaneously, like traffic in a long-exposure photograph. I am at once wiping makeup off my face in the Albertsons parking lot and unbuttoning my suit jacket to walk to my next Mandarin lesson, falling in love and getting dumped, praising God and embracing a life of sin.

But for the first time, these memories feel muted—as if they belong to somebody else. In a sense, I suppose, they do. That young man down in Provo seems like a Playmobil person now, darting pointlessly around the perfectly square city blocks, too scared to see beyond that grid, let alone to imagine hiking the Y one day as a woman.

I feel not just pride in who I have managed to become but a deep certainty that Happy Valley will soon live up to its name more than it does today—because somewhere down there, although I can't quite spot the block, queer youth are sharing freshly baked peanut butter cookies with LGBT-friendly Mormons right across the street from the downtown Temple.

I know there are still kids like Jeannie down there right now for whom it all still feels so big: the Church, the Temple, this Y, the city. I hope that one day they can see it this small.

The sun dips below the cloud cover and starts to climb up the slope, bringing the sagebrush to life, differentiating the brown of the grass into various shades of amber, yellow, and orange. I am dazzled in a way that makes me believe—if not in God, then at least in goodness.

Emmett told me that the mountains saved his life. From up here, I can see why.

# Chapter 3

# TEXAS OUTRAGEOUS

Gay marriage is not fine with me.
> —*former* Dancing with the Stars *contestant*
> *Rick Perry*[1]

The last time I was in Texas, I was on my way to get a vagina.

Corey and I were driving from Atlanta to San Francisco via Los Angeles, cutting across the South on the interstate in three brutal days so we would have time for a more leisurely trip up the Pacific Coast Highway right before the operation. My impatience made the Lone Star State wider. "We're *still* in Texas?" I'd whine as we passed yet another Highway 287 ghost town.

Back then—in April of the now-innocent-seeming year of 2014—I had no idea that Republican-controlled states like Texas would soon develop an incurable obsession with my genitals.

---

1 "Texas Gov. Perry: 'Gay Marriage Is Not Fine with Me,'" http://political
ticker.blogs.cnn.com/2011/07/28/texas-gov-perry-gay-marriage-is
-not-fine-with-me/

At the time, the GOP was still fighting a losing battle against same-sex marriage in order to keep their evangelical base rallied and their fund-raising coffers full. Transgender people weren't on their radar the way we are today. *Time* magazine hadn't yet declared "The Transgender Tipping Point" with a photo of Laverne Cox on the cover.[2] Film and TV were still in the courting phase of their love affair with women like me. Sure, we were less visible back then, but I now know that visibility is often the forerunner of backlash more than it is a sign of true progress.

In the naïveté of my mid-twenties, though, I thought that all my rights would fall into place like dominoes: I would get the long-anticipated surgery, quietly update the gender markers on my identity documents, marry Corey whenever it became legal, and just *live*.

Three years later, Donald Trump is president, I have spent most of my reporting career writing about the endless onslaught of idiotic bathroom bills, and I'm back in Texas because state lawmakers are trying—*again*—to force women like me to use the men's room and bearded men like Billy to use the ladies' room.

Billy and I head for Texas on July 15, 2017, because the state legislature is considering Senate Bill 3—a bill that would require transgender people to use restrooms in

---

2 "The Transgender Tipping Point," http://time.com/135480/transgender-tipping-point/

public schools and government buildings that match our birth-certificate gender markers.[3] Were it not for bigoted lieutenant governor Dan Patrick, the legislature wouldn't even be in session now.

Patrick, who has called transgender-bathroom protections in schools "the beginning of the end of public education as we know it,"[4] was so hell-bent on getting SB 3 passed that he and Governor Greg Abbott forced the state legislature to return to Austin for a special summer session after it failed to pass a similar bathroom bill during the traditional legislative calendar.

That means transgender Texans don't get a summer break from defending their rights; they get Saturday detention at the statehouse instead—and I want to hang out with the cool kids.

As Billy and I drive from Dallas to Austin, we start to see ads for the legendary Texas gas-station chain Buc-ee's, famous for its house-made jerky and for the sheer size of its locations. Any given Buc-ee's looks like someone copy-pasted 7-Eleven until it filled up a football field. The billboards—all of which feature the same smiling cartoon-beaver mascot—boast about how clean the "fabulous restrooms" are. They inform us that the best two reasons to stop at Buc-ee's are "number one and number two."

---

3 "Senate Committee Passes 'Bathroom Bill' After 10 Hours of Testimony," https://www.texastribune.org/2017/07/21/watch-hundreds-texas-testify-bathroom-bill/
4 https://youtube.be/urk50A1CL4A

It's funny to me, in a sardonic way, that most people on road trips worry more about restroom cleanliness than they do about restroom safety. My top priority is not getting beaten up.

Even though I've never had a problem in a bathroom, the fear of assault is always on my mind, especially in states where bills like SB 3 are being discussed on local news and conservative talk-radio stations. As a transgender person, you never know when some self-appointed potty vigilante is going to spot you and decide to make a scene.[5]

Early on in my transition, when I was less confident in my appearance than I am now, figuring out where to go to the bathroom on a long road trip felt like planning a bank robbery. I liked one- or two-stall restrooms in chain restaurants that had enough foot traffic to feel safe but weren't so busy that there would be a line. A Starbucks or a Panera was ideal. Often I would hold it in for long stretches until I found an exit that looked promising. And as nearly a third of transgender people reported having done in the 2015 U.S. Transgender Survey,[6] I avoided food and water—even when I was hungry or thirsty—just so I would have to use the bathroom less frequently.

---

5 "Self-Appointed Bathroom Cop Catches Dallas Woman Using Women's Restroom," http://www.dallasobserver.com/news/self-appointed-bathroom-cop-catches-dallas-woman-using-womens-restroom-8259104

6 2015 U.S. Transgender Survey, http://www.transequality.org/sites/default/files/docs/usts/USTS%20Full%20Report%20-%20FINAL%201.6.17.pdf

When I did find the right spot, I was all business, in and out of there like lightning: no fixing my hair in the mirror, no waiting around to use a frustratingly slow hand dryer, nothing.

Nowadays I don't think twice about pulling into Buc-ee's for a pit stop. We fill up the big SUV that we have rented for the Texas leg—"When in Rome," right?—and walk into a gas-station convenience store the size of a large supermarket. It is breathtaking. If Willy Wonka de-hydrated meats for a living, his factory would look like the inside of this place: an endless supply of beef jerky on one side, carousels full of beaver-themed Buc-ee's mer-chandise on the other, and seemingly every beverage known to man stored in school bus–length fridges along the walls.

In the bathroom, I do what any other decent woman who cares about her fellow women would do: try to find a toilet that *hasn't* already been ruined by a hoverer, sit down on the goddamn seat, pee, and leave. The bath-rooms at Buc-ee's are indeed as advertised: sparkly clean, with stall doors that run almost floor to ceiling—a fea-ture that reportedly makes the gas station a favorite stop for Lou Weaver, the Transgender Programs Coordinator at Equality Texas.[7] Being transgender turns you into

---

7 "The Deal with Transgender People and Bathrooms," http://www.houstonchronicle.com/local/gray-matters/article/Transgenders-and-bathrooms-6613673.php

something of a restroom connoisseur—the Yelp Elite Squad of urination.

I think about it sometimes while I'm peeing: how bizarre it is that some people are afraid of me—or at least the *idea* of me, a caricature that they've been fed through propaganda. I don't feel like the "beginning of the end" of anything.

I'm a person, not the harbinger of some cultural apocalypse.

Intellectually, I can tell myself these bathroom bills are the product of cynical backroom scheming: when same-sex marriage became legal nationwide in 2015, anti-LGBT hate groups needed a new scapegoat to stay relevant and keep raising money. It's not a coincidence that there were over double the number of anti-transgender bills filed in state legislatures in 2016 as there were in 2015:[8] when you're fighting a lucrative culture war, it's a savvier choice to simply change the target than to surrender.

But when I remember that I'm not just a pawn on a political chessboard but a flesh-and-blood human being, the prevalence of bills like SB 3—and the persistence of politicians like Patrick who try to pass them—feels surreal, and far from the easy future I once anticipated.

By the time Billy and I are able to tear ourselves out of Buc-ee's an hour later, we have both bought T-shirts with

---

8 "State Legislation Targets Trans Community Like Never Before," http://www.thedailybeast.com/state-legislation-targets-trans-community-like-never-before

that grinning mascot on them, half a pound of turkey jerky, a bag of something crunchy called "beaver nuggets," and two bottles of the sparkling Mexican mineral water Topo Chico. We sit in the car together, washing down the peppery jerky with long pulls of the fizzy drink. I'll have to pee again before we get to Austin.

Dan Patrick will have to deal with it.

When my waffle comes out of the iron at the Austin Best Western in the shape of Texas, I feel blessed, like I found Jesus Christ on my toast.

*I must not have used enough batter,* I think, as I rush my plate over to Billy so that he, too, can witness this golden, griddled sign from above.

But upon closer inspection, I realize that the waffle maker itself is Texas-shaped—and, with some web searching, I learn that many Texas hotels and motels use this same model. I have never been to a state as obsessed with itself as this one. Sure, other states have "pride," but I have never eaten a Vermont-shaped waffle. Just saying.

We are up early enough for hotel breakfast on July 18 so we can protest the beginning of Dan Patrick's special session. Transgender bathroom rights aren't the only thing on the chopping block this summer: Planned Parenthood funding and health insurance coverage for abortions are also being threatened. Meanwhile, progressive activists are urging the legislature to use the special session for a nobler purpose: to repeal Senate Bill 4, a law forbidding Texas municipalities from serving as "sanctu-ary cities"—safe havens for undocumented Americans during a time of rising deportations.

As Billy and I walk up the tree-lined sidewalk that leads to the south steps of the Capitol, volunteers from half a dozen advocacy groups are handing out signs and—more impor-tant, given the hundred-degree weather—bottled water. There are signs for women's rights and signs for LGBT rights and signs for immigrant rights, with a smorgasbord of messages to choose from: "My Faith Does Not Discrim-inate," "Y'all Means Y'all," "Just Wash Your Hands," or— my favorite—"Build *This* Wall," with a line pointing to the separation between church and state.

I'm wearing a shirt that says "1987," which a stranger assumes is a political slogan. ·

"What does that mean?" she asks me.

"It's the year I was born."

The unrelenting heat hasn't deterred turnout, so it takes me a few minutes of wandering through the crowd to find the people I'm here to meet: Jess Herbst, the first openly transgender mayor in Texas history, and Am-ber Briggle, the proud cisgender mother of a transgender boy named Max. Once again, I've made the mistake of not dressing for the weather: Jess and Amber are both wearing airy, light-colored skirts; I left the hotel in black fleece-lined leggings.

Together we work our way up the steps while the scheduled speakers line up behind the podium at the top. Jess excitedly introduces me to a dizzying number of transgender Texans. Amber hands me her "Stop Bullying Trans Kids" sign and tells me to hoist it up, freeing her to hold a Transgender Pride flag and a framed photograph of Max. (*Someone* came prepared.)

The speeches begin as the sun bakes my lifted arms. Every so often the door to the Capitol opens behind us and an air-conditioned breeze rushes out of the building—but it doesn't provide enough relief to stop us from eventually relocating to the shade, where we can make more comfortable introductions.

Jess Herbst and I first bonded when I interviewed her over the phone in February 2017—shortly after she had come out as transgender in a letter to the 673-person town where she, her wife, and their two daughters have lived since 1999. That town is New Hope, Texas, a rural suburb of Dallas just north of McKinney.

A longtime city councilor before her transition, Jess became the new mayor in May 2016 when the previous mayor died of a heart attack. At that point Jess had already been taking estrogen for a year and a half, quietly coming out to her loved ones, living as herself much of the time but still presenting as male during town business.[9]

Nine months later she decided to simplify her bifur-

---

9 "The Trans Mayor of a Texas Small Town," http://www.thedailybeast.com/the-trans-mayor-of-a-texas-small-town

cated life, posting an online message to the government website and addressing it to "the citizens of New Hope."

"As your Mayor I must tell you about something that has been with me since my earliest memories," she wrote. "I am Transgender."[10]

By the time I reached out to her, Jess had already given dozens of interviews and her inbox was full of requests for more. But I said the magic word: I told her that I was also transgender.

Cisgender reporters are often so fascinated by the mere existence of transgender people that they treat us more like exotic zoo animals than human beings. They ask boilerplate questions like "When did you know?" or "How does it feel?" or the ever-popular but remarkably invasive "Do you want the surgery?" When I interview other transgender people, I treat them like equals, not science experiments. So when I got Jess on the phone, we skipped past the sensationalizing questions and just talked. I wasn't interested in the simple fact that she was transgender— whoop-de-doo, so are 1.4 million other Americans[11]—I was interested in New Hope, in her life as a member of a marginalized community in a county that chose Trump over Clinton by a margin of 56 to 39 percent.

---

10 "An Open Letter to the Citizens of New Hope," http://newhopetx.gov/important-message-from-the-mayor
11 "How Many Adults Identify as Transgender in the United States," https://williamsinstitute.law.ucla.edu/research/how-many-adults-identify-as-transgender-in-the-united-states/

Jess told me that the people of her town don't seem to care about what name she goes by or which gender pronouns she uses; they care about eliminating public eyesores, like the rusty cars sitting on cinder blocks that some residents have left on their lawns.

"Being transgender has nothing to do with my job," she told me. "The car on blocks and the house next door are way more important than what I'm wearing."[12]

When we hung up, I knew I had to meet her in person one day.

And now here she is before me, looking like she's ready to pick me up from soccer practice.

I kid, but Jess does have a maternal air about her, which makes sense because she's now a second mom to her two daughters. She has short, layered blond hair falling just above her shoulders, clear blue eyes, and expertly drawn brows. Like my actual mother, she is an Apple addict, as evidenced by the watch on her wrist—held in place by a rainbow Pride band, no less. She is gregarious and charming, instantly making me feel like I'm part of her pack of friends.

Her wife, Debbie, is decidedly more reserved—the brunette to Jess's blonde—but she still carries herself with the forceful resolve of a lifelong Texan who will not abide any more of this bathroom-bill bullshit. Debbie has lived

---

12 "The Trans Mayor of a Texas Small Town," http://www.thedailybeast.com/the-trans-mayor-of-a-texas-small-town

in New Hope since age two and knows the town even better than its famed Madame Mayor. In the year and change since Jess came out to her constituents, Debbie has become a professional at occupying the Capitol Rotunda.

I can tell from her mild impatience to get inside the statehouse that this protest is an obligation for her—not one she fulfills grudgingly, mind you, but rather a duty that she feels to protect her wife from a bill so stupid she can barely believe it's being considered.

"I'm here to write a book about LGBT organizing in red states," I tell Debbie as the last speaker wraps up and the crowd filters toward the statehouse, forming neat lines outside the doors so that we can get through the metal detectors as quickly as possible.

"Well," Debbie deadpans, "this is it."

The room-temperature air inside the Texas State Capitol is so refreshing that I wonder why this protest had an outdoor portion in the first place: Couldn't we have come straight here, to this beautiful rotunda with its terrazzo floor and its lofty domed ceiling? Back in 1955, Texas taxpayers footed a half-million-dollar bill for installing central air conditioning in this historic building, so isn't it a waste of their money, really, to sweat it out under the hot sun first? [13]

---

13 Mike Cox, *Legends and Lore of the Texas Capitol* (Stroud, UK: History Press, 2017).

But Texans are tougher than I am. They have to be.

The single word that best describes the nonsense LGBT Texans have to deal with is *still*. Texas *still* has a "no promo homo" law requiring any sex-education programs to "state that homosexual conduct is not an acceptable lifestyle and is a criminal offense."[14] Even though the state has a trillion-dollar economy, Texas *still* doesn't have employment nondiscrimination protections for LGBT workers. And Texas *still* has a law criminalizing sodomy, even though the 2003 Supreme Court decision *Lawrence v. Texas* rendered it obsolete. As the *Texas Observer* reported, every attempt to formally repeal the sodomy ban has since failed.[15]

Transgender Texans have an especially hard lot. In addition to dealing with Dan Patrick's seemingly never-ending bathroom-bill crusade, anyone born here must obtain a court order to change the gender marker on their birth certificate—a challenging process because, as the National Center for Transgender Equality notes, "some Texas officials and judges are averse to issuing" one.[16] I changed my California birth certificate with a doctor's note; a transgen-

---

14 "Utah Says No to 'No Promo Homo' Law, But Other States Lag Behind," http://www.thedailybeast.com/utah-says-no-to-no-promo-homo-law-but-other-states-lag-behind

15 "Seven Anti-LGBT Laws That Remain on Texas's Books," https://www.texasobserver.org/seven-anti-lgbt-laws-that-remain-on-texas-books/

16 National Center for Transgender Equality, https://transequality.org/documents/state/texas

der minor born in Texas would have enormous trouble doing the same—and the religious right here knows it.

That's why SB 3 aims to restrict bathroom use by birth certificate: without even using the word *transgender*, the Republican-controlled legislature can effectively single out kids like Amber Briggle's little boy, Max.

The Rotunda quickly fills with people and sound. The crowd turns toward the center of the room—marked by the star-shaped state seal on the floor—and the chants begin: "We are together as one Texas resistance!" followed by "Hey hey, ho ho, hate has got to go!" And then in Spanish: *"¡Texas, escucha! ¡Estamos en la lucha!"* ("Texas, listen! We are in the fight!") There's a woman in a blue dress standing on the star whom I eventually recognize as Wendy Davis, a former Democratic gubernatorial candidate and Texas state legislator best known outside the state for her eleven-hour-long filibuster against abortion restrictions in 2013.

Asked about Dan Patrick's attempt at a bathroom bill back in 2016, Davis said, "I've seen bad things die a quiet death; I'm hoping this will be among them."[17]

If what Billy and I are witnessing now is indeed the *last* death of the horror-movie villain that is the Texas bathroom bill, it is a decidedly noisy final blow.

---

17 "Wendy David Predicts Legislature Would Kill Transgender Bathroom Bill," http://www.mystatesman.com/news/state--regional-govt--politics/wendy-davis-predicts-legislature-would-kill-transgender -bathroom-bill/KwW6vPBefNzNNl0Mcy84gJ/

This rotunda is renowned for its acoustics. The website for the Texas Senate recommends that kids "clap [their] hands while standing in the middle of the Rotunda" and listen to the sound bounce off the ceiling. *Austin Monthly* claims that "if you whisper something while standing in the center of the main rotunda, people in the outer passages can hear you."[18] And a veteran Capitol tour guide told *Texas Monthly* that the "perfect echo" in the middle of the room still shocks him after decades on the job: "As a matter of fact," he said, "I'll walk through there sometimes and forget about it while I'm talking and then boom!"[19]

So just imagine what the room sounds like when a hundred protesters are shouting in unison, at a volume that communicates how much they have on the line.

The chants grow louder. The fists pump faster and some people even start dancing to the rhythm. Soon the echoes have echoes. The strength of this group is thunderous, deafening. I have never encountered politicians more determined to hurt my community, but then again I have never been surrounded by people more determined to protect that community. Rock icon Janis Joplin once said that "Texas is okay if you want to settle down and do your own thing quietly, but it's not for outrageous people." I

---

18 "Say a Famous Saying in the Capitol's Echo Chamber," http://www .austinmonthly.com/AM/January-2016/Bucket-List-Say-a-famous- saying-in-the-Capitols-echo-chamber/
19 "Smitherman's 'Independent Texas,'" https://www.texasmonthly.com /the-culture/giving-a-tour-of-the-capitol/

wish she were alive to see these beautiful, outrageous queers. We are as powerful as Dan Patrick is awful.

"We do everything big in Texas: bigotry *and* love," Amber had told me before I arrived. "We got them both in spades."

She's right. A recurring theme in comic-book movies is the idea that superheroes and supervillains need each other. Whether it's Heath Ledger's Joker in *The Dark Knight* telling Batman, "You complete me!" or Gene Hackman's Lex Luthor saying that "to commit the crime of the century, a man naturally wants to face the challenge of the century," the general idea is the same: concentrated forms of good and evil define each other through contrast.

Maybe in some cosmic sense, LGBT Texans are so resilient because they've had to survive the Tea Party—or maybe Texas bigots feel the need to be as heinous as they are because the LGBT people here are so vexatiously persistent.

But real life is not a comic book. And the fight for full equality is not entertainment.

The truth behind social conservatism in Texas is far more banal:[20] the districts are gerrymandered, the evangelical Christians are influential, and the Republican Party controls the white vote.[21]As the *Austin American-*

---

20 "America's Future Is Texas," https://www.newyorker.com/magazine/2017/07/10/americas-future-is-texas
21 "Texas: Harbinger of the Future," http://www.pbs.org/wgbh/pages/frontline/shows/architect/texas/realignment.html

*Statesman* reported, Trump beat Clinton by only 9 percent in Texas, but exit polls showed that among the state's white voters he crushed her 69 to 25. Nationally, Trump won white voters by a disappointing but less lopsided margin of 58 to 37.[22]

However they came about, the present dangers in Texas are greater than any child should have to face. For some kids in this rotunda, SB 3 could literally be a life-or-death issue: a 2016 study published in the *Journal of Homosexuality* found that, among transgender college students, experiencing "denial of access to bathrooms" was "statistically significantly associated with lifetime suicide attempt," suggesting "a distinct relationship between the stress of not being able to use bathrooms...and one's mental health."[23]

I can't decide what's worse: knowing that Republicans must be aware they are endangering people's lives when they try to pass a bathroom bill or realizing that they don't care.

As the cacophony continues, I try to convince myself that SB 3 won't pass, remembering that Joe Strauss, the Republican Speaker of the Texas House of Representatives— and an all-too-rare voice of reason on this issue—has al-

---

22 "Behind Trump's Victory: Divisions by Race, Gender, Education," http://www.pewresearch.org/fact-tank/2016/11/09/behind-trumps-victory-divisions-by-race-gender-education/

23 Kristie L. Seelman, "Transgender Adults' Access to College Bathrooms and Housing and the Relationship to Suicidality," *Journal of Homosexuality* 63, no. 10 (February 2016).

ready said, "I don't want the suicide of a single Texan on my hands."[24] But in the Trump era, you can never predict when Republican moderates are going to cave to extremists.

The sound of the crowd grows so loud that my ears start to fuzz out. I slip away from Jess and company to find a quiet place to sit for a minute. Why not the women's room? Half of the ladies in here are transgender; half aren't. Everybody's peeing; nothing bad is happening. I take my time, fully aware that I am using a restroom in Dan Patrick's office building.

Between all of these protests, I realize, Patrick has probably *caused* more transgender people to use restrooms in government buildings than he will ever be able to keep out. I linger for one more peaceful moment, knowing that the second I step out of this stall and through the door into the din on the other side, I'll be back in a world where my body is controversial.

"I want to come down to Austin because I want to see friends—not because of bullshit like this," Nicole Lynn Perry tells me as we walk down the stairs in the statehouse.

I strike up a conversation with Nicole, a black transgender activist from Dallas and a former Marine, after reading the eye-catching slogan on her T-shirt: TRANSGENDER VETERAN: I FOUGHT FOR YOUR RIGHT TO HATE ME.

---

24 "America's Future Is Texas," https://www.newyorker.com/magazine/2017/07/10/americas-future-is-texas

Nicole served in the military in what now seems like another life: in 2009, three weeks after she turned twenty-one and shortly before being stationed in Japan, a pre-transition Nicole married a straight cisgender woman whom she would be with for five years.

Nicole says she stayed deep in the closet during her time in the Marines because it was a "male-dominated service and any sign of weakness gets you looked down upon." She left at the end of her active-duty contract in 2013 with an honorable discharge so that she could transition. At the time, transgender service members were not allowed to serve openly. ("If I'm wanting to be myself, I'm going to have to get out of here," Nicole reasoned. "I can't stay in.")

And then, to make a long story short, Nicole transitioned, her marriage ended, and now she is a polyamorous pansexual transgender woman bringing the same discipline she had as a Marine to her activism.

Like so many of the people I meet at the State Capitol, Nicole sees protesting here as an almost unavoidable part of living in Texas, like dealing with the summer heat. Indeed, the only good thing about an anti-LGBT bill like SB 3 is how many queer people converge on an already progressive city like Austin to protest it. After the bullshit, there's always time for friendship.

Jess, Debbie, Nicole, Amber, Billy, and I all head to Scholz Garten, a downtown German pub dating back to 1866, for some post-protest beverages. At my urging, we also order something called a "giant Bavarian pretzel" served with sides of queso, garlic butter, and spicy mustard.

Sitting across from Amber, I think about how much her life must have changed for her to find herself at a table like this. "I'm a cisgender middle-class white lady who lives in suburban Dallas—I don't really fit the bill, ya know," she tells me.

Amber and her husband, Adam, moved to Texas in 2009. She grew up in the Upper Midwest; Adam is from Colorado. Their son, Max, now nine years old, transitioned from female to male when he was nearly seven. In photos they look like the quintessential all-American heterosexual picket-fence family: square-jawed husband, blond wife, a couple of cute kids. Indeed, one of the unexpected and wonderful side effects of transgender people coming out at younger ages is that they bring loved ones into the queer fold who might never have expected to become a part of it.

Amber tells me that she's been blown away by the welcome she's received in this state as the parent of a transgender child: "I can't really compare it to anywhere else that I've lived, but I'm really encouraged and uplifted by the community we have in Texas. You saw today—on a workday in the middle of summer—how many people were out there."

Max began exhibiting "weird behaviors" as early as preschool, Amber says—or, at least, they were weird to her without any context. When he was two years old—

and going by a feminine name—Amber praised him for being a "good girl" and he shouted, "Mom! I not a girl! I a boy and I like Spider-Man!" At age four, he asked: "Mom, can scientists turn me into a boy?"

That question sent Amber on a desperate hunt through mommy blogs, looking for anything that could help explain how Max was behaving. But most posters used euphemisms like "gender creative" to describe kids who could be transgender. There were almost no reliable resources to help a mother like her: she certainly didn't stumble across the American Academy of Pediatrics' full-throated statement of support for transgender youth, because it wouldn't be written until 2017.[25]

"No one was admitting their kids were transgender because that wasn't a thing a kid could be," Amber recalls.

But in the first grade, after Amber discovered that Max had been holding it in all day at school to avoid using the girls' restroom, she had a conversation with him in which he made his identity clear, and indicated that he would prefer "he" to "she."[26] The newly out boy, Amber says, "went back to school on a Monday with new pronouns and a new name and a new bathroom and he lost zero friends because kids don't give a fuck." Nor did Amber

25 American Academy of Pediatrics, https://www.aap.org/en-us/about-the-aap/aap-press-room/Pages/AAP-Statement-in-Support-of-Transgender-Children-Adolescent-and-Young-Adults.aspx

26 "Boyhood Found," http://www.dentonrc.com/news/news/2016/06/05/boyhood-found

give any fucks about how she would be perceived as a parent, immediately smoothing things over with school officials to ensure they used his new name and allowed him to use the boys' bathroom.

"It's your job to love your kid," she says. "It shouldn't be hard."

If caring for your children is a job, Amber deserves a corner office: after Max effectively came out to her, she connected with a local group for parents of transgender children, got involved with LGBT activism on a local and national scale, and became the fiercest defender of transgender youth I've ever met. It used to be the case that the LGBT community had just bears; now we've got Mama Bears too.

When Texas attorney general Ken Paxton filed a lawsuit opposing the Obama administration's inclusive guidelines for transgender restroom use in public schools, Amber invited him over for a family dinner—and he accepted.[27]

"He never misgendered Max, like even accidentally," Amber tells the table. "He was wonderful. He was everything you'd want a dinner guest to be: they brought a dessert, they told jokes. And then as they drove away—I shit you not, it was a stormy season—there was a rainbow and we were like, 'We did it!'"

---

27 "Texas Attorney General Dines with Local Mother of Transgender Child," http://www.dallasobserver.com/news/texas-attorney-general-dines-with-local-mother-of-transgender-child-8667691

But Paxton went on to support Dan Patrick's bathroom bill anyway. Amber hopes that Paxton still thinks about the evening he met Max—that the memory of that dinner is lodged in his brain somewhere, even if it didn't end up changing his behavior.

Jess, joining the conversation, says she is certain it helped.

"It is so easy to discriminate [against people] when they are not real to you," the mayor chimes in from across the table. "When they are flesh and blood, it makes a difference."

I wish that politicians treated their transgender constituents as they would want their own children to be treated—a sort of LGBT version of the Golden Rule. For now, though, I am glad we have allies like Amber in our corner. I think about what Adam Sims once said to me in the Encircle house in Provo—that "oppression and opposition can build the most beautiful connections"—and I feel lucky that I now have a transgender friend who used to be a Marine and a friend who is a mother of two in a Dallas suburb.

"I own a business, my husband is the president of our church, we own a minivan, I love Jesus and country music; I'm just a regular Texan, ya know," says Amber.

"Oh wait, you drive a minivan?" Jess fires back with feigned disgust. "You need to leave. Transgender child? That's fine. But a *minivan*?"

We all laugh. Nicole told me that she wanted to come

to Austin for friendship, not for "bullshit," and I agree—but sometimes the best friendships come from dealing with bullshit together.

The Bavarian pretzel we ordered finally arrives. It's as big as a vinyl record. God bless Texas.

"The Valley is actually *not* a valley," Natalia Rocafuerte informs me. "They just use that name to trick people to come down here."

Natalia and I are sitting together at the Green Owl Deli in McAllen, the second-largest city in the Rio Grande Valley at the southern tip of Texas.

"Down here" is an apt way to put it. To get to McAllen from Austin, you have to drive south to San Antonio and then travel 160 miles even farther south on a worn-down local highway as the traffic fades and the dragonflies martyr themselves on your windshield. And then suddenly there are palm trees and you find yourself in a cluster of low, sprawling cities along the U.S.–Mexico border that 1.3 million people call home.

A "valley" would imply mountains, or at the very least hills. But the landscape is flat.

Natalia, a fine arts student who uses the gender-neutral pronoun "they"—and who cleverly lists their gender on Facebook as "unavailable"—explains the false advertising: in the early 1900s, developers re-branded this completely mountainless South Texas floodplain as "Magic Valley" to make the real estate more appealing.[28] The "Magic" part went away; the "Valley" stuck.

Growing up right alongside the border in Brownsville, Natalia says they felt "lucky" to have a green card. Tens of thousands of people in the area are undocumented and law enforcement officers are everywhere.[29] Natalia's mother worked across the street from the Rio Grande River itself at an elementary school that would go on lockdown whenever someone was spotted wading across the water. The area is defined by the constant pressure of the Border Patrol.

"It's always boiling down here," Natalia explains. "That's the best way to express it."

With an increasingly militarized border to the south and interior border checkpoints to the north, the Rio Grande is more like a vise than a valley, trapping undocumented Americans and their loved ones in one of the country's most impoverished areas. Queer Chicana scholar Gloria Anzaldúa, who was born in nearby Harlingen in 1942, described the Rio Grande Valley in 1987 as "still struggling to survive."[30] Thirty years later, that remains the case; as the *Texas Tribune* recently re-

28 South Texas, 1905–1941," *Geographical Review* 91, no. 2 (April 2009).
29 "Estimates of Unauthorized Immigrant Population, by Metro Area, 2014," http://www.pewhispanic.org/2017/02/13/estimates-of-unauthorized-immigrant-population-by-metro-area-2014/
30 Gloria Anzaldúa, *Borderlands / La Frontera* (San Francisco: Aunt Lute Books, 1987), 90.

ported, one in three people in South Texas now live in poverty.[31]

Even sitting in this café with Natalia, ten miles north of the nearest crossing, the border *feels* as if it's right outside the window. The river courses through every conversation here, winding its way through every life.

Anzaldúa famously called the U.S.–Mexico border *"una herida abierta,"* "an open wound."

"Borders are set up to define the places that are safe and unsafe, to distinguish *us* from *them*," she wrote. "A border is a dividing line, a narrow strip along a steep edge."

But Anzaldúa also understood from personal experience that the border wasn't just a physical boundary but a socioeconomic and psychological space—a "borderland" that leaves a lingering "emotional residue" on anyone who crosses it, no matter how far away they travel.

"Living in a no-man's borderland, caught between being treated as criminals and being able to eat, between resistance and deportation, the illegal refugees are some of the poorest and the most exploited of any people in the U.S.," she wrote—and she's still depressingly right.[32]

Being queer or gender nonconforming in the Rio Grande Valley only compounds that exploitation. Al-

---

31 "Latest Census Data Shows Poverty Rate Highest at Border, Lowest in Suburbs," https://www.texastribune.org/2016/01/19/poverty-prevalent-on-texas-border-low-in-suburbs/

32 Gloria Anzaldúa, *Borderlands / La Frontera* (San Francisco: Aunt Lute Books, 1987), 4, 12.

though the area has long voted Democratic—and turned out solidly against Trump in November 2016[33]—the population is largely Catholic, still tightly wed to traditional gender roles and macho culture. There is one abortion provider in the area and it is surrounded by antichoice signs. Men here are expected to be men, Natalia says, and women women.

"I never wanted to shave my legs, and in gym class I would get teased for it because there is a very high femme standard for women down here," Natalia tells me.

Natalia remembers feeling a "little weird" at a young age, presenting as a tomboy and developing crushes on their girlfriends. The kids at school spread rumors that they were a lesbian—and, after Natalia dyed their hair blue, they were given the demeaning nickname Care Bear. But Natalia didn't have access to information that would help them make sense of their identity until they got an internet connection. Natalia eventually found "openly queer friends" in high school but didn't truly find their people until they left the Rio Grande Valley to attend college near Austin.

When Natalia comes back to visit the Valley—now a confident and self-possessed visual artist—they are as surprised as I was when I went back to Utah Valley by

---

33 "Majority of Votes for President in RGV Were Democratic," http://www.krgv.com/story/33682718/majority-of-votes-for-president-in-rgv-were-democratic

the sheer number of LGBT people who have been here all along—and how much louder they are now.

"I never allowed myself to call the Valley a home because I was never myself here," they tell me. "And coming back here, [I realize] that was kind of my choice. But it's also a different environment now."

One of the primary forces changing this Valley is Aquí Estamos, a youth-run LGBT activist organization founded in May 2015.[34] Aquí Estamos fights against wage theft, protects undocumented queer folks, and even hosts an annual Queerceañera, an LGBT-friendly dance in the spirit of a quinceañera. The day after my talk with Natalia, Billy and I head over to the MoonBeans coffee shop in the city of Pharr to meet up with one of the group's founding members: Eduardo Martinez, an affable queer bisexual man who is also, judging from his EDDIE GUER-RERO IS MY FAVORITE WRESTLER T-shirt, a big fan of the wrestler Eddie Guerrero.

The name of the organization that Eduardo helped found with local activists like Dani Morrero comes from a popular immigrant-rights chant: *"Aquí estamos / y no nos vamos / y si nos sacan / nos regresamos."* ("We're here / and we're not leaving / and if they throw us out / we'll come back.") The name is meant, in part, to serve as a reminder that there are indeed queer peo-

---

34 Aquí Estamos, http://www.aquiestamosrgv.org/about/

ple in the Rio Grande Valley—an overlooked part of the United States that, as Eduardo says, "a lot of people have heard of...through the news but don't really know exactly what it is."

As a white American who grew up on the coasts, I had never devoted much thought to the Rio Grande Valley until I became a reporter. That's the only way I knew that I should come here for *Real Queer America*. There is a queer community here as overlooked as the Valley itself.

"We don't think about the LGBTQ people in these populations, in certain populations," Eduardo says. "That's something people who maybe aren't connected don't know—that there's LGBT people here. Like, how can there not be?"

Eduardo loves it here. He loves it as much as Emmett loves Utah. He loves it so much that some people around here know him better by his punny web handle: "Pharr from Heaven." He loves the tacos, and the raspas— Mexican snow cones topped with fruit—and the accordion stylings of Esteban "Steve" Jordan, who was born in the nearby town of Elsa. Like so many queer activists born in the Valley, he loves Gloria Anzaldúa and wishes her writing were taught in local high schools. Eduardo tells me that he has "walked through all these streets so many times" and that he gets homesick whenever he leaves, which isn't very often.

Through Aquí Estamos, Eduardo and his fellow organizers hope to make the Rio Grande Valley a place where queer people want to stay—or, at least, where staying out of necessity doesn't feel like being caught in a trap. (Everywhere I have gone on this trip, I have asked people, "Why do you stay?" Here the answer is often "Because I can't leave.")

"If we're going to be investing and working toward something, we want it to be for the community we grew up in," Eduardo says.

With a winning smile, he adds: "I think it's getting better. Little by little. It's a process. It's a lot of conversations we're having with family or friends."

And much like Utah's Happy Valley, the Rio Grande Valley is made richer by the people who stay. As George Longoria, a nonbinary genderqueer person who uses the pronoun "they," tells me at a coffee shop in Edinburg later that night, "If our most creative and adventurous and innovative and whatever-the-fuck people leave, how are we supposed to ignite change?"

George came back to the Valley after what they describe as "a spectacular fall from grace as an ex-model," and now they work to change the culture of the region alongside their partner, Kurt, a transgender man. They make a gorgeous couple: George, tall and statuesque with short, buzzed hair; Kurt beside them, dark-haired and scruffy-chinned, with a captivating twinkle in his eye.

Both of them seem at ease tonight, sipping coffee at our corner table, but they generally avoid going out after dark for fear of verbal violence—or worse. George has had to endure shouts of *"Maricón!"* at gas stations where people assumed they were a gay man; other times, people assume that George is a transgender woman and adjust their dirty looks accordingly.

"Sometimes it's just people shouting at you from the cars, but other times it's deadly, so we just don't want to have any close calls," George says. "We've actually modified our life schedule to avoid that."

Despite the harrowing experiences of discrimination and marginalization that both George and Kurt have faced here—like being aggressively patted down by a bouncer, fielding stares at the bank, or having their application for an apartment inexplicably denied even though their combined income was three times the rent—they like living in the Valley. Here they can be on "the ground floor" of LGBT activism, as they call it, even if it sometimes feels like they are invisible to the rest of the country.

"When I used to work at call centers, people would be like, 'Where am I calling?'" Kurt remembers. "And I'd be like, 'South Texas.' And they'd be like, 'San Antonio?' And I'd be like, 'No, bro, four hours south, keep going.'"

At his previous job in a restaurant, Kurt went "stealth," meaning he kept his transgender status secret at work. On the one hand, being open would have allowed him to live more authentically—and to be more friendly with his coworkers. On the other hand, he knew that if he came out to his coworkers, "it would have definitely been talked about a lot"—and then he would have feared physical assault during the long walk back to his car after a late-night shift.

"It's a rock and a hard place, right?" I ask.

"But us," George says, "we are *nopalitxs*" — using the gender-neutral Spanish ending in lieu of a masculine or feminine vowel, before translating for me: "We are cactuses. Between a rock and a hard place, cactuses will grow anywhere, so I'm saying we're Valley people, we'll be okay."

"We'll kind of wiggle through," Kurt agrees.

Before Billy and I leave the Rio Grande Valley, I scour the map for a place where we can see anything even remotely approaching the river in its natural state. The best option, coincidentally, is called Anzalduas Park. An online review warns that it is "the skeletal remains of [an] immigration policy gone wild," a mostly deserted park "inhabited by more border patrol vehicles than wildlife or families."[35]

The description fits. A helicopter hovers over the area near the park entrance as we drive up. The only vehicles we see nearby are law enforcement. The park is abandoned in the middle of the afternoon on a beautiful summer day, the grills unused, the playground empty. The river itself is picturesque, an earth-tinged greenish color, the reeds on either side tickled by a warm breeze.

But in the five minutes it takes me to stop the car near the bank and take some photographs of the water, two

35 https://goo.gl/maps/6UhChvVY4632

different cop cars pointedly drive by. There's a park on the Mexican side where children are playing on the riverbank but here, on the American side, there is no sound.

Anzaldúa wrote that the U.S.–Mexico border is "an unnatural boundary."[36] She dreamed of a day when her people could be "on both shores at once," "see[ing] through serpent and eagle eyes." Where the helicopter above sees a border, a snake in the grass or a bird in the air sees only water. If Trump builds his wall here it would, as the *New York Times* reported, "bisect several major wildlife refuges"[37] in an impoverished area that relies in part on ecotourism to stay afloat. An already unnatural boundary could soon become even more so.

In 1987, the year I was born, Anzaldúa challenged white Americans like me to come to terms with this place—with this line across which we project our fears and prejudices.

"Admit that Mexico is your double, that she exists in the shadow of this country, that we are irrevocably tied to her," she wrote. "Gringo, accept the doppelgänger in your psyche."

The man currently in the Oval Office began his campaign by calling Mexican immigrants "rapists." As president, he has threatened to send the U.S. military into Mex-

36 Gloria Anzaldúa, *Borderlands / La Frontera* (San Francisco: Aunt Lute Books, 1987), 3, 78–79, 86.

37 "In South Texas, Threat of Border Wall Unites Naturalists and Politicians," https://www.nytimes.com/2017/08/13/us/in-south-texas-threat-of-border-wall-unites-naturalists-and-politicians.html

ico to take care of "bad hombres."[38] According to the Pew Research Center, 79 percent of his supporters said that illegal immigration is a "very big problem," with half of Trump voters believing the racist lie that undocumented Americans are more likely to commit crimes.[39, 40]

White people put Trump in office, which means I put Trump in office, even though I didn't vote for him. His presidency is a collective failure of white America to confront its own racism.

The people I met here will continue to pay the price for that colossal injustice while I walk away clean. They all love this Valley. Eduardo is obsessed with it. Kurt told me that he "digs it." Natalia called it a "weird, special place." Anzaldúa herself wrote, "How I love this tragic valley of South Texas," waxing rhapsodic about "the Mexican cemeteries blooming with artificial flowers, the fields of aloe vera and red pepper, [and the] rows of sugar cane."[41]

Queer people in the Rio Grande Valley deserve better than our nightmarish present. Like cactuses, they are

38 "Trump Threatens Mexico over 'Bad Hombres,'" http://www.politico.com/story/2017/02/trump-threatens-mexico-over-bad-hombres-234524

39 "Trump Voters Want to Build the Wall but Are More Divided on Other Immigration Questions," http://www.pewresearch.org/fact-tank/2016/11/29/trump-voters-want-to-build-the-wall-but-are-more-divided-on-other-immigration-questions/

40 "Contrary to Trump's Claims, Immigrants Are Less Likely to Commit Crimes," https://www.nytimes.com/2017/01/26/us/trump-illegal-immigrants-crime.htmltt

41 Gloria Anzaldúa, *Borderlands / La Frontera* (San Francisco: Aunt Lute Books, 1987), 89, 90.

finding ways to thrive in the heat. But even cactuses need water.

Billy and I drive away, heading north to Houston. As we approach the Border Patrol checkpoint south of Falfurrias on State Highway 281, I ask Billy to grab my driver's license from my purse, and he pulls his own out of his wallet. I have no idea what to expect—and the fact that I can drive up to it not knowing what to expect is proof of how privileged I am. I roll down the window of our SUV as we approach, and the Border Patrol officer looks at us just long enough, it seems, to notice that we are both white.

"Are you a citizen?" he asks, hurriedly.

I nod.

Then, to Billy: "Are you a citizen?"

Billy nods.

And just like that, he waves us through.

I know I have the right house in Houston because the minivan parked in the driveway has been decked out with pro-LGBT bumper stickers. The car belongs to Kathy and Bob, the boomer parents of my friend Kaylee Christine, a fellow transgender woman I met online who made it eminently clear to me that I couldn't come to Texas and skip her city.

Billy and I have spent all of July 22 driving up the Gulf Coast in intermittent thunderstorms, arriving just after the rain lets up for the day.

"We're almost as good as the Motel 6," Bob says as we walk in, but he's underselling the place.

The twin beds in Kaylee's old room upstairs have been topped with pastel flannel quilts. The towels are fresh. Bob ferries the Wi-Fi password to me right away, thinking that I'm some high-powered writer type who will need to get online immediately. Kathy asks whether we want coffee or tea in the morning. The hospitality makes me feel like I'm at the Four Seasons.

Their house is a comforting, controlled mess, filled with the sort of knickknacks and bric-a-brac that semi-retired middle-class couples collect over time: carved wooden angel figurines, blocks that spell out F-A-M-I-L-Y, signs with cute sayings about how cats actually own humans and not vice versa. The kitchen-cum-living-room has big picture windows all the way around one wall—the "selling point," Kathy tells me, of the whole house.

Family photos from the seventies to the present are arranged in a collage on the wall, all of them noticeably aged except for a single canvas print in the upper left corner: a post-transition photo of Kaylee, long-haired, smiling, wearing a dress. The wall tells a story that doesn't have to be spoken—a story about a transgender daughter asking for an old picture to be taken down, her taking a replacement herself, then hanging it with permission in the family home. It is the second indication—after the bumper stickers—of how strongly Kathy and Bob support Kaylee. Pictures can be sticking points for some parents of transgender children; Billy remembers repeatedly asking his mother to take his high school senior picture off the wall until it stayed down.

Kaylee arrives with her partner, Michelle Alvarez, an adorably shy transgender electrologist, to drive us to Walter's Downtown, the industrial venue where the riot grrrl band Giant Kitty will be playing a show tonight. We step outside just before twilight, in the cool but still-humid aftermath of the thunderstorm, to find a fantastically full double rainbow spanning the suburb. But of course, instead of staring in awe, we spend five minutes trying to get a selfie, figuring out whose phone has a "white balance" setting good enough to capture both our faces and the display in the sky. Michelle's phone does the trick. Everything is beautiful and gay.

You would be hard pressed to find a more underestimated city than Houston. Compared with Austin, it is seen as "uncool." Culinary critics continue to overlook it, as *Eater* recently observed, [42] even though its multi-ethnic food scene continues to wow foodies in the know. [43] (Restaurateur David Chang of Momofuku fame recently wrote for *GQ* that Houston was the first city where he

---

42 "Esquire Critic Admits Houston Is Underrated as a Food City, Places It Above Dallas," http://houston.culturemap.com/news/restaurants-bars/02-20-12-esquire-critic-john-mariani-admits-houston-is-underrated-asa-food-city-places-it-above-dallas-in-wake-of-top-chef-snub/#slide=0

43 "Terrible Listicle Declares Houston a Third-Tier Food City," https://houston.eater.com/2016/12/7/13873206/houston-best-food-cities-in-america

felt like he was tasting "the food in a *Blade Runner*–like future."[44]) The city has an unexamined reputation for being a boring, unhip sprawl.

Certainly no one could accuse Houston of being small. It is the country's fourth-most-populous city. But that's all the more reason to dig beneath its spread-out surface and find the LGBT threads running through it. From 2010 to 2016, for example, the mayor was an out lesbian: Annise Parker, who, as the *New York Times* reported, made Houston "the largest city in the United States to elect an openly gay mayor."[45]

It's true that the LGBT community is relatively small here as a proportion of the city's overall population[46]— and it's sadly the case that voters here repealed the trans-inclusive Houston Equal Rights Ordinance, or HERO, in 2015—but Houston is still an underappreciated queer hot spot.

"The majority of the city is honestly, realistically, pretty much fine with the trans community," Dee Dee Watters, chair of the Houston-based organization Black Transwomen, Inc., informs me over the phone, chalking up the death of HERO to the transphobic smear

44 "The Next Global Food Mecca Is in…Texas," https://www.gq.com/story/david-chang-houston-food-city

45 "Houston Is Largest City to Elect Openly Gay Mayor," http://www.nytimes.com/2009/12/13/us/politics/13houston.html

46 "The Metro Areas with the Largest, and Smallest, Gay Populations," https://www.nytimes.com/2015/03/21/upshot/the-metro-areas-with-the-largest-and-smallest-gay-population.html

campaign that preceded it: "The downer is the picture that was painted for them.... Their campaign was a really good campaign because it embedded fear into a lot of people."

Anti-HERO television commercials showed a little girl entering a restroom stall only to have a grown man follow her inside and slam the bathroom door shut.[47]

Former Houston Astro Lance Berkman also recorded a message claiming that keeping HERO in place "would allow troubled men who claim to be women to enter women's bathrooms, showers, and locker rooms."[48]

The imagery was visceral and brutal—and it hit Houston voters hard. They voted 60 percent to 39 percent to kill HERO. Of course, HERO didn't make it any easier for sexual predators to enter a women's room than such a crime had been before the ordinance existed; repealing the civil rights legislation was explicitly about keeping transgender people out. But the "men in women's bathrooms" messaging was so effective that some Houstonians didn't realize what they were voting for until it was too late.

As Dee Dee tells me, "Since that battle, I've had more women come up to me and tell me, 'Hey, I have no problem

---

47 "The Anti-Trans Bathroom Nightmare Has Its Roots in Racial Segregation," http://www.slate.com/blogs/outward/2015/11/10/anti _trans_bathroom_propaganda_has_roots_in_racial_segregation .html

48 "Houston Baseball Legend Stokes Trans Bathroom Panic," http:// www.thedailybeast.com/houston-baseball-legend-stokes-trans -bathroom-panic

with *you* using the restroom with me; I just have an issue with having a man coming into the women's restroom.'"

Houston certainly doesn't *feel* like a city where 60 percent of people think that I'm a potential bathroom predator. On our way to see Giant Kitty in a car full of queer and transgender people, it feels like I'm in a better version of San Francisco—one where the median home price isn't $1.5 million.[49]

The backbone of Giant Kitty, fronted by Syrian-American punk singer Miriam Hakim, is a transgender wife-and-wife duo on guitar and drums named Cassandra and Trinity Quirk—and all three of them are friends of Kaylee's. We park in an industrial stretch of downtown Houston, walk along the sidewalk where Kaylee and Michelle shared their first kiss—which I beg them to reenact—and arrive at Walter's, where a prominently displayed sign at the entrance indicates that neo-Nazis and KKK members are banned from entering. We duck into the green room with the band while a hard-core punk group opens the show.

And when Giant Kitty finally takes the stage, the vibe of the venue changes in an instant: the hard-core punk bros fall into the back to wait for the headliner while an ever-growing number of queer women step right up to the base of the stage, sashaying and bobbing to the

---

49 "SF Median House Price Rises to $1.4 Million," https://sf.curbed.com/2017/7/31/16069776/san-francisco-median-home-price-2017

beat as the band begins to play. Cassandra and Trinity aren't holding up signs announcing that they're transgender, but an attentive fan will notice that the sweatbands on Cassandra's guitar straps are in the colors of the Transgender Pride flag: white, pink, and baby blue. It's a subtle code that lets me know I am welcome here—that the band would have my back if anything bad went down.

("We've kind of made our own scene, I think," Trinity tells me the next day, over Topo Chicos in the house she owns with Cassandra, while a small Keanu Reeves standee watches over us from the mantel and their cat Tomboy vies for our attention.)

It is obvious that Giant Kitty has no interest in conforming to more masculine norms of punk culture. They revel in their quirky riot grrrlness, playing songs like "Old People Sex" that celebrate geriatric intercourse and "Don't Stop That Bus," a tribute to Keanu Reeves's tour-de-force performance in the 1994 action thriller *Speed*.

"Quick scientific poll: Who thinks girls are hot?" Cassandra asks, herself a hot girl in a denim dress with Zooey Deschanelesque bangs. "This song is for anyone who thinks girls are hot."

That sentiment is something that the punk bros in the back of the house and the queer-girl posse in the front mostly agree upon, as evidenced by the loud cheers before the band launches into a sultry little number called "Like Girls Do."

But as soon as Giant Kitty wraps, the punk bros loudly

"whoo" and reclaim the front of the venue, so Kaylee and the rest of our crew abscond to an all-night diner, House of Pies. Billy has a slice of lemon meringue. Michelle has a grilled cheese, plus a milk shake that looks like a stock photograph of a milk shake. Kaylee, a vegan, springs for the odd combo of onion rings and a bowl of strawberries, while I order an indulgent patty melt that makes me even fonder of Houston.

The next day, when the band is awake, I pay a visit to Cassandra and Trinity. The pair have been dating since 2010 and transitioned long before then—so long ago that, like me, they falsely believed that we had escaped the notice of the religious right.

"It's hard now that trans people are the new Big Bad," says Cassandra. "It's weird because I felt like for a while we were under the radar and people didn't give a shit anymore and now it's kind of flipped."

Now in their forties, neither Cassandra nor Trinity is particularly loud about the fact that they're transgender, although they're not actively trying to hide it.

"I'm a strong believer in just living my life and being who I am and then if people find out that I'm trans, that's a more impactful thing socially," says Cassandra. "Like, 'Oh, she's cool. That makes me think about trans people. Maybe they're not all crazy and I'll let them pee at Target now.'"

But the political environment lately has forced them to take a stand. When the founder of Houston's Whatever Fest wrote a transphobic Facebook post in February of

2017, Giant Kitty numbered among the bands that pulled out of the event in response.[50] The fact that Giant Kitty had two transgender members got mentioned in news write-ups; a "double-edged sword," as Cassandra calls it, because they want fans to love them for their music, not for being transgender.

"I've been approached after a couple of shows, like, 'Why don't you guys advertise your trans-ness more?'" Trinity recalls.

And then Cassandra, in her best commercial-announcer voice, jokes, *"Ten percent more trans!"*

These two are happy here in Houston in their house full of records. They believe that coastal queers overlook their city because they deem it "guilty by association," unfairly equating Houston with the regressive legislation that comes out of Austin. Cassandra has lived all over the country, and her official review is that Houston is "pretty hip" and "about as liberal" as any other metropolis, which makes the stigma around it all the more mystifying to her.

"When I was moving down here, I had some friends who were really upset with me," Cassandra remembers. "They were like, 'You'll be back in a year!' or 'Oh, they're gonna shoot you!' But Houston has been a really good

---

50 "Hari Kondabolu, Giant Kitty, More Pull Out of Houston Festival After Founder's Transphobic Remarks," https://www.spin.com/2017/03/whatever-fest-transphobic-bands-pull-out/

time. We could never afford a house like this living in New York, there's a lot of friendly people here, and the commute is nothing."

Indeed, what LGBT people lack in numbers here they make up for in friendliness. I spend the rest of my time in Houston inside Kaylee's three-bedroom apartment, which she opens to a revolving cast of transgender tenants, many of them in the process of finding and securing work. They come and go all day, while *Mario Kart* and *Super Smash Bros.* cycle through the Wii. Gender pronouns are exchanged casually and respected instantly. On the floor of the family room, propped up against the bottom of the kitchen counter, are old signs from the fight to protect HERO—a reminder of a lost but not forgotten battle.

For a second, though, I am able to forget about the transphobic bullshit that brought me to Texas. I feel giddy—fifteen years younger, even—among these new friends. There is something miraculous about being with a group of people who have to wear emotional armor everywhere else but here, where they can be authentic and unguarded. It is miraculous—although it shouldn't be—that we can feel *this* human. That we can cobble a space like this together and own it.

When I leave—and I don't want to—I notice a small sign hanging in the foyer.

TEXAS, MOTHERFUCKER, it reads. THAT'S WHERE I STAY.

★　　★　　★

When I ask Jess Herbst how large her property is, she tells me instead how long it would take to walk to the edge of it.

The beautiful family home she and her wife built sits on property inherited from Debbie's parents: fifty acres of pastoral land, complete with cows grazing around a small pond. If you stand on the porch and look out at the field on the other side of the barbed-wire fence, you can even spot the occasional roadrunner scurrying through the grass. (Much to the disappointment of a city dweller like me, they do not go "Beep beep!" as they run by.)

Jess tells me that when people find out she's the mayor of a small town called New Hope, they "think of the little town in *Gilmore Girls,* with the diner, the downtown, and the square."

But New Hope is no Stars Hollow: "No," Jess says, "we are just a bunch of people, spread out."

Billy and I are spending our last night in Texas here at Jess and Debbie's place. Jess was born in 1958, less than a decade after my parents, but she transitioned a few years after me, so she feels simultaneously like a mother and a little sister. Either way, she is family—and she treats us as if we're her college kids who have come back home for the holidays, listing off the contents of the fridge. I greedily grab a yogurt as we talk.

Jess met Debbie long before transition, while they were both undergraduates at East Texas State University. In 1978 they went to a campus showing of *The Rocky Horror Picture Show* with the same circle of friends; two years later they were married. Debbie knew that Jess "cross-dressed" from the very beginning of their relationship—and that is indeed how they understood it at the time, lacking all of the information about transgender identity at our fingertips today.

"We didn't know what the word *transgender* was," Jess says. "Not in 1978."

Finally, about a decade ago, Jess says, she started to realize that she was transgender and began the process of coming out, not just to Debbie but to an expanding circle of family members and friends. First she told her oldest daughter, then her youngest. Her best friends found out next, then a handful of colleagues were brought into the loop. Quietly, with Debbie's support, Jess began physically transitioning. But not until January 2017 did she pen her now-famous digital epistle to the city of New Hope: "I am Transgender."[51]

The ensuing media firestorm, Jess remembers, initially unnerved Debbie, as did the sense of permanence that came with it: Jess was just going to be Jess from now on, 24/7.

"She had to do a little soul-searching, because she told me that she had this vision in her mind of growing old with a man and now that wasn't going to happen," Jess remembers. "But fortunately she came to the conclusion that it's me she loves."

---

51 "An Open Letter to the Citizens of New Hope," http://newhopetx.gov/important-message-from-the-mayor

While we wait for Debbie to come home, Jess gives us the grand tour of the house, showing off the remodeling they have done over the last few years. When we reach the kitted-out closet in the master suite, she boasts that it is "eight months void of any male clothing"—except, she admits, for the old pair of overalls she occasionally must wear to drive the tractor and spear new hay for the cows. (I still remember the day in Georgia when I finally got rid of all the cargo shorts I wore before transition; I didn't exactly have the best fashion sense as a boy.)

The home office is a tech lover's dream, with professional-grade Macs and a 4K monitor, which Jess recently used to edit an advertisement for last week's rally against SB 3. Jess enjoyed a successful career in graphics at the dawn of the personal computing era before starting her own company. She and Debbie live comfortably but not ostentatiously.

When we turn away from the toys, I notice a large safe with a vault-style door.

"Of course, I *am* a Texan," Jess says, catching my gaze with a grin, entering the combination, spinning the wheel, and opening the door to reveal a collection of hunting rifles—some family heirlooms, others more recent acquisitions.

But the real masterpiece in Jess's house is the small ventilated compartment that she built in the closet for her cat's litter box, featuring a pressure-sensitive switch on the floor that turns the fan on for five minutes after

Ms. Katy Kitty has done her business. Would that every transgender person in the country could always relieve themselves in such secure and luxurious conditions!

I love the house so much that I want to quit my job, move into the guest room, and earn my keep as a maid—so it surprises me when Jess says that she considered giving it up after Trump won.

"In November, I seriously thought about selling everything and fleeing to Europe, but I decided to stick it out and see if I can make a difference," she tells me.

"Is that what kept you here?" I ask, trying to gauge how serious she was about expatriating.

"Yeah, I just didn't feel like I could leave," she replies. "This is North Texas. I got fifty acres. I could sell everything and move to Europe and live comfortably and eat cheese. But that's not how things get better. You don't make things better by running away from them."

Besides, Jess still has duties here, like tonight's city council meeting. Debbie comes home just as we are getting ready to head to the town hall. But before we leave, we gather around the kitchen counter to watch the live feed of the SB 3 debate on Jess's phone.

The author of the bill, Senator Lois Kolkhorst, is talking about how much she cares about the "privacy and protection of our small children and our young girls." I can't watch any more. No matter how many times I see a bigot try to pass a bathroom bill, I never get inured to these mealy-mouthed justifications for discrimination; it still makes my skin crawl to listen to someone pretend that attacking transgender people is about protecting kids when in fact it hurts them.

I tune out Kolkhorst and fantasize about teleporting back down to Austin and shouting on the Senate floor that 59 percent of transgender students have been barred from using the appropriate restrooms,[52] or that bills like SB 3 affect the mental health of a vulnerable population, 75 percent of whom already don't feel safe at school.[53] I want to read the state senators the entire text of Janet Mock's *New York Times* op-ed about how "young people overwhelmingly get it," whereas adults like Dan Patrick and Lois Kolkhorst "insert themselves—their politics, their fears, their prejudices, their ignorance—into [transgender children's] lives."[54]

But I know from years of reporting experience that facts don't matter to our enemies. Hatred doesn't need data to fuel itself. Prejudice isn't trying to pass peer review.

Right before we leave, the State Senate holds its initial vote on SB 3. Every Republican supports it. The bill is ap-

---

52 "LGBTQ Students Experience Pervasive Harassment and Discrimination, but School-Based Supports Can Make a Difference," https://www.glsen.org/article/2015-national-school-climatesurvey

53 "Report: Trans Youth and School Facilities," https://www.glsen.org/article/new-report-details-extensive-harms-denying-transgender-students-access-school-facilities

54 "Janet Mock: Young People Get Trans Rights, It's Adults Who Don't," https://www.nytimes.com/2017/02/23/opinion/janet-mock-young-people-get-trans-rights-its-adults-who-dont.html

proved 21–10.[55] After the vote is formalized later tonight, the House, led by Speaker Joe Strauss, will be the only hurdle the hateful bill has left to clear.

We drive the half mile to the New Hope town hall in Jess's Volkswagen Passat as the sun starts to set. The interior of the building is unremarkable: beige marble tile, beige walls, even a beige dais, in a room no bigger than a two-car garage. With no hard edges for my eyes to hang onto, this would be an ideal place for a nap. But I shake off the sleepiness to watch my friend at work.

In side conversations before the meeting begins, I overhear a man misgender Jess; she waves it off as the man immediately fixes his mistake. She bangs the gavel to begin the proceedings, jolting me upright, but the meeting itself is boring, dreadfully so, and mostly drowned out by the constant thrum of the air conditioning. The highlights—and I really have to stretch the definition of that word to use it—are some minor local drama over the naming of the town hall and a twenty-minute discussion about how far back from the edge of the road the trees should be trimmed and whether or not property owners should pay for it. Not exactly riveting stuff.

The top priority for many New Hope residents seems to be reducing the number of commuters who clog the

55 "Senate Votes Again to Advance 'Bathroom Bill,'" https://www .texastribune.org/2017/07/25/texas-senate-votes-advance-bathroom-bill-again/

roads: Can the speed limit be lowered? Could speed bumps be built to deter them?

Absolutely no one is concerned about where transgender people go to the bathroom. Nothing could matter less to the people of New Hope. If it would persuade commuters to pick another route, they would probably allow transgender Texans to flood the streets with urine.

"If I could do something about the traffic that comes through here I would be a hero," Jess had told me earlier. "But unfortunately that's a state-controlled road."

Granular local issues like this are what got Jess into politics in the first place. She didn't set out in the early 2000s to become a closeted sleeper agent for the Texas transgender community.

When Jess and Debbie first built their New Hope house, many of the roads in town—including the one to their house—were unpaved, so Jess started going to city council meetings and asking, "When are they going to do something about the gravel roads?"

She was repeatedly told there wasn't a budget for it, so she ran for a city council seat, won, and found money in the budget to start paving.

"It took me about eight years and I got rid of all the gravel roads," she tells me. "By that point, I was really hooked. I was used to going there and having a say on the town."

Billy and I spend the rest of the night with Jess and

Debbie, first at a new American restaurant in the nearby town of McKinney—which reminds me a lot of Stars Hollow, actually, albeit with a Texan twist—and then back in their home. Over drinks, Debbie tells us that staying with Jess after she started transitioning was a no-brainer: "Well, of course—why wouldn't I?" And Jess reminisces about how she was once petrified to do precisely this—socialize, go out in public—and how normal it now feels. They have both made many new friends since Jess went public with her transition—and have had more excuses to travel the state to see them.

"Texas has become a lot smaller and a lot bigger at the same time," Jess says.

At the end of my time in Texas—after a thousand miles of driving between spaces that feel as warm as the hug goodbye Jess gives me the next morning—I know exactly what she means.

Billy and I are just starting the long, multiday drive to Indiana on the morning of July 26, 2017, when President Trump picks up his phone and, as is his habit, starts to tweet: "After consultation with my Generals and military experts, please be advised that the United States Government will not accept or allow transgender individuals to serve in any capacity in the U.S. Military."

He goes on to tweet that the military can't be "burdened" with the "medical costs" of including us in the armed forces—even though, as the press later reports, the government spends five times more on Viagra for soldiers than it does on medically necessary transition-related health care.[56]

My phone starts to buzz with people asking whether I've seen the news. But I'm already driving by then, so I can't respond—and even if my hands *were* available, I feel too morose to be as outraged as I was over SB 3 last night.

This is exactly the kind of dystopian development I could feel coming the night Trump was elected, but anticipating evil doesn't make it any less dispiriting when it materializes. My heart is stuck on the "burdened" part of Trump's tweetstorm, with its particularly vicious insinuation that transgender people only weigh down those around them. I have never wanted to serve in the military—and medically, I wouldn't be able to anyway—but that language still wounds me, preying on my long-standing fear that my transgender status is a burden on my cisgender wife.

Billy stews in the passenger seat, thinking about the people in his immediate family who voted for Trump: *How could they support a man who would do something like this to people like him?* He writes a text to them about the news, then deletes it, then writes it again and presses *Send*.

---

56 "The Military Spends 5 Times More on Viagra Than It Would on Trans Soldiers' Care," https://tonic.vice.com/en_us/article/mbazpv/military-spends5-timesmore-on-viagra-than-it-would-on-transgender-soldiers-care

I see a message from Jess come across my screen and make a mental note to read it later.

After a dozen or so miles on State Highway 75, I manage to table my gut reaction and think about the transgender veterans I know instead. The words on Nicole Lynn Perry's shirt—I FOUGHT FOR YOUR RIGHT TO HATE ME—run over and over in my brain. When I find some time to call Nicole later, she tells me that, as a black transgender woman and former service member, she was hit particularly hard by the timing of Trump's cruel tweets—on the sixty-ninth anniversary of Truman's order to desegregate the military.[57] Her unfiltered reaction: "What the fucking hell."

That night, by coincidence, Billy and I were already planning to stop near Fayetteville, Arkansas, to talk to my internet friend Teri Dawn Wright, a Desert Storm veteran who transitioned after she left the army.

We pull into her gravel driveway, in a riverside town about an hour outside the city, sometime after 10 p.m. She greets me with the sort of embrace that only two transgender women who have never met in person can share: tender, knowing, instantly familiar. Her hair fades from blond to pastel blue at the shoulders. The rhinestones on the front of her pink shirt catch the

---

57 "Trump Announces Transgender Military Ban on Anniversary of Truman Ordering Equality in Armed Services," http://time.com/4874333/donald-trump-transgender-military-truman-anniversary/

porch light as her new Labrador puppy plays around our feet.

As we talk, Teri's voice is an almost-whispered, tremulous alto.

"The fact that he did it over Twitter was kind of demeaning and just dehumanizing," she tells me, as we sit together on a bench by the small fishpond she built in her backyard.

Teri remembers the paranoia she felt when she served—back before she had the language to make sense of her identity: "You're constantly wondering if someone's going to figure out that you're hiding the fact that you're trans, even though you don't know the name for trans."

We talk for an hour about everything and nothing: Arkansas and astrology, kayaking and gardening, eventually looping back to the morning news. The mood is as somber as the night is warm. Teri tells me the tweets made her feel "subhuman," and I can see why: she suffered so much trauma in the army, Veterans Affairs will not cover her sex-reassignment surgery, and now the President of the United States himself has enlarged the target on her back.

Before we leave, in an effort to cheer us all up, Billy pulls out his phone and opens an augmented reality app that shows us the constellations as he pans across the sky. I am awed by the brightness of the stars here in northwest Arkansas—the brightest I've seen them since I was a child, camping with my family at Big Bear Lake in the San Bernardino Mountains. We tilt our heads back, let our pupils dilate, and find our signs in the sky before hugging goodbye.

Billy and I get off I-49 at our exit in Fayetteville and stop at the traffic light.

The entire day has been a reminder that no matter how amazing queer people are—no matter how much energy we expend trying to convince other people that we're human—the bad guys win too often and inflict too many casualties along the way. Progress has a painfully steep cost. History will not be kind to leaders like Trump and those who share his anti-LGBT positions, but that's cold comfort in a present like this one.

Billy and I process it all together between long stretches of silence at that traffic light. And then the driver behind us angrily cuts into an opposing lane of traffic to pass me. That's when we realize that we have actually been sitting not at a traffic light, but at a stop sign at an empty intersection for five full minutes, too gutted by the events of the day to notice.

Back at the hotel, exhausted, I look at the text Jess sent me: "We have faced disappointment and discrimination before. We are transgender and we are stronger and far more resilient than Donald Trump or the far-right Texas legislature understand. We will persist."

I want to believe her. Tonight, I don't know if I can.

# Chapter 4

# BOO-MINGTON

There is a tendency to consider anything in human behavior that is unusual, not well known, or not well understood, as neurotic, psychopathic, immature, perverse, or the expression of some other sort of psychologic disturbance.

—*Alfred Kinsey*[1]

**E**strogen is not made out of sugar and spice. In pill form, it is synthesized from two decidedly unsexy ingredients: soy and yams.[2] But that's only fitting because, when I first started taking prescription estradiol in the fall of 2012, I felt like a yam: ugly, hairy, and awkwardly shaped.

I had been popping those pills for six months at graduate school in Atlanta when I received some welcome news: the renowned Kinsey Institute had awarded me a fellowship to study at their Indiana University sex library that summer. Like any nerdy humanities graduate student would, I fantasized about meeting a sexy someone in the archives and spending long afternoons admiring

---

1 "What Are Bioidentical Hormones?," https://www.ncbi.nlm.nih.gov/pmc/articles/PMC1447861

2 Alfred C. Kinsey et al., *Sexual Behavior in the Human Male* (Philadelphia: W. B. Saunders, 1948).

each other's, um, research before sneaking off to make love in the stacks. But who was going to look at a gross yam like me and see a juicy peach, ripe for the picking? And could I really hope to find that someone in Bloomington, Indiana?

I knew by then that Atlanta was essentially the queer headquarters of the American South, but I still had preconceptions about Indiana. The state seemed like a less-than-ideal setting for a visibly transgender woman to spend the summer, let alone find summer love.

This was a state then governed by a man named Mike Pence, who strongly opposed same-sex marriage and had once proposed diverting federal HIV/AIDS money to "institutions which provide assistance to those seeking to change their sexual behavior"—a proposal widely regarded as an endorsement of "conversion therapy," or the discredited practice of trying to change someone's sexual orientation or gender identity.

But I *did* fall in love in Indiana—not just with Corey but with Bloomington.

On July 28, 2017, I feel that same affection bubbling back to the surface as I take the exit off State Road 45 and head toward downtown Bloomington. I have wanted to come back here ever since the day I left it four years ago—and after the disorienting feeling of watching Trump try to tweet transgender troops out of the military, I need to spend a few days somewhere familiar.

As we drive down North College Avenue, I point out

personal landmarks to Billy: there, to the right, is Lover's Playground, the adult-toy store where Corey and I bought vibrators together at two in the morning—and there, just off to the left, is the turn-in for the cocktail bar where we first held hands a few days before that. (Yes, we moved fast; queer women often do.) Soon we are driving a lap around the picturesque Courthouse Square, where Corey and I whiled away lazy afternoons browsing book-shops and trying out new lunch spots.

This is the opposite of returning to Provo, where I felt so much initial dread and unease. But that's what love does to a place, I suppose: if love could make Corey look at me in 2013 and see a beautiful woman instead of a lanky tuber of a transsexual, then love can make an Indiana town into a queer wonderland.

"Are you *so* excited?" Billy asks, bouncing in his seat. My giddiness is apparently contagious.

I am indeed excited—even more so because my wife will land in nearby Indianapolis later tonight. I haven't seen Corey in a month and, after she flies out to visit me this weekend, I won't see her again until I am done re-searching this book in late August. And much as I enjoy Billy's company, I miss spooning Corey every night.

Bloomington has changed in the last four years: the ho-tel near the Courthouse Square where Billy and I drop off our bags, for one, wasn't here back in 2013; it was built as part of an effort to accommodate the many parents and football fans who make frequent pilgrimages to the col-

Emmett Claren (foreground), Billy, and me at Battle Creek Falls in Provo, Utah

Me on Y Mountain in Provo

Billy on Y Mountain

Billy being a nature hunk in Provo's Rock Canyon

The Mandan Summit trail at Sundance

Billy and me with Jacob Cook and Carlos Garcia (left) at the Encircle house

The view from inside Encircle

The City Limits drag show in Provo

Billy in his Buc-ee's shirt in Temple, Texas

Texas-shaped waffle in Austin

The protest over the bathroom bill at the Texas State Capitol

A double rainbow all the way across the sky in Houston
*(Michelle Alvarez)*

A creepy bird in the Hagerman National Wildlife Refuge in Sherman, Texas

View from the U.S. side of the Rio Grande at Anzalduas Park in Mission, Texas

The world's largest rocking chair, in Casey, Illinois

The fateful elevator in which Corey and I met

Corey and me returning to the scene of the crime in Bloomington, Indiana

Smoove G. and
Brick Kyle at the
Back Door

Coloring-book night at the Back Door

The epic bacon cheese fries at Mid City Grill in Johnson City, Tennessee (*Justin Mitchell*)

Jenn and me on Roan Mountain near the Tennessee–North Carolina border (*Justin Mitchell*)

Zelda the tortoise, keeper of all the gay secrets

Me pushing Jenn on a makeshift pool noodle raft *(Justin Mitchell)*

Billy and my rendering of him at the figure-drawing party

Billy being a dork transcribing interviews by the Carnegie Hotel pool in Johnson City

Justin Mitchell, me, and my fanny pack at Dollywood (*Justin Mitchell*)

Lunch with Temica Morton at Cracker Barrel in Jackson, Mississippi

The Sensational Nicole Lynn Foxx at WonderLust in Jackson

Billy as the orange stripe in the crosswalk at 10th and Piedmont in Atlanta

Lunch with Kayley Scruggs in midtown Atlanta

Hanging out with Charles Stephens by the Mechanical Room at the Phillip Rush Center

Corey at Indian Rocks Beach, Florida

lege town.[3] Other places are gone, like my favorite burger spot, and the café owned by Rachael Jones, a fellow transgender woman and something of a local legend.[4] The city seems larger now, but not because it magically acquired more surface area; memory has a funny way of editing out the time it took to traverse a place and holding on only to its bright spots. In my mind's eye, Bloomington looks like a map of Disneyland, with outsize attractions connected by tiny walkways.

The main attraction is the Kinsey Institute—the library founded by pioneering sex researcher Alfred Kinsey, creator of the Kinsey Scale, which measures sexual orientation on a gradation from zero ("exclusively heterosexual") to six ("exclusively homosexual"). If you're an American who has had good sex, you owe a debt to Kinsey. He has been called the "father of the sexual revolution,"[5] a man who breached now-antiquated bedroom taboos decades before his time.

"The living world is a continuum in each and every one of its aspects," Kinsey once wrote. "The sooner we learn this concerning human sexual behavior, the sooner we shall reach a sound understanding of the realities of sex."[6]

---

3 "Hotel Developers Still Looking to Expand in Bloomington," http://indianapublicmedia.org/news/hotel-developers-expand-bloomington-67832/

4 "Rachael Jones: Transgender Insurance Agent," http://www.magbloom.com/2017/04/rachael-jones-transgender-%E2%80%A8insurance-agent/

5 "Father of the Sexual Revolution," http://www.nytimes.com/books/97/11/02/reviews/971102.02rhodest.html

6 Alfred C. Kinsey et al., *Sexual Behavior in the Human Male* (Philadelphia: W.

Today that sounds like something any college student could tell you about human sexuality; Kinsey wrote it in 1948. It was a powerfully queer way of looking at sexuality long before the academic field of queer theory existed.

Kinsey rejected "discrete categories," which he said were rare in "nature" but all too common in the "human mind," with its nasty habit of "[trying] to force facts into separated pigeon-holes." Almost sixty years later I studied queer theory, which taught me to reject black-and-white categorization and embrace life in the gray. So it's only fitting that my queer romance with Corey began at the institute that Kinsey founded here in 1947.

I was one week into my research when she showed up—a college senior with a grant from the City College of New York to come here and study feminist pornography. I didn't know that from the start, of course; I felt too gross even to say hi to her, although we were often alone together in the institute's cramped third-floor reading room. But I knew from glancing at her that she was gorgeous; that she bit her lip when she was concentrating, and that, if she had decided to come here, we must have a few common interests.

We spent three silent days together in that room. But then, as I left to go back to my rented basement apartment on the third afternoon, Corey followed me into the

---

B. Saunders, 1948), 147.

elevator. I may have been a yam, but she wanted to eat me up. I felt gross. I said hi anyway.

That elevator ride was the prelude to a friendly dinner at an Indian restaurant, followed by a platonic sleepover. We shared a bed as friends that night—and then as lovers every night after that until we left Bloomington a month later, which was much longer than I was originally planning to stay in Indiana. I was held captive by her mischievous sense of humor, her sexual energy, and the way she challenged me—intellectually, politically, and emotionally—to be better.

This college town became our queer jewel, surrounded by more conservative country on all sides. We were both aware of the state's reputation. But inside Bloomington we felt about as welcome as one visibly queer cisgender woman and one early-in-transition transgender woman could feel. Rachael's Café was our hangout of choice. Other establishments could be a dice roll: sometimes we walked into a restaurant together and walked right back out when we got nasty looks. But often we could hold hands—and holding hands with my wife isn't something that I take for granted to this day.

Coming back now, I'm curious to find out if Bloomington will still feel like the red-state LGBT oasis that it did in the summer of 2013. Was my perception of this place softened by the rose-colored glasses of my love for Corey? Or is Bloomington just good in and of itself?

Billy and I pick Corey up late that night and she showers me with kisses. She too feels the electricity of returning to the place where we first met. That night, walking around the Courthouse Square, she tells Billy that coming here made her realize that queer life could find a way outside New York City. Raised on Long Island and educated in Harlem, she was pleasantly surprised by the liveliness of this Midwestern town.

Corey realized that she could exist somewhere like Indiana and feel, if not perfectly safe, then as safe as any queer American could hope to be. But what makes Bloomington that way? Are laws and policies responsible for its becoming an LGBT oasis? Are organizations? What, exactly, makes an oasis an oasis?

Before I came to Bloomington for the first time in 2013, I sent an email to Lauren Berlant, the social theorist who coined the concept of "queer world-making" with fellow scholar Michael Warner in a famous 1998 essay called "Sex in Public."

At the time that essay was being written, the New York City Council had overwhelmingly approved zoning changes that threatened to close several gay-themed adult businesses on Christopher Street in Greenwich Village.[7]

Berlant and Warner were concerned not only with

---

7 "Council Approves Package of Curbs on Sex Business," http://www.nytimes.com/1995/10/26/nyregion/council-approves-package-of-curbs-on-sex-businesses.html

protecting public space for queer people but also with carving out cultural space for queer life in a society they deemed "heteronormative," meaning that almost everything about it—from government to religion to "His" and "Hers" towels—favored heterosexuality as the only "right" way to live. The term "heteronormative" has since passed into popular parlance; at the time, however, it was breathtakingly radical to consider how persistently heterosexuality pervaded every facet of public life.

"Heterosexuality involves so many practices that are not sex that a world in which this hegemonic cluster would not be dominant is, at this point, unimaginable," Berlant and Warner wrote. "We are trying to bring that world into being."[8]

Some twenty years later, queer people are still "trying to bring that world into being." But queer worlds are hard to build and even harder to define. Neighborhoods like the Village are easy to label as "queer" based on the concentration of LGBT establishments alone. ("After a certain point," as Berlant and Warner noted in their essay, "a quantitative change is a qualitative change. A critical mass develops. The street becomes queer.") But how do you find a queer world in a place like Bloomington, Indiana, which isn't exactly West Hollywood?

I emailed Berlant for recommendations because she

---

8 Lauren Berlant and Michael Warner, "Sex in Public," *Critical Inquiry* 24, no. 2 (winter 1998): 547–66.

works four hours north of Bloomington at the University of Chicago. Her response was as brief as you'd expect an academic rock star's to be: "There's a new gay bar: The Back Door... Cafés: Rachael's, Soma (queer p[eople] hangouts)." But that was all I needed. A single point of entry is like a passport into any town's queer world; three was plenty.

On my second night in Bloomington I went to the Back Door—which, in addition to the sex pun in its name, could literally be accessed only through an alleyway entrance. The foyer was decorated with old Kinsey Institute memorabilia, but the nostalgia it evoked was quickly replaced with visions of an even queerer future when I entered the bar itself: the walls were zebra print. The décor consisted mostly of elaborate paintings of unicorns—and one portrait of Dolly Parton—hung up in gaudy, gilded frames. If a rainbow could gain sentience and become an interior decorator, I thought, this would be her greatest creation.

But the kitschiness of the space was balanced out by the hominess of the bar's vibe. I rarely drink—a Mormon habit still dying hard a decade later—so it was a relief to be able to sit down at a table and watch a drag show that featured a gut-bustlingly funny performance of Isaac Hayes's "Chocolate Salty Balls" from *South Park*. I could tell this bar wasn't just a place to find someone to bring to bed; it was also a gathering space for a community. Any remaining jitters I had about being in Indiana faded as the night wore on.

Berlant's recommendations kept paying dividends as I built connections of my own. Rachael's Café had provided an early gateway into Bloomington's queer subculture, giving me a quiet place to study and stay on top of local events. An employee at the Kinsey Institute introduced me to a bookstore where I could catch a screening of a mid-nineties lesbian romance film.

And not too long after I arrived, my queer housemate, Megan—who lived in the room above the basement apartment that I had rented for the summer—took me and her friends out for a night on the town that began at a straight club, moved to a now-closed lesbian bar called Uncle Elizabeth's that was tucked away in a drab shopping center, and somehow ended at a local strip club called Night Moves that is locally famous for its playful roadside signs with messages such as LET'S BE NAUGHTY AND SAVE SANTA A TRIP.[9]

I remember almost none of that night except a feeling of absolute bliss and belonging on the cab ride home, jammed in the backseat between two queer women; I had made the excellent decision to drink that night. Somehow, through a handful of chance connections and a twenty-five-word email from Lauren Berlant, I had found Bloomington's queerer side.

---

9 "Will the Show Go On? Strip Club Faces a Changing City," http://www.limestonepostmagazine.com/will-the-show-go-on-strip-club-confronts-a-changing-city/

Queer culture is slippery in precisely this way: the visible world is for straight, cisgender people, but the queer world courses through every secret crack in its facade. The only thing Berlant could do from her computer was point me to places like Rachael's and the Back Door because, as she and Warner wrote, the queer world "necessarily includes more people than can be identified [and] more spaces than can be mapped beyond a few reference points."

To explore the queer world—and thereby to help create it—you have to show up and see where the night takes you. Queer culture, Berlant and Warner noted, often has to be pieced together from "mobile sites" such as drag shows, dances, and parades, so joining in its rhythm requires flexibility and curiosity. Bringing an itinerary along would be pointless.

"The queer world," they wrote, "is a space of entrances, exits, unsystematized lines of acquaintance, projected horizons, typifying examples, alternate routes, blockages, incommensurate geographies."

This slippery quality means that queer people will always find new ways to congregate when bigots try to shut down our gathering places. But that doesn't mean they can't make life difficult for us. As Berlant and Warner noted, the New York City Council's attempt to shut down gay businesses on Christopher Street in the midnineties threatened to send queer people either to the internet or to "small, inaccessible, little-trafficked, badly lit areas remote from public transportation and from any residences." Still, they would have survived.

You can try to exile queer people from public life, you can send us into the shadows of the world, but we are resilient. Much like cactuses, as George Longoria reminded me in Texas, we find purchase in the most extreme environments—and so we keep creating queer worlds wherever we can. Even in south-central Indiana college towns.

At its best, queer world-making can be thrilling, like knowing a secret handshake or being on the inside of a juicy secret. Queer world-making is the excitement of being able to find a single door—a back door, even—that you can walk through and find your people, waiting.

A mere four years later, I discover that many of my reference points in Bloomington are gone.

Under the Saturday sun, Corey, Billy, and I walk through the lush green paths of the Indiana University campus, spotting two rabbits, a pair of deer, and more chipmunks than we can count along the way. We are hoping to revisit the entrance to the Kinsey Institute, provided that the door to the campus building in which it is located is unlocked on a summer weekend.

I pull the handle of the door to Morrison Hall and feel a wave of relief as it gives way. The musty smell of the building overwhelms me with its forgotten familiarity, resurfacing old sensations as if I'm experiencing them for the first time: the rush I felt when I said hi to Corey in the elevator, the excitement of her agreeing in this very lobby to go to dinner with me. I think back to the skittish version of myself that pulled open that same door in 2013, excited to take the elevator to the Kinsey Institute and start my fellowship but nervous about how I looked: I had decided to stop wearing my wig that summer after months of growing out my hair, but I was still wearing breast forms as I waited for the estradiol to change my figure.

I look at us now, four years older, married, holding hands. For us, this is holy ground.

Corey hits the elevator button and it lights up. The doors slide open and we step inside. Unlike the city of Bloomington itself, the elevator is *smaller* than I remember it—and its size explains why a shy little yam like me had no choice but to talk to Corey. For two people to ride together, we must have been almost touching. With three people it is downright claustrophobic.

The Kinsey Institute is still on the third floor and is closed for the weekend, but we expected that to be the case. Instead we take a dozen pictures in front of the gold-colored hallway sign, trying to get a selfie of us kissing that doesn't look too gross to post on Instagram. A visiting researcher who is working on the weekend awkwardly passes us on his way to the elevator, wondering aloud what we are doing.

"Can we see the reading room?" we ask him, after sharing a brief version of our love story.

The answer is no. A burst pipe last summer damaged much of this building; the reading room—the space where Corey and I first laid eyes on each other—is still closed for repairs.[10] There's no way for us to see the spot where (I later learned) Corey ogled my butt as I bent over the photocopier or to sit at the table where I watched hours of fetish pornography—for science, of course.

We go back to the lobby instead and Corey starts making out with me so passionately that Billy gets uncomfortable and steps outside to wait for her ravenousness to run its course. Corey's hands begin to wander. But not ten seconds pass before the door opens again and the same visiting researcher from earlier catches us in flagrante. We giggle at the awkwardness of being caught and scamper outside like teenagers. Why hadn't Billy been a better lookout?

"I'm sorry," he says, laughing. "I could have stopped him but I thought it would make a better memory."

In the late afternoon, Corey and I go on a driving tour of our old haunts to see if any of them have had better luck than the flooded reading room at surviving the last four years.

On the second day my wife and I spent together in 2013—when we were still "just friends" but suspiciously

---

10 "Kinsey Institute Closed Temporarily Due to Flooding," http://indianapublicmedia.org/news/kinsey-institute-closed-indefinitely-due-flooding-100069/

close ones for having known each other so briefly—we went to a cocktail bar called the Rail. It was there that I lightly brushed my pinky against hers on the table between us. For me, that was a heart-stoppingly bold move. Sitting in the parking lot of the Rail now, Corey remembers the "mini-orgasm" sensation she had when I touched her—when she realized that our already intimate friendship would evolve into something physical later that night.

But the Rail itself doesn't exist anymore. It is now an empty building perched on a hill by the railroad tracks. The patio where we sat that night is bare. This parking lot, where we once walked to my Honda Fit together, hand in hand, knowing that we were about to have sex, is empty.

We drive by my old basement apartment, where we went together after the Rail—and where Corey responded to my admission that I hadn't yet undergone sex-reassignment surgery with the reaffirming whisper, "I don't care." It was here, in a split-level house behind two fast-food places, that we spent long days cuddling, watching reality TV, and blowing off work to spend more time studying each other. But my housemate is long gone by now, and judging from the pile of boxes in the driveway, the latest in a long line of basement tenants is moving out today.

Finally we drive by Rachael's Cafe, now a Chinese restaurant called Gourmet Garden. I knew this heartbreak was coming because I had read about it online; the rent had gotten too high for Rachael, so she closed up shop.

Corey and I are saddened by the loss of our favorite spots, but we expected some casualties.

All places change, of course, but queer worlds are especially defined by their "fragility," as Berlant and Warner put it.

The sites of queer culture are "ephemeral," to borrow another word from the scholars, popping up and shutting down with the same hurried persistence of the rodents in a frantic game of Whac-A-Mole.[11] After all, Stonewall— the most well-known gay bar in the world by name—has closed and reopened more times than the mouth of a mechanical alligator on a mini-golf course.

Corey and I found our version of queer Bloomington, plumbed its depths, and consigned it to memory. It feels as if we walked across this town four years ago on a queer suspension bridge that fell apart as soon as we crossed it. But it's a thought as warming as the summer night that there will always be queer people here, mapping their own reference points, building beautiful worlds that may collapse behind them—but still carry them where they need to go.

After Corey goes home, Billy and I set out to find queer Bloomington anew.

Rachael's Café might not be open anymore, but Hopscotch Coffee has sprouted up since I left—and it's there

---

11 Lauren Berlant and Michael Warner, "Sex in Public," *Critical Inquiry* 24, no. 2 (winter 1998): 154

on the afternoon of August 1 that we meet Janae Cummings, the chair of Bloomington Pride, who strolls up the stairs in a black power T-shirt and kickass sunglasses to match. The first thing she tells us after ordering is that she never expected to live here.

"Bloomington is so rural, you know, and I'm a black queer woman," she says. "Coming to Bloomington seemed like the *opposite* of something I should do."

Having grown up on the outskirts of Indianapolis, Janae saw Bloomington as "this sort of hippie enclave in Indiana," albeit one "where you have to drive through a Klan-heavy area to get to [it]." This is often the case with red-state LGBT oases: when passing through Arkansas, for example, everyone we met told Billy and me to visit a gay resort town called Eureka Springs—and we did—but we passed just as many Confederate flags on the journey as we saw rainbow flags at our destination. Had we not been white, the unease wouldn't have been worth the payoff.

"I'm supposed to be in this liberal utopia, which it's not at all," Janae tells us, recalling how she recently stopped at a traffic light and discovered that the two trucks on either side of her both had Confederate flag bumper stickers. "People who are honest about that know it's not that way at all."

It is a luxury to be able to *get to* a place like Bloomington without feeling personally targeted for your skin color—and even then, white supremacy makes its presence known within the city—which is why Janae was nervous to *move* here. Only an attractive job offer doing communications for Indiana University persuaded her to chance it, for a brief time.

"I thought I'd be here for a year and then I would get back to a bigger city," Janae remembers, but then something changed. "I kind of slowly but surely fell in love with Bloomington. It surprises even me."

Janae moved here when the lesbian bar Uncle Elizabeth's was "on its last breath," as she describes it, and just as the Back Door was getting off the ground. With no surefire way to tap into the city's queer culture, she felt rootless and alone upon arrival. ("I had a hard time finding community," she recalls, "because I didn't know it was here.") But through the Kinsey Institute—and through the woman who would become her wife—Janae was "able to kind of find my place here." Like me, all she needed was a point of entry.

"And the kind of quaint 'Bloomington thing' starts to grow on you, I guess." Janae laughs.

Sitting on the patio at Hopscotch, our iced drinks melting in the sun, it's easy to be seduced by this place. Bloomington does not quite approach Bay Area levels of granola but is still pretty hippie-dippie for the Midwest, making Janae feel out of place driving her Jeep around amid all the Priuses. Bloomington is to Indiana what Missoula is to Montana: a college town whose steady influx of progressive young adults has attracted a year-round population that largely seems to share their politics. Its quiet charm feels real, earned—the furthest possible thing from Brooklyn twee. I have only ever been here in the summer but in the winter, Janae says, the Courthouse Square gets "lit up like Hill Valley in *Back to the Future.*"

The town does have a certain cinematic quality to it. The 1979 coming-of-age movie *Breaking Away* was famously filmed here but I've always compared Bloomington to fictional River City, Iowa, from *The Music Man.* Life here passes so slowly that the arrival of the Wells Fargo wagon would indeed be breaking news.

"If it could be a little faster-paced here, I would appreciate it," Janae says. "But it's a good place to call home."

Janae is bisexual and was dating a man at the time her now-wife—a fellow employee of Indiana University—started pursuing her "super hard," inviting her to lunch and to hang out after work. ("Oh, what a wonderful friend I have!" Janae remembers thinking. "She's actively flirting with me and I'm just obtuse.") Two and a half months, a few drunken text messages, and one false start later, the pair finally connected—and they have "been together ever since."

Not only has Janae made Bloomington her home, she became the chair of Bloomington Pride to help make the city more welcoming for other queer and transgender people of color. Under her leadership—and after some dramatic board turnover—the organization has become more expressly political, adding educational workshops to the annual Pride celebration in the summer, hosting new support groups, and challenging the local police to improve their relationship with the city's queer community if they want to march in the parade, as many departments in progressive cities do.

Janae has seen "a little pushback" from people who think they have "gone too political." But in the Trump era, I would argue, there's no such thing as too political.

Because as progressive as Bloomington might be compared with other parts of Indiana, it still needs radical work. Red-state LGBT oases like this one are not uniformly welcoming. Corey and I can come back here for a visit and feel comfortable; I'm white and my wife is white-passing, born to a Puerto Rican mother and an Irish father. But Janae lives here, works here, even chairs Bloomington Pride, and she has to check herself before displaying public affection.

"Even now, there are times when I'm nervous holding hands in public," Janae says. "Some of that is racial and some of that is being in a same-sex relationship. But we can be walking and there are times when I am absolutely apprehensive and I'm anxious about what people are going to do or what they are going to say."

Our contrasting experiences in this city are proof of black feminist scholar Kimberlé Crenshaw's theory of intersectionality—the idea that "the violence that many women experience is often shaped by other dimensions of their identities, such as race and class,"[12] as Crenshaw

---

12 Kimberly Crenshaw, "Mapping the Margins: Intersectionality, Identity Politics, and Violence Against Women of Color," *Stanford Law Review* 43, no. 6 (July 1991).

put it in a 1991 article for the *Stanford Law Review.* In other words, black women don't face misogyny in one corner of their lives and racism in another; they experience both of them at once, blended together in a particularly virulent prejudice cocktail. As the black feminist Combahee River Collective famously wrote, it is "difficult to separate race from class from sex oppression because in our lives they are more often experienced simultaneously."[13]

Crenshaw argued that although "racism and sexism" and other bigotries "readily intersect in the lives of real people," scholars still have a hard time understanding the struggles faced by people who experience multiple forms of oppression that "interact" and "overlap."[14]

Janae and I have several identities and demographic categories in common: we are both women, both queer, both married, both gainfully employed. But racism is such a strong form of hatred—one from which I am exempt—that Janae and I can walk down the same Bloomington street and come away with contrasting experiences. I can reach for Corey's hand without a second thought. But Janae feels that gut-level hesitancy—in part due to her blackness, in part due to her sexual orientation, but realistically due to both in ways that would be impossible to disentangle.

---

13 Combahee River Collective, "A Black Feminist Statement," *Women's Studies Quarterly* 42, no. 3–4 (2014): 210–18.
14 Kimberly Crenshaw, "Mapping the Margins: Intersectionality, Identity Politics, and Violence Against Women of Color," *Stanford Law Review* 43, no. 6 (July 1991): 1241–99.

I ask Janae if she would ever leave Bloomington. After all, she had been planning on staying here only a year. Would she ever want to go to some "storied liberal metropolis?" I ask.

"Do they really exist?" she wonders in response. "Where is that?"

"New York, Los Angeles...?" I suggest.

"Maybe I'm a little cynical but I've had enough experiences here to show that *this* is not a liberal utopia," she says. "That's why I question whether they exist. Because I've been shouted at on the street enough times—and people cross the street on me—and that has everything to do with my identity in this wonderful town that's supposed to be so safe and loving."

There is a difference, it seems, between an oasis and a utopia: when you're in a desert, an oasis can be a single well of water in the sand—or, in this case, one college town with an incredible queer bar. A watering hole doesn't make the desert safe; it just makes it habitable. Even then, when you arrive at the refuge that is Bloomington, so much of your experience here depends on the particular identities you bring with you. And utopias—well, utopias don't exist. If one did, every LGBT person in the country would move there and queer world-making would end.

Queer people, as Berlant and Warner phrased it, are always "conscious of [our] subordinate relation" to a heteronormative world. We rely on "zones and other worlds estranged from heterosexual culture" because, even in places like Bloomington that get labeled "safe," we are still a marginalized minority, albeit one with varying levels of privilege.

That's why businesses like Hopscotch—which Janae says filled the vacuum left by the closure of Rachael's Café—matter. As Berlant and Warner wrote, "If we could not concentrate a publicly accessible culture somewhere, we would always be outnumbered and overwhelmed."[15]

Janae and her wife have traced their own queer trajectory through this town. Their Bloomington love story follows different reference points than the one I shared with Corey: Darn Good Soup, Cardinal Spirits, the Bluebird Nightclub, a Shovels and Rope folk concert where Janae felt "a feeling of closeness and intimacy" with her wife back when they, too, were still "just friends."

"I remember feeling her hovering over me and I'm like, *She's awfully close*," Janae recalls. "And I remember really loving that feeling and wishing I would be embraced."

Their queer romance—like ours or anyone's here—is a constellation of memories drawn across this town. And as constellations once did before astronomers formally divided them up, they can overlap and share stars.[16] There is one star in particular that Janae and I both love. It is inarguably Bloomington's queer Polaris.

---

15 Lauren Berlant and Michael Warner, "Sex in Public," *Critical Inquiry* 24, no. 2 (winter 1998).
16 "Constellation Guide," https://stardate.org/nightsky/constellations

"As long as the Back Door is standing," Janae says, "we'll be okay."

The Back Door is easier to find today, thanks to a new mural painted in the alleyway, featuring Daffy Duck dressed in stewardess drag and pointing to the bar. It is also easier to locate in the overcast light of day than it was in the middle of a June 2013 night, looking at my smartphone screen and wondering where the hell my navigation app was taking me.

Just after 3 p.m.—an hour before the Back Door officially opens—Billy and I walk inside to meet Brick Kyle, a soft-spoken fine arts student who stayed in Bloomington after graduation to become the bar's graphic designer, and Smoove G., a self-described "big dyke" with a crew cut and sporting a black T-shirt that says SOLID GOLD CLIT—written in gold lettering, of course. Brick mixes us a green-coffee-and-ginger concoction to give us a midafternoon kick as Smoove picks out a table in the middle of the empty bar where we can sit and chat.

Smoove starts to explain her job title. "I am sort of the, I don't know, I don't like to call it *daddy*, but…"

Brick makes it official: "You're the daddy of the bar, for sure."

Twelve years ago, Smoove was working for a major bank in the Bay Area, doing what she describes as "trap[ping] people in endless cycles of debt." Feeling as if she was selling her soul to the devil, Smoove ditched the corporate career, the six-figure salary, and the hour-long commute to come back home to Indiana. At the time, her friends in San Francisco thought she was "crazy," warning her that she was "going to die here." With George W. Bush in the White House, they figured, conservative parts of the country couldn't possibly "get worse" for gay people—a laughable thought today, of course, as anti-LGBT bills sweep through red states.

Smoove reassured her friends, "I'm not going to die there, it's fine—plus we can't *all* live here. We need to spread the wealth a little bit in terms of this bubble."

Bloomington definitely needs a Smoove more than the Bay Area needs a Smoove. Her fatherly duties include writing checks, taking care of the inventory, and managing other Back Door business. Together with co-owner Nicci B., she has shaped this place into something special: the rare bar where you can find queer people of every stripe dancing and drinking together. Go to New York City, with its taxonomic nightlife scene, and you can find a bar for each different variety of bear; here, everybody has to get along.

"From the beginning, I wanted it to be a queer bar," Smoove explains. "I wanted to use that language because to me, it was just more inclusive. Historically, gay has been for, you know, [cisgender] white guys."

Look a little deeper than the zebra-print walls and the unicorn paintings and you can see what she means by "queer bar." In lieu of gendered signage on the two bathroom doors, one has a drawing of two toilets on the front and the other has a drawing of a toilet and a urinal. Through the door I pick is the most political restroom I have ever seen. Signs on the walls proclaim NO MERCY FOR THE PATRIARCHY and BLACK LIVES MATTER. The back of the door has been stenciled repeatedly with the words Fight, Fight, Fight, Fight—and on the wall is a framed poster of Zoe Leonard's famous poem beginning, "I want a dyke for president."

But my favorite piece of décor is a blown-up photo of lesbian socialist intellectual Angela Davis with a speech bubble saying, "Radical simply means 'grasping things at the root.'"

Janae had reminded me of the Davis photograph in the bathroom the other day at Hopscotch, telling me that she sometimes overhears people asking, "Who's that?" or cracking wise about the picture. But then, as Janae had said, "There's usually someone in the Back Door who is like, 'Hey, this is who that is and this is what you need to know. Shut up.'"

"It's actually a really remarkable place," Janae had added, citing how "activist-minded" it was.

Indeed, although socializing is the primary purpose of the Back Door, anyone who can't do that respectfully will have Smoove to answer to.

"You don't just get to leave," Smoove elaborates. "You're gonna get a little lecture about how this isn't cool and if you want to come back in here, you better not ever do that again."

Persistent bad apples, as Brick puts it flatly, "get banned."

The Back Door is a perfect example of the red-state queer ethos that being politically active is a responsibility, not a choice.

"I don't think being queer, you can be neutral or not political," Smoove says. "I mean, you have to take a stand because we still don't have full rights or protections."

Few know that better than LGBT people in Indiana. In March 2015, then-Governor Mike Pence signed the Religious Freedom Restoration Act, essentially opening the door for business owners to discriminate against LGBT people based on religious beliefs.[17] That shameful law was immediately followed by widespread calls to boycott the state. The tech company Salesforce announced that it would end travel to Indiana.[18] Indianapolis-based Angie's List canceled a $40 million expansion project.[19]

At the time, I wrote an op-ed asking Americans outside the state to consider the fact that queer people still live here before deciding to boycott Indiana in toto—because in

---

17 "Gov. Mike Pence Signs 'Religious Freedom' Bill in Private," https://www.indystar.com/story/news/politics/2015/03/25/gov-mike-pence-sign-religious-freedom-bill-thursday/70448858/

18 "Salesforce Packed a Punch in Galvanizing RFRA Opposition," https://www.indystar.com/story/money/2015/04/02/salesforce-packed-punch-galvanizing-rfra-opposition/70842680/a

19 "A Year After RFRA, Angie's List East-Side Expansion Is Still Off," https://www.indystar.com/story/money/2016/07/08/year-after-rfra-angies-lists-east-side-expansion-still-off/86435652/

places like Bloomington, businesses were slapping THIS BUSINESS SERVES EVERYONE stickers on their doors to signal their disagreement with Mike Pence's license to discriminate. I hated the thought of businesses like Rachael's Café or the Back Door losing revenue because someone had canceled a conference to punish the regressive Indiana state legislature. As feminist blogger Melissa McEwan bluntly put it on Twitter, "Anyone saying #BoycottIndiana can kiss my fat ass. You'll just hurt the most vulnerable Hoosiers."[20]

Fortunately, Governor Pence was forced to essentially neuter the law mere days later in one of the most decisive demonstrations of LGBT political power in recent history[21]—although it seemed like much of the country forgot that episode when Pence got the vice-presidential nomination in 2016. Queer people in Indiana didn't forget.

On election night, the watch party at the Back Door took on a funereal mood as the electoral map turned red—in part because the crowd's longtime adversary Mike Pence would now be a heartbeat away from the presidency.

"There were a lot of tears," Brick recalls.

"You see the look of shock and disbelief on people's

---

20 "Stop," http://www.shakesville.com/2015/03/stop.html
21 "Gov. Pence Signs Revised Indiana Religious Freedom Bill into Law," https://www.washingtonpost.com/news/post-nation/wp/2015/04/02/gov-pence-signs-revised-indiana-religious-freedom-bill-into-law/?utm_term=.5170bdb24111

faces," Smoove adds. "I'm like, 'Even if we get rid of Cheeto, Pence is not that much better.' And I guarantee you [that] he's the one behind rolling back all the rights for everyone in our community."

Smoove's hunch is right. As the *Daily Beast* reported, citing sources in the White House, Pence had been "pushing hard" to kick transgender troops out of the military before Trump's late-July 2017 tweetstorm on the subject.[22] Anyone who saw Pence as just another bland Republican white guy was ignoring the extreme threat he posed to the LGBT community.

But as Brick soberly notes, life in Bloomington has moved on out of necessity. The news cycle will continue to be terrible. Trump will do something awful almost every day. Pence's behind-the-scene machinations will continue. There is nothing to do but carry on. That doesn't mean ignoring oppression, Brick explains—it means recognizing the limits of your reach.

"You can't stop everything just because idiots are taking control of the country," he says. "You just have to focus on community."

This bar has been Brick's passion since college. Originally from the small town of Seymour, Indiana, Brick started working here as a coat-check boy after transferring from the New Albany campus of Indiana University

---

22 "Trump Bows to Religious Right, Bans Trans Troops," https://www.thedailybeast.com/trump-bows-to-religious-right-bans-trans-troops

to Bloomington. Soon he started bartending; not long after that, he was recruited to do all the bar's marketing—or, as Brick puts it, "I kind of just stuck around until I forced them to make me do everything." Bloomington is where he came out as gay and "blossomed," as Brick describes it with a small flourish, after enduring a religious childhood and the relative isolation of life in small-town Indiana. He doesn't just pour drinks; he pours himself into the bar because he knows what this place means to the community here.

The passion pays off. I am not the only out-of-towner who cherishes the Back Door, who still thinks about it years after leaving. Smoove has had one woman tell her that "she hasn't had this much fun since Studio 54," the seventies celebrity hot spot widely regarded as the best nightclub in history.[23] Folks visiting from the coasts are constantly surprised by the Back Door—many of them, Smoove notes, openly wishing that New York City had an LGBT bar *this* good.

Even the difficulty of finding it after dark adds to its charm. As Smoove explains, the back-alley entrance is a "nod to old-school queer bars where you had to know a password.

"You literally were going to back doors and basement doors," she says.

---

23 "The 25 Best Nightclubs of All Time," http://www.complex.com/pop-culture/2012/01/the-25-best-nightclubs-of-all-time/26

And if you hang out here long enough, you might just brush shoulders with LGBT royalty.

Brick lights up when I ask him for his favorite memory here: "There was one time when I first started working here. I had on this eighties ski jacket and running shorts that were a little too tight, and weird hair, and probably like a 'baby doll' necklace. And I was smoking outside and Kyan [Douglas] from *Queer Eye for the Straight Guy* was out there with me, and I was having a mental breakdown, a panic attack."

Smoove, when asked the same question, tells me that *RuPaul's Drag Race* legend Shangela once "ended up in my hot tub," leaving the story at that.

"Indiana kind of sucks but Bloomington is great," Brick sums up.

"I love this little town," Smoove agrees. She can remember but a single bad experience here: "Only once walking down the street someone called me a 'big dyke.' And I'm like, 'Yeah, you're right! I am! Congratulations! Goodbye!' I'm like, 'Great, it's working.'"

"The shirts help," Brick chimes in.

"Are there more like this one?" I ask, still in awe of SOLID GOLD CLIT.

"Oh yeah," Smoove says, with a grin. "I have a whole closet full of this shit."

Later that night, Billy and I return to the Back Door and post up at the bar. Tuesday nights like this one are coloring-book nights. A small but steady stream of local queer women filter in, grab a coloring book, and sip on something sweet. I pick out an Avengers book and go to work on a picture of Black Widow with some pink crayons; Billy opts to color Hello Kitty. I order a "Citron on My Face" and Billy chooses the "Pink Taco," because apparently even the drink names here have to be puns. The bartender—a different person named Brick, if you can believe that—takes good care of us, keeping our glasses full, sneaking in a slice of pizza with a friend between refills. Johnny Cash plays on the stereo. For a gentle hour, it feels as if there is no world outside, no nightmarish dystopia where politicians are plotting to strip us of our rights.

We leave happy, as buzzed as the sides of Smoove's head, and go back to the hotel. If Corey were here, I'd be tempted to quit my job and build a life here. I could become a Back Door regular, if not to drink then to see what Smoove's shirt says each night.

When I first came to Bloomington, Rachael's Café was my daytime sanctuary: the bathrooms were gender neutral. The homemade quiche was delicious. And the friendly fifty-something transgender woman working the cash register was a walking reminder that I was welcome. That woman was Rachael Jones herself, standing radiant and tall behind the counter in a blond wig and thick-rimmed librarian glasses. Just *seeing* her changed my life.

When I started transitioning in 2012, I didn't know how being transgender would affect my job prospects other than adversely. Fifteen percent of respondents to the 2015 U.S.

Transgender Survey said they were unemployed—three times the overall U.S. unemployment rate. Almost a third of us were living in poverty, compared with less than 15 percent of American adults.[24] (It's important to note that white and Asian transgender people had the lowest unemployment rates—12 and 10 percent, respectively—but those rates were still multiple times higher than respective figures for the white and Asian populations at large.)

Watching Rachael run her own small business in south-central Indiana was my first vision of a future in which I turned out okay. Like too many young transgender people, I didn't know anyone over the age of thirty in our community when I first came out; I have since remedied that—and it was important that I did. I needed to see someone like her being accepted somewhere like here.

Sitting across from Billy and me on a wrought-iron chair outside Bloomingfoods—a local grocery store about half a mile from where her café used to be—Rachael tells us that she started her beloved local business after coming out in 2007 because she felt like she had no other options as a transgender woman. A former salesman, Rachael had no "preplanned design" to create a queer-friendly coffee shop; rather, she was "grabbing at straws out of desperation."

"I don't think that anybody would have hired me

---

24 2015 U.S. Transgender Survey, http://www.transequality.org/sites/default/files/docs/usts/USTS%20Full%20Report%20-%20FINAL%201.6.17.pdf

[based] on the energy I put off, which was so afraid and so ashamed," she remembers. "So having a place where people come to me—and providing a place where people can just be—seemed like the only solution."

Even the gender-neutral restrooms were simultaneously for her—"Where was I gonna go then?" she asks—and for her customers. By carving out her own space, she made one for everyone else.

Rachael's energy today is the furthest thing from afraid and ashamed. She looks happy. It's too hot outside for her to comfortably wear her wig, and she's dressed in thin, comfortable clothes so that she can ride her motorcycle around town. Her hair is drawn back in a ponytail and there are two swatches of eyeliner on the rims of her eyelids. As we sit and talk, she waves to the locals who recognize her. After closing the café two years ago due to rising rents, Rachael found a job as an insurance agent for New York Life—a gig that provides more stability than operating a restaurant. She shares joint custody of her three kids with her ex-wife; the youngest just graduated from Indiana University.

From 2007 to 2015, Rachael was the friendly face presiding over Bloomington's best-known queer destination. Upon closing, her café was heralded by the local press as "an institution of acceptance" even though it was also acknowledged that the business itself had had a bumpy history.[25]

---

25 "Rachael's Café Closes After 8 Years of Fostering Acceptance," https://www.heraldtimesonline.com/news/local/rachael-s-cafe-closes-after-

"I almost lost my house several times, my car was repossessed, my heat was turned off, the power was shut off at the café a couple of times," Rachael tells us, pulling back the curtain on troubles that she did her best to hide from customers. "It was a big struggle. *Jeez*, it was hard, you guys."

The Rachael that Corey and I met in 2013 showed no sign of being under duress. She was composed, approachable, and generous.

When Corey and I wanted to go hiking in the woods, she recommended a spot in nearby Brown County State Park called Ogle Lake—and when she found out I hadn't packed any footwear for the summer other than flats, she insisted that I borrow a pair of her sparkly silver Converses to wear on the trail. Our walk around the shimmery lake remains one of my fondest memories from my first summer with Corey, even though the shoes were half a size too small.

Rachael's Café was one of the only places in town where Corey and I could feel like an ordinary couple—where our dreamlike summer romance felt rooted and real. A sex library and a dark basement have their place in any good queer fling but, to envision a fully fledged relationship, we needed to know what it was like to be Samantha and Corey in public, having lunch and getting coffee. When Corey and I went back to separate cities at the end of the summer (she to New York and I to

---

years-of-fostering-acceptance/article_b1110ae9-2a68-5317-a5e0
-11b4a67acba3.html

Atlanta), it was that everyday stuff—not the fireworks—that made me want to give long-distance a chance.

"The café was such a special place to me," I tell Rachael, showing her a present-day picture of Corey and me. She had remembered both of us when I asked her to meet up for this interview.

"Oh, thank you, honey," she says. "Thank you."

Other people have told her the café changed their lives—and Rachael tells me, "It always makes me feel blessed that that was the case."

Over the course of the café's operational years, Rachael hosted wedding receptions for couples who had met there. In 2008 the café served as de facto headquarters for Barack Obama's team—and the night Obama won, she hosted an "elbow-to-elbow" election-watch party that culminated in a thank-you phone call from the big man himself. Obama narrowly took Indiana that year, with Monroe County's 65-to-33 percent vote in his favor helping to tip the scales. And in 2010, an Indiana University exchange student named Lucy Danser wrote a monologue based on interviews with Rachael that would become *Rachael's Café—The Play,* a 2014 production at London's Old Red Lion Theatre.[26]

Danser described Rachael better than I ever could: "What makes Rachael special," she told the Indiana Uni-

---

26 "IU Exchange Student Creates a One-Woman Play About Rachael's Café Owner," http://archive.inside.indiana.edu/features/videos/2014-02-13-iniub-video-rachael-cafe.shtml

versity news site, "is the fact that she neither forces people to notice her but doesn't hide away. She just is."[27]

I can only add that Rachael herself is what made Rachael's Café special. Rachael is the sort of person who draws people in, and who doesn't seem to know why she draws people in, but her obliviousness to her own charisma only amplifies it. I didn't go to her café for the bathrooms or even the quiche; I went there because *she* was there.

I remember something Janae told me when I had bemoaned the loss of my favorite Bloomington hangout: "Rachael's still here, just not the café."

At this point, just before I have to leave Bloomington, I am realizing that this city—or any red-state LGBT oasis, for that matter—doesn't just exude safety. There is nothing in the water, no invisible mist in the air that makes queer people happier here. Even places like the Back Door are just drywall and concrete at the end of the day. But Bloomington is still an oasis—"It's Mecca," Rachael agrees.

"What makes it like that?" I wonder aloud. "Is it places? Sort of, but I think it's mostly the people you meet and the connections you make—and you are one of those people for me."

That's the important thing, isn't it? The Back Door

---

27 Ibid.

without Brick, Smoove, and Nicci B. would just be four zebra-print walls. The Rail without Corey would have been another craft cocktail spot in a country that already has too many of them. The reason queer people build worlds—and the reason Rachael built her café—isn't just to be free from bigotry; it's to be with one another. What made her struggling business worthwhile, Rachael tells me, were the "wonderful people" of this city that she met while running it.

"There's a lot of happy memories there, honey," she says. "A lot of beautiful people, a lot of happy memories. Now you're making me sad."

I tear up, too, but Rachael assures me that "it was not my talent to be a restaurateur."

Untethered from her small business, Rachael is free to spend more time riding her motorcycle around the country, visiting friends and family. She has not physically transitioned, so she's somewhat self-conscious about her appearance as she travels. But she has plenty of tales about having her expectations of an American region subverted—about expecting to get beaten up by two "rough guys" at a bar in Key Largo, for one, only to have them help her find a place to stay.

She knows there are dangers out there. But like so many people I have met on this trip, she wishes there were more awareness of the cultural change that has happened over the last decade—change that has been driven by unapologetically out people like her.

"America has come a long way," she informs us. "Indiana has come so far, you guys."

And she wishes national reporters like me did more to call attention to that change. "I think there's a huge disservice done by the media. There's so much negativity reported. And it's so much better, you guys. I mean, if I was passable, I couldn't say that because no one would know [I'm transgender], but *everybody* knows. It's so much better. It's so much freer. It needs to be reported."

It's work so necessary that Rachael half seriously volunteers to help me with it.

"We should collaborate," Rachael tells me before getting up to hug me goodbye and ride her motorcycle away into the night. "Because I got an old, beat-up motor home and I have had so many ideas of what to do with it."

I hope one day I can take it across the country with her. It would feel like being back in Rachael's Café every day. Maybe we could start a food truck?

In Antoine de Saint-Exupéry's classic fable, *The Little Prince*, a wise fox tells the eponymous prince that the pair of them ought to "tame" each other—to "establish ties," as he defines it.

"To you, I am nothing more than a fox like a hundred thousand other foxes," the fox explains. "But if you tame me, then we shall need each other. To me, you will be unique in all the world. To you, I shall be unique in all the world."

I know almost everyone who grew up with *The Little Prince* feels as if Monsieur de Saint-Exupéry wrote this passage just for them—but feeling a bit cliché hasn't stopped me from revisiting it whenever I need to remember what love is about.

In the cognitive dissonance that so often accompanies attraction, we tell ourselves that the people we love have unique properties that compel us to love them. Maybe they are beautiful or funny or their hair falls just so around their shoulders. We see them from across a room and hear Elvis Presley in our heads crooning at slow tempo: "But I...can't...help..."

I do believe that no two people are alike; I could meet millions of queer women and never find someone who excites me in the same way Corey did in Bloomington, and still does today.

But it's probably *less* true than we would like it to be. Lots of people are beautiful or funny or blessed with a good head of hair. Whenever we meet an attractive person, they are—as the fox might say—one attractive person like a hundred thousand other attractive people we could have met that day. Who knows? Maybe if I had come to Bloomington a month later, I would be married to someone else who stepped into that Kinsey Institute elevator at the same time as me.

That might not seem like a very romantic notion. But Saint-Exupéry's fox understood that love is work—that we have agency to decide whether to invest our love in the people whose paths we cross. The "ties" of love must be "establish[ed]"; they don't just happen. In other words, love is the result of the process of loving someone. The little prince had to "sit a little closer" to the fox every day "at the same hour" to tame him. He could have tamed another fox, but he tamed *his* fox—and that is what made the little creature "unique in all the world."

The same principle, I think, applies to loving places.

I love Bloomington, but I have been to dozens of similar towns across the country—many of them while writing *Real Queer America*. It's not hard to find a small city with a cute downtown area, a queer-friendly coffee shop, and a neighborhood gay bar. You can eat the same fancy maple-bacon doughnut from a hundred different boutique bakeries in a hundred different American municipalities. The geography surrounding these towns is varied, of course—maybe your favorite place to visit is by a lake or an ocean or a prairie—but the underlying structure is more or less the same. That doesn't make these towns ordinary; it just means they need to be tamed.

I made Bloomington mine the same way Corey made me hers: by establishing ties. I didn't just buy coffee from Rachael; I walked a mile in her shoes—literally. I didn't order pizza from a chain; I went to local spot Mother Bear's Pizza on the regular for my favorite pie: the "Dante's Inferno," with mozzarella, sausage, and a generous scattering of jalapeño peppers. Together, Corey and I explored every corner of Bloomington as thoroughly as we explored each other: the fields north of campus, the boutique video-rental shop with incredibly specific categories like "Non-Satanic Malevolent Children," the cookie shop that stays open late for people who get the munchies called—pun alert—Baked.

And like the little prince did every day with the fox, we came back—and we'll keep coming back every few years, even if it seems strange to some people that two queer ladies would want to go on vacation to Indiana. In one of my favorite episodes of *Parks and Recreation*, Aziz Ansari's character, Tom, is scandalized by the fact that sad sack Jerry likes to vacation in Muncie.[28] But why *not* Muncie? Why not any place you make yours?

Like everyone else, queer people don't always choose the places where we forge our worlds so much as they choose us. Would my bisexual friend Liz travel all the way to Bloomington for a slice of Dante's Inferno? Probably not, the same way I wouldn't buy a ticket to her hometown of Fargo, North Dakota, just to have the chicken cordon bleu sub she has raved about for years—unless, of course, I could be with her, seeing the city's queer culture through her eyes.

There are so many Bloomingtons in America that queer people call home, whether the states they are in

---

28 "The 15 Best Hoosier Moments in 'Parks and Recreation,'" http://www.indystar.com/story/entertainment/movies/2015/01/05/hoosier-moments-in-parks-and-recreation/14116321/

seem welcoming or not. Muncie, to pick one example, is a lot more than a punch line: that town added sexual orientation and gender identity to its antidiscrimination legislation right after Mike Pence signed the Religious Freedom Restoration Act into law.[29]

And I'm sure Muncie has a Rachael.

When Corey proposed to me in October of 2013, I was in a New York City hospital bed recovering from heart surgery. The hour was late. I was urging her to go home and get some rest. Corey got up as if to leave but instead pulled a small box out of her bag.

The ring was simple: a tiny diamond embedded in a gold band with *Little Boo,* her pet name for me, engraved on the inside.

I told her then what I still believe today: "The diamond is Bloomington."

To me, it is "unique in all the world," a glittering gem in our golden forever.

29 "A List of Local LGBT Anti-Discrimination Ordinances in Indiana," http://www.indystar.com/story/news/politics/2015/09/23/a-list-of-local-lgbt-anti-discrimination-ordinances-in-indiana/72627926/

# Chapter 5

# NOT THE FAMILY
# THAT YOU'RE IN

You choose your lovers, you pick your friends
Not the family that you're in, nah
They'll be with you 'til the end.

*—Dolly Parton*

**J**ennifer Culp was the first woman ever to treat me like her sister.

Her husband, Justin Mitchell, was the first man to call me "sweetheart."

I can't remember exactly when their little A-frame house in east Tennessee first started to feel like my second home. It could have been back in 2013, while I was playing Xbox on the couch with Jenn's brother, Joe, joyriding virtual Jeeps around an expansive level of *Halo*, completely ignoring our objective. Or it could have been the afternoon that I played *Resident Evil 6* with Jenn the following year, as we idly discussed the hotness of built men in Henley T-shirts. But it was probably the morning after the first night I stayed over in Jenn and Justin's small guest room, when I woke up covered in rainbows.

In the morning light, I learned that Jenn collects hundreds of prisms and hangs them everywhere, so when the sun slants through the windows, the whole house becomes a queer wonderland.

Jenn and the Johnson City, Tennessee, crew were the first group of friends I found after transition and, perhaps not coincidentally, they became what queer people like to call a "chosen family":[1] a close-knit network of loved ones who—despite not being related to you by blood—support you as if they are. Like a lost baby bird that imprints on the first person to pick her up, I made them my own, indelibly and irreversibly. I started making four-hour pilgrimages from Georgia up to their house whenever I could, ditching grad-school obligations to spend more time in Tennessee.

It's not that my friends in Atlanta disrespected my gender. They were quite kind. But through no fault of their own, they had too many memories of me before transition, wearing cargo shorts, dating a straight girl, and trying to grow out a scraggly beard. So yes, they called me "Samantha" and used female pronouns. But I also knew they saw flashes of my old self every time they looked at me—which is why it felt so amazing to come to Johnson City, where I knew I wasn't being seen as the "after" in a before-and-after photo spread.

And besides, none of my relationships at the time were

---

1 "Queer 2.0: The Importance of 'Chosen Family,'" https://www.nbcnews .com/video/queer-2-0-the-importance-of-chosen-family811533891617

strong enough to support me in the way that I needed so early in transition. Compared to many transgender people, I got lucky with my immediate family. Over a quarter of respondents to the 2015 U.S. Transgender Survey said that a nuclear-family member "stopped speaking to them for a long time or ended their relationship altogether" after they came out. One in ten reported experiencing family violence. Eight percent said they were kicked out of their homes.[2] None of that happened to me. But after I came out as transgender, my relationship with my blood family grew strained.

I behaved awkwardly around my parents because I knew how their religion—once my own—viewed people like me. They behaved awkwardly around me because I insisted they use my new name and pronouns, and they felt—as many parents of adult transgender children do—that this was all coming out of nowhere and moving too fast.

My relationships with my siblings were less troubled, but still, the weight of our mutual history was almost too much to bear. How do you practice your feminine voice around people who spent a decade listening to your baritone? How do you share space with the sister whose clothes you used to steal? My answer, at first, was that I didn't. I preferred having a sister to whom I had never been a brother. I preferred having a home where I had never had to hide.

---

2 2015 U.S. Transgender Survey, http://www.ustranssurvey.org/

I avoided my family of origin—and I built a family of my own in Johnson City.

We have a routine every time I come into town—and the night of August 3, 2017, when Billy and I arrive in Johnson City, sadly sans Corey, is no different.

First, we greet the animals: Doc, an affection-hungry German shepherd who has no idea how enormous he is; his more docile female counterpart, Red; and a tiny terrier mix named Lilly, whom Justin found abandoned in the middle of the night, shivering in a cold corner of the nearby dog park. Last but not least we say hello to Zelda, an energetic red-footed tortoise whose homemade—and artificially humidified—wooden habitat has a rainbow Pride flag for a backdrop. Billy falls in love with "Zelly" at first sight, tenderly brushing the top of her scaly head with his index finger.

. Then we head straight over to an all-night diner called Mid City Grill to share a plate of house-cut bacon cheese fries with a big side of drippy ranch, washing it all down with a six-pack of Yee-Haw beer brewed right across the street. Out of all the places to eat in Johnson City's 1920s-style downtown—sometimes referred to as Little Chicago[3]—this BYOB joint is undeniably the best. The food here doesn't have to be good—many of the people

---

3 "Little Chicago," http://www.stateoffranklin.net/johnsons/chicago/chicago.htm

eating it are either drunk or rapidly on their way to inebriation—but it *is*. My favorite burger, the "Heater," is topped with pickled jalapeños that have been marinated in sriracha. It is sinfully scrumptious.

After sustenance, it's back to the house for video games—*Resident Evil 7* this time around—with a side of homemade bourbon slushees. Justin has always been cagey about the ingredients in this beverage, but I've managed to piece most of the recipe together by now: Jim Beam bourbon, Earl Grey iced tea, San Pellegrino blood-orange soda—and one final, still-mysterious ingredient.

Before we get too tipsy, though, we receive a visit from Jenn's brother, Joe—an illustrator who worked as an international male model for several years after Jenn submitted his headshot to an agency as a joke[4]—and Joe's equally photogenic wife, Hannah, who commandeers the Xbox controller and begins shooting zombies in the head with a terrifying degree of precision.

At some point in the night Joe and Hannah head home, *Resident Evil* gets swapped out for a movie, and we start dozing off—some of us on the couch in a pile of dogs, others upstairs on beds. The dogs will need to be walked in the morning, out to the sinkhole in the stalled housing development half a mile from here. But for now I am full

---

4 Encyclopedia of Fashion, "Joseph Culp," http://www.fashionencyclopedia.com/wiki/joseph-culp

and happy, drunk and loved. I stumble upstairs to my air mattress and sleep better than I have in weeks.

Queerness is as much about friendship as it is about sex.

In his 2005 book *In a Queer Time and Place,* cultural theorist Jack Halberstam wrote that we should try to "detach queerness from sexual identity" and pay attention to "queer friendships" and "queer networks" instead.[5]

That might seem like a radical notion at first: after all, the fact that I have sex with another woman seems to be a big part of what makes me queer in society's eyes. But most of my life takes place outside the bedroom—and my queerness seems to come with me wherever I go. As Halberstam argued, what makes queer people a "perceived menace" to the "institutions of family, heterosexuality, and reproduction" has at least as much to do with the unusual ways in which we connect to each other as it does with the actual Leviticus-banned intercourse itself.

My queerness doesn't exclusively stem from my relationship with my wife; it is also an alternate way of existing in the world that has improbably allowed me to acquire a second family in an overlooked corner of Tennessee. So if you want to understand LGBT life in America, you need to know something about queer friendship.

Halberstam's 2005 argument drew from an influential

---

5 Jack Halberstam, *In a Queer Time and Place* (New York: New York University Press, 2005).

1981 interview given by gay French philosopher Michel Foucault—published under the title "Friendship as a Way of Life"—in which the thinker argued that it is the "homosexual mode of life" that makes homosexuality "disturbing" to the world, "much more than the sexual act itself."[6]

When I first read that interview back in graduate school, younger and spunkier than I am today, I didn't understand the philosopher's point. What makes an entire "way of life" homosexual or queer? Wasn't queerness itself about forbidden sexual desire? Nope—at least not for Foucault.

Foucault warned that when we hypersexualize homosexuality—when we think about it as "two young men meeting in the street, seducing each other with a look, grabbing each other's asses and getting each other off in a quarter of an hour"—we gloss over everything else that can be "troubling" to a "sanitized" heteronormative world about "affection, tenderness, friendship, fidelity, camaraderie, and companionship."

What about the intense relationships, the philosopher wondered, between young men in the military?

What about female friendships in the United States, he observed, in which women "do each other's hair, help each other with makeup, dress each other," "put their

---

6 Michel Foucault, "Friendship as a Way of Life," trans. John Johnston, *Gai Pied*, April 1981.

arms around each other, [and] kiss each other"—
friendships much like the one I share with Jennifer Culp?

"To imagine a sexual act that doesn't conform to law
or nature is not what disturbs people," he insisted. "But
that individuals are beginning to love one another—
there's the problem."

The kind of category-defying love Foucault describes
is a "problem" only because love is supposed to stay inside the proper social channels in our heteronormative
culture. The family you're born into is the family you're
supposed to be content with—and we are told repeatedly, without any explanation or supporting evidence,
that we are meant to "love them no matter what." To fit
into such a culture, your friendships ought to be lesser
bonds than your familial ties—which, in turn, are second
only to the sexual contract you share with your spouse.
Probe that unspoken ordering too insistently and you will
receive only tautologies in return: "Because they're your
*family*," or "Because he's your *husband*—that's why."

But when you're queer, you learn how arbitrary that
way of looking at the world can be. The people with
whom you grew up can become strangers in a single,
heartbreaking instant.

You discover as a queer person that there's nothing
stopping you from imbuing your friendships with the
same meaning that most people attach to their familial
relationships. You stop looking for the truth about your
identity in your sexuality and instead, as Foucault ad-

vised, "use [your] sexuality henceforth to arrive at a multiplicity of relationships."

That is what has happened to me since coming out as queer and transgender. The heady feeling of finally being myself and loving who I want to love didn't last forever; what has sustained me in the long run is the deep ties that I built with friends.

A woman like Jenn didn't just start to feel "*like* a sister" to me. She was transformed, through some kind of queer alchemy, into an actual sister. And I love her now with what Foucault would call a "dense, bright marvelous love"[7]—a love so strong that it refuses the binary checkboxes of friendship and attraction to become, simply and indescribably, its own thing.

All the experiences I have shared with Jenn are bound up together in a single thick knot.

We have danced together in a cloud of bubbles dressed like R2-D2 from *Star Wars* and Leeloo from *The Fifth Element*. We have made ourselves up to look like fancy space aliens from an all-female humanoid species that we invented (naming it "Neebo" after Johnson City's now-defunct college bookstore), then taken bizarre photos together in the ornate lobby of the Carnegie Hotel for no other reason than it was Saturday night. We have wan-

---

7 Ibid.

dered arm in arm through the seven rooms of the Miami Beach gay club Twist until the gray predawn. We have swayed together to Lana Del Rey's languorous voice in an Atlanta amphitheater and held hands on the chain lift of a Dollywood roller-coaster. She and I have swum and cuddled and laughed and grilled and sipped on frozen margaritas for breakfast.

Jenn is a writer, a visual artist and—like my wife—a Scorpio who believes in astrology mostly because it seems to explain her own charms so well. I am the dull and dutiful Capricorn, drawn to her dazzle but not dumb enough to be completely duped by it—and, as a result, Jenn has written that I am one of two people on earth with whom she feels "most comfortable" being her "not-trying-to-entertain-anyone self."[8] Between being one of Jenn's best friends and Corey's wife, I have come to think of myself as something of a Scorpio whisperer, one of the chosen few permitted to see behind the curtains of their often-mercurial moods.

But Jenn's intensity—like Corey's—is more than worth any trouble it might cause.

Since she and I first met at a fan convention at nearby East Tennessee State University in 2013, she has never asked me a question about being transgender that felt exoticizing or "othering," nor has she ever made me feel

---

8 "How to Look Like Every Sign of the Zodiac," https://theestablishment.co/how-to-look-like-every-sign-of-the-zodiac-e210efe9952e

like my womanhood was somehow less than her own. Her acceptance was immediate and unspoken, so matter-of-fact that it didn't even register as an event.

That's why it's hard to picture Jenn as a young Republican and self-described "true believer" who got baptized into her Bible Belt Christian faith at age twelve—a time of her life she recalls for me as we float together in the Carnegie Hotel pool on the afternoon of August 5. But maybe it shouldn't be: as a former suit-and-tie-wearing Mormon missionary who used to cite the Bible to denounce homosexuality, I know firsthand that personal change can be, shall we say, thorough.

Jenn shifted from Republican to libertarian in high school, which is also when she started to acknowledge—if only to herself at first—that she was bisexual.

"I didn't want to say anything [about being bi] at the time, not because I was ashamed of it per se—I was starting to break with the church a bit by then," Jenn remembers, explaining the real reason she stayed closeted: "The attitude at our school was that you're doing it for attention."

Jenn knew exactly what her fate would be if she came out: she would be branded an "attention whore." Classmates would hound her about whether she had ever been with a woman, and if she said no they'd tell her she wasn't bisexual—even though, as Jenn informs me, she hadn't slept with *anyone* at that point, male or female. So Jenn managed to convince herself that she was straight—even though her behavior in college would go on to suggest otherwise.

"I made out with a bunch of women and was like, 'Well, this is just what straight girls do,'" Jenn jokes now.

"That phrase," she adds, laughing, "just a straight girl who is obsessed with *The L Word!*"

Jenn's first husband, whom she married shortly before turning eighteen in what she now sees as an ill-advised rebellion against "the limited agency of adolescence,"[9] definitely "thought it was hot when I would mess around with women," she remembers.

But he would have felt threatened if she had asserted a bisexual identity more forcefully than random make-out sessions in college. Instead, her bisexuality kept brewing behind the scenes as her worldview expanded. She met liberal professors at East Tennessee State, where she was studying art. She became a regular reader of the women's blog *Jezebel.* And she befriended lots and lots of queer people, many of them fellow bisexual women. It was widely assumed that Jenn was bisexual, too, but she would correct people, "No, but I *am* attracted to girls"—as if that weren't the very definition of their shared sexual orientation.

At age twenty-two—as Jenn memorably writes in the essay collection *Split*—she came home to find her hus-

---

9 Jennifer Culp, "Oathbreaker," in *Split: True Stories About the End of Marriage and What Happens Next* (ebook collection), ed. Katie West and Jasmine Elliot (Fiction and Feeling, 2017).

band "in flagrante eating-Arby's-roast-beef-melts-and-watching-*Borat* with another woman in the home we'd shared for four and a half years."

"Oathbreaker!" she shouted at him—and then filed for divorce the next day.[10]

She had no intention of settling down with the next person she met, vowing to sleep around a bit instead, but six months later she found herself dating her current husband, Justin Mitchell, a man with dimples so deep you could fit pennies inside them when he smiles. And not only was Justin stupidly handsome, he had a mind so sharp that Jenn couldn't hide her inner life.

One day Justin told her, "Jenn, you're pretty bi."

"I guess you kind of have a point there," Jenn replied, but the theory took a while to sink in.

My friend has come out to me privately in several conversations over the course of our long friendship, often borrowing Justin's phrase "pretty bi."

But on June 11, 2016, to mark Pride Month, she wrote a makeup tutorial that doubled as a coming-out essay for the feminist website *The Establishment*.[11] In it Jenn captured all the complicated feelings she had about being publicly bisexual—about how she didn't want to "make a point of announcing it" but then felt "horrified at the thought of

---

10 Ibid.
11 "How to Make Yourself Look Like Rainbow Pride," https://theestablishment.co/how-to-make-yourself-look-like-rainbow-pride-f9128fce38bc

some openly queer lady" seeing her rainbow-themed Pride makeup and accusing her of "jacking our shit."

"My sexual identity is super mundane," she wrote. "It's not particularly deviant; it's just...normal. Just the way things are! It's just my life. And we are *legion,* we invisi-bi femme women in committed opposite-sex relationships with straight or bi men."

Bisexual people are indeed everywhere. In fact, according to the most recent estimates from the Williams Institute at the UCLA School of Law, bisexual people "comprise a slight majority" of the LGBT community, at 1.8 percent of the total U.S. population, compared with the 1.7 percent who identify as either gay or lesbian.[12] One recent study in the *Archives of Sexual Behavior* found that 12.2 percent of millennial women reported having had a same-sex sexual experience.[13] But you might not realize how prevalent bisexual people are because of the social pressures that keep them in the closet—and because, according to 2013 Pew Research Center data, the "overwhelming majority of bisexuals have opposite-sex partners" and therefore often get falsely perceived as straight.[14]

---

12 "How Many People Are Lesbian, Gay, Bisexual, and Transgender?" https://williamsinstitute.law.ucla.edu/wp-content/uploads/Gates-How-Many-People-LGBT-Apr-2011.pdf

13 Jean M. Twenge et al., "Change in American Adults' Reported Same-Sex Sexual Experiences and Attitudes, 1973–2014," *Archives of Sexual Behavior* 45, no. 7 (2016): 1713–30.

14 "A Survey of LGBT Americans," http://www.pewsocialtrends.org/files/2013/06/SDT_LGBT-Americans_06-2013.pdf

Bisexual people are so ubiquitous that Jenn didn't real-ize until her mid-twenties "that some women actually are just straight-up heterosexual and solely sexually attracted to men."[15] Now that I'm a part of Jenn's extended John-son City family, I can see how she missed that memo.

"Tennessee—I have such a strong community of queer friends here," she tells me, as the afternoon sun obliterates the last sliver of shade left on the pool. "I don't know if it's the majority, but a good friggin' half of my close friends."

But even though she is surrounded by fellow red-state queers, Jenn sometimes doubts her place in the LGBT community. The day after she wrote her essay for *The Es-tablishment,* an armed gunman walked into the Orlando LGBT nightclub Pulse, killing forty-nine people and wounding dozens more. It was—for a time, anyway— the worst mass shooting in modern American history. Jenn knew that Corey and I weren't regular club goers, but the thought occurred to her that we *could* have been there. To process her feelings, she drew a picture of Corey and me, holding hands and wearing the same glittery dresses we wore when we all went dancing together at Twist in Miami Beach. It hangs over my desk to this day.

Jenn tells me that the Pulse shooting "definitely took me from this kind of celebratory place" where she felt

---

15 "How to Make Yourself Look Like Rainbow Pride," https://theestab-lishment.co/how-to-make-yourself-look-like-rainbow-pride-f9128fce38bc

like "stepping out" and claiming her identity right back to feeling invalid—back to an emotional state where she didn't feel "queer enough to be mourning this with everyone else in the LGBT community."

"That rattled me back in the closet a little bit, if that makes any sense," she says, adding that there are still days when she asks herself, "Do I really count? Because I'm married to a man."

"Fight that bad voice," I whisper to Jenn, wanting to squeeze her more gracefully than I can while treading water in the Carnegie pool.

She counts. *Of course* she counts. And if we could literally count every queer person in America—if we could wake up one day and see *everyone* whose lives or desires cut across the heteronormative mainstream, whether they are currently in a same-sex relationship or not—we would never look at our country the same way again.

I have never been to Paris, but I have been to Johnson City—and that feels good enough for me. This is my far-away land of artists and libertines and weirdos.

In the week that Billy and I spend here, we attend a figure-drawing party held above a storage unit, where my pansexual illustrator friend Brett Marcus Cook poses nude with a bunny mask held over his crotch—and where the bisexual manager of a sex-toy shop puts on a Wonder Woman costume and whips a transgender woman in a frilly Victorian dress. I try to sketch them, but *scrawl* might be a more apt verb given my skill level. We hang out in Joe and Hannah's loft, drinking La Croix and eating caprese crackers topped with basil grown on the balcony, all while playing with their tailless cat Hodu, whose name means "walnut" in Hannah's native Korean.

We scale Roan Mountain near the North Carolina border under the full sun, a thin line of clouds the only interruption in the blue sky. We have dinner with Jenn's eccentric parents—and Jenn's mom, Jane "Peppi" Culp, compliments Billy on finishing his slice of key lime pie as if he had just brought home a report card with straight As. We talk loudly about our formative queer experiences— about Billy and Jenn's shared love of *A Shot at Love with Tila Tequila,* for example—over enormous frozen margaritas at my favorite strip-mall Mexican restaurant, El Charolais. (A little *too* loudly, judging from the uncomfortable stares of the other patrons.)

Time is mostly measured in dog walks. By day we take Doc, Red, and Lilly around the neighborhood in the musty aftermath of the summer rain. By night we go to the flooded quarry in neighboring Elizabethton, under an overcast sky illuminated by a full Aquarius moon.

Sometimes I wish I could put this life in a bottle and send it to my queer friends in New York.

Or they could just move here and save for retirement. In 2017, Johnson City made WalletHub's list of the one hundred best small cities in America, out of a pool of over twelve hundred, based on affordability and quality of life.[16] It is now number nine on the *Forbes* list of "Best Small Places."[17] You could put a down payment on a house here for a year or two's worth of rent in a big city—and believe me, I've considered doing just that; there's a house for sale on Corey Drive that literally has my wife's name on it.

But it's not just the financial cost of living in Johnson City that makes me want to staple flyers for it all over Brooklyn; it's the emotional cost of *not* living here—or at least somewhere like it.

When I ask people what they like about New York, I hear that it's the "cultural capital of the world," an inexhaustible fountain of unique experiences. But what good is a city that has "so much going on" if the people who live there are miserable? I'm generalizing here, but there's solid data to back me up. In 2014 the National Bureau of Economic Research (NBER) declared New York City the unhappiest city in America based on answers to the question, "In general, how satisfied are you with your life?" That study puts a quantifiable cap on a qualifiable sensation I have always felt when hanging out in big-city queer circles: not ennui, not mere sadness, but what Thoreau might call "quiet desperation."

Yes, I may be surrounded by masses of like-minded people when I visit an LGBT-friendly megalopolis like

16 "Best Small Cities in America," https://wallethub.com/edu/best-worst-small-cities-to-live-in/16581/

17 Forbes Best Small Places List, https://www.forbes.com/lists/2006/5/2943.html

New York City. But because no one besides millionaires can *really* afford to have a stable, long-term existence there, we end up spending money that we don't have at bars where the booze is marked up 400 percent—all because we can't properly host each other in tiny shared apartments full of laundry that we haven't done yet.

So why should I get excited about the prospect of a gay bar on every corner when I can just roll up to New Beginnings in Johnson City with a car full of my ride-or-die friends? And why should I care about which cool people are going to your even cooler friend's show if the people I'm going to meet there are also unhappy denizens of the same godforsaken asphalt island?

Big-city LGBT life, to me, is proof that more can be less. As pop legend and gay icon Britney Spears famously told Sabrina the Teenage Witch in 1996, being surrounded by people is sometimes "the loneliest place to be."[18]

New York City may have four times as many LGBT people as Johnson City has people, period, but finding happiness as a queer American is not a mere numbers game.

And yet the sheer inertia of a place like New York City can make it feel almost inescapable. There is a perpetual existential gloom hanging over Manhattan, but so many people I know are unwilling to get themselves out from

---

18 "No Place Like Home," http://www.melissazone.com/sabrina/transcript.php?id=076

under it. As NBER noted, one obvious but depressing conclusion we can draw from its 2014 study is that "individuals do not aim to maximize self-reported well-being." In other words, they must care about *something else* more than happiness.

Often, I've found, my big-city acquaintances are looking for a job title, a boost to their social capital, or—most vexing of all—a certain sense of being "in the middle of everything."

I have almost been pulled into New York City's gravity, despite my loathing for it. A good chunk of LGBT media jobs require you to live there—even in an age when I can write anywhere with a Wi-Fi connection. But the last time I was offered a position there, I seriously considered it—and then turned it down. World-renowned museums and Zagat-rated restaurants are great and all, but there is no sculpture awe-inspiring enough, no tapa tasty enough to persuade me to move into a glorified shoebox of an apartment and ride to work every day in a dysfunctional system of underground tin cans. As long as I can figure out how to make a living literally anywhere else, I will stay away forever.

More and more LGBT people seem to be operating on a similar wavelength. I asked Gary J. Gates, the most widely cited demographer of the American LGBT community, what evidence he has seen of queer demographic shifts away from coastal big cities over the last decade.

He pointed me to his recent Williams Institute analysis

of U.S. Census and Gallup polling data, which compared the concentration of same-sex couples in American cities in 1990 to the percentage of their LGBT population from 2012 to 2014.[19] (It's an imperfect comparison, but given how hard it is to gather data on a small population like the LGBT community, it's one of the best available.) And the results are striking: Salt Lake City leapt up *thirty-two spots* in the overall rankings between 1990 and the 2012–2014 time period. Louisville, Kentucky, rose thirty slots over the same period. Norfolk, Virginia, and New Orleans, Louisiana, both jumped more than twenty places. Meanwhile San Francisco remained static, Los Angeles fell two slots, and New York had a staggering eleven-place slump.

Gates believes that this discrepancy speaks to the social change happening in many red-state cities. As he wrote in the analysis: "Substantial increases in LGBT visibility in more socially conservative places like Salt Lake City, Louisville, and Norfolk likely mean that these areas are not as different from cities like San Francisco, Austin, and Seattle (all with long histories of fostering social climates where LGBT people felt more comfortable) in their acceptance of the LGBT community today than they were twenty years ago."

Indeed, an "important explanatory factor" for that

---

19 "Comparing LGBT Rankings by Metro Area: 1990 to 2014," http://williamsinstitute.law.ucla.edu/wp-content/uploads/Comparing-LGBT-Rankings-by-Metro-Area-1990-2014.pdf

data, as Gates acknowledged in the analysis, is the increased "willingness" of LGBT people in conservative areas to come out of the closet. In other words, although the analysis probably indicates some degree of population shift, it doesn't mean that *every* queer person in New York City has packed up and moved to Norfolk instead.

But the data also fits in with general U.S. migration patterns toward the South and the West, as an earlier Williams Institute analysis observed.[20] And given the fact—noted by Gates—that only 12 percent of LGBT adults say they factor levels of LGBT social acceptance into their moving decisions, less and less is stopping us from moving south or west—and plenty of attractive midsize American cities are calling our name.

The emerging truth is that LGBT people have been building beautiful lives away from the coasts for years in places like Johnson City. Progressive laws and policies may help queer people thrive but they are not, on a gut level, what keeps us going; friendship is our fuel. You could re-ban same-sex marriage in Tennessee and make it illegal for me to use the women's restroom here, but I would still probably choose it over New York. I'd be a law-breaker, sure, but at least I would have fresh air to breathe and pleasant company to share it with.

---

20 "Geographic Trends Among Same-Sex Couples in the U.S. Census and the American Community Survey," http://williamsinstitute.law.ucla.edu/wp-content/uploads/Gates-Geographic-Trends-ACS-Brief-Nov-2007.pdf

Because love is what does the heavy lifting in queer survival. It may not be "all you need," as the Beatles sang—or as Ewan MacGregor once crooned over Baz Luhrmann's computer-generated Paris—but it's pretty damn close.

Chosen families are what make queer life possible in places like the Bible Belt.

And when it comes to LGBT issues, this state might be the Bible Belt's buckle. According to the Transgender Law Center, Tennessee is the only state in the country that "specifically forbids" transgender people from updating the gender markers on their birth certificates—even if they have undergone sex-reassignment surgery—thanks to a statute passed in 1977, long before the issue was on most bigots' radars.[21] There are also no statewide nondiscrimination protections for sexual orientation and gender identity; indeed, a 2011 law bans cities and towns from passing LGBT-inclusive nondiscrimination ordinances of their own.[22] This is a state that forces queer people to be vulnerable to harassment and abuse.

That's why having a network of loved ones is so important to queer people in Tennessee. Yes, being in a city teeming with openly LGBT people might provide a sense of

---

21 "State-by-State Overview: Rules for Changing Gender Markers on Birth Certificates," http://transgenderlawcenter.org/wp-content/uploads/2016/12/Birth-Cert-overview-state-by-state.pdf
22 "LGBTQ Non-Discrimination in the States," https://www.freedomforallamericans.org/category/states/tn/

safety in numbers—and it might come with certain formal protections, too—but a small chosen family can punch well above its weight. As Cole Davis, a transgender man who first came out into the Christian evangelical community in rural Deep Run, North Carolina, once told me, even though only 15 percent of white evangelicals believe that someone's gender can be different from the one they were assigned at birth,[23] a few allies can be enough: "When you have [even] a handful of people who accept you fully as trans, it definitely helps you get through a lot of dark times."[24]

Love, it seems, is like dish soap: a little bit goes a long way. So, if it strikes you as insane that 88 percent of LGBT adults do *not* think about social acceptance when we choose a place to live, it's because most of us know we can build a chosen family almost anywhere—even in Tennessee.

The concept of "chosen family" was first popularized by anthropologist Kath Weston in her 1991 book, *Families We Choose: Lesbians, Gays, Kinship,* in which she suggested that tight-knit queer friend groups were "an alternative form of family" in a country where "the nuclear family clearly represents a privileged construct."

"Gay (or chosen) families dispute the old saying, 'You

---

23 "Views of Transgender Issues Divide Along Religious Lines," http://www.pewresearch.org/fact-tank/2017/11/27/views-of-transgender-issues-divide-along-religious-lines/

24 "Will Evangelicals Ever Get Over Their Anti-Trans Prejudice?," https://www.thedailybeast.com/will-evangelicals-ever-get-over-their-anti-trans-prejudice

can pick your friends, but you can't pick your relatives,'" Weston wrote. "Not only can these families embrace friends; they may also encompass lovers, coparents, adopted children, children from previous heterosexual relationships, and offspring conceived through alternative insemination."

The fact that I'm traveling with Billy is a prime example of chosen family in action: this is a guy who dated my wife before he transitioned in college. Not a lot of straight people would willingly spend two months with their spouse's ex-partner. But he is my road-trip buddy and Corey's best friend. The three of us are all bound together in a complex network of intimacy, history, and affection.

Billy is like a sibling to me — the transgender brother I never had. We have both known from an early age that our genders did not match the sexes we were assigned at birth, but we lacked the vocabulary to write a sentence like that until we made queer friends in college and graduate school, respectively. In parallel-but-still-disconnected lives, he and I both had realizations about being transgender that had to do with the length of our hair.

Billy cut his short in college and thought, "Wow, I didn't realize how badly I wanted this — or how good this feels."

I buzzed my head in the first years of graduate school — when I was still in denial about being transgender — and all I could think about was how long it would take to grow out if I ever did find the willpower to transition.

And we both came out in waves: first to ourselves, then to close friends at school, and finally to family. (Or rather, Billy's formidable Italian mother found out last, discovering that her son was transgender when she saw him mentioned by name on his college website. "What's going on?" she asked him. "Who's Billy?")

At this point in the trip, after hours spent conversing in the car about our transitions, Billy and I readily tell each other that we love each other. The tenderness and immediacy of our friendship are almost untranslatable to some of the straight cisgender people we meet, many of whom assume that we must be romantically involved—even though it was my wife he once dated. I harbor no jealousy over that fact, though. And Corey saw no reason why their breakup should be the end of their friendship.

When you're queer, you can't always afford to dispose of people—nor do you always want to. We experience enough rejection within our faiths and our families that we think twice before pressing the eject button on a relationship. And with the cultural odds stacked against us, our friendships can take on the urgency of blood bonds. Billy is an irreplaceable part of my chosen family now—a strange little elf of a man who, from time to time, gives me peerless advice.

Friends like Billy—friends like the estimated "friggin' half" of Jenn's circle who are also queer—can instantly make a place feel safer.

But because the media overwhelmingly focus on the tragic things that happen to queer people in red states, that kind of community building often goes unnoticed by people on the coasts. As Jack Halberstam wrote in *In a Queer Time and Place,* "Too often minority history hinges on representative examples provided by the lives of a few extraordinary individuals"—among them LGBT people who have been murdered in conservative parts of America.

"[In] relation to the complicated matrix of rural queer lives, we tend to rely on the story of a Brandon Teena or a Matthew Shepard rather than finding out about the queer people who live quietly, if not comfortably, in isolated areas or small towns all across North America," Halberstam wrote.

But how can people find out about those quiet—and I would say *often* comfortable—lives?

"BREAKING: Bisexual Tennessee Woman Has Large Queer Friend Circle" doesn't exactly make a catchy headline. But I think it's vital for our country to realize just how true—and how common—statements like that are. That won't happen as long as we remain stuck in a media environment that associates queerness with the metropolis and bigotry with red states.

As a longtime LGBT reporter, I feel qualified to say there are two broad types of red-state LGBT stories that mainstream outlets like to publish: either they want a story about a backward law engineered by evangelicals to

punish queer people, or they want a fluffy, deeply indi-
vidualistic human-interest piece about, say, a transgender
homecoming king in Texas.[25]

What's missing in that dichotomous media environment is attention to the quotidian fabric of queer life in a
place like Johnson City, Tennessee. Even in the face of the
demographic shifts I have described in this book, we still
have little cultural understanding of queer sociality outside
major urban centers because so little is written about it.

"Most theories of homosexuality within the twentieth
century assume that gay culture is rooted in cities [and]
that it has a special relationship to urban life," Halberstam wrote, noting that this focus "made sense" at first
due to the "great gay migrations of young queers from
the country to the city in the 1970s."[26]

But I would argue that focusing inordinately on queer
urban life didn't make sense even back then given how
many small-town queers "recount[ed] complicated stories of love, sex, and community in their small-town
lives," as Halberstam himself noted—and it especially
doesn't make sense now that we know just how quickly
midsize American cities are becoming the country's new
queer hubs.

---

25 "Meet the First Trans Homecoming King in Texas," https://www
   .thecut.com/2014/10/meet-the-first-trans-homecoming-king-in-
   texas.html
26 Jack Halberstam, *In a Queer Time and Place* (New York: New York University Press, 2005).

I don't know how to reorient the media to pay closer attention to LGBT life between the coasts—nor do I know how to make chosen families into click-grabbing articles.

But I can devote an entire brief chapter of this book to my friends. Jenn and Justin are not household names. They are not well-known activists. But wherever you live in this country, there are Jenns and Justins in your zip code.

Justin Mitchell is the kind of man who can make you unironically say, "It's so nice to have a man around the house."

He makes a mean vanilla milk shake. He taught me that the best way to slice a pizza is to skip the rolling cutter and use a pair of scissors instead. The last time he came over to our apartment, he unclogged the shower drain with no prompting, then pointed out the exact spot to spray the door hinge with WD-40 to get rid of the squeak. I had been too lazy to do it. To be honest, I'm waiting for Justin to come back.

His sheer capability almost frightens me. In the amount of time that I spend talking myself into doing a chore—like washing the blender after making milk shakes, for example—Justin has finished it and moved on to the next one.

Justin always had an anti-authoritarian streak while growing up in Tennessee, which I imagine helped shape him into the politically progressive guy I met in 2013. Back then, the devilishly handsome twenty-something young man would spend hours playing video games on Xbox Live, talking on his headset to people around the world, chastising them whenever they used sexist language or dropped a homophobic slur.

These days—when Billy and I come into town—Justin is ramping up to return to school so he can eventually become an optometrist. He is splitting his time between finishing financial-aid applications, working part-time as an usher at the Carnegie Hotel, and taking odd jobs from older folks for spare cash. And somehow he still finds an hour in the mornings to walk the dogs, feed the tortoise, and play *Dragon Age: Inquisition.*

I tell Justin that I want to interview him while I'm in town and he gets endearingly nervous.

"What would I say?" he asks me one day as we drive past El Charolais. "What do you want to ask me about?"

I give him some off-the-cuff response about "growing up in Tennessee" and "becoming an LGBT ally," but the more I think about it the less I want to demystify my best friend's husband.

I like Justin better as a mystery. Jenn and I often joke that neither of us has ever been able to plumb the depths of his mind—that he contains so many multitudes that he must be living a double life around Johnson City, the way Phil Connors in *Groundhog Day* spends his time going around Punxsutawney changing flat tires, rescuing boys who fall from trees, and performing the Heimlich maneuver on choking diners. I would rather Justin's second life remain a secret. I suppose he's a lot like his homemade bourbon-slushee recipe: I don't need to know all the ingredients to know it tastes delicious.

Instead I enjoy spending a week watching Justin be Justin. To get away from the dog-filled house for a few nights, he negotiates a low rate for the four of us at the Carnegie and we have several sleepovers in luxurious, nineteenth-century style.

One day while Justin is working—and Billy and I are idling away the morning hours watching the Food Network—he bursts into our room in his old-fashioned bellboy uniform with a Diet Coke in his hand that I did not request but that he already knew I wanted. (As Tracy Jordan yells in *30 Rock* when he asks about the French fries he never ordered, "You guys need to anticipate me!") But Justin's "peak Justin" moment is him driving down a rural road on the way to Roan Mountain with Lilly nestled on his lap, one-handing a burger from Pal's Sudden Service.

A day or two before we skip town, Jenn and Justin take us to Dollywood, the amusement park opened by country-music legend Dolly Parton in the middle of the Great Smoky Mountains.

When we arrive at the park, I learn that Dolly's road-trip skills put my own to shame: Her $750,000 tour bus—which I would happily visit over the Met any day—was built to her specifications, with a full-sized bathtub and refrigerator and a fuel tank big enough to go several hundred miles without stopping.[27] Would that my rented SUV had that kind of range—or at least a tub for Billy to lounge in as I drove across the country.

Dolly herself, of course, is one of the most well-known celebrity LGBT allies. She has reportedly helped some of her own family members come out as gay—and she employs transgender people in her company.[28] Her bold, rhinestone-studded style comes across almost like a dare to drag performers to imitate her. And after North Carolina passed its bathroom bill, she spoke out—in rhyme, no less—saying, "I just know if I have to pee, I'm gonna pee. I don't care where it's gonna be."[29]

Justin speaks of Dolly—as many folks in this state do—with a tone bordering on worship. After wildfires ravaged some eastern Tennessee towns in November 2016, her fund donated more than $8 million to those left homeless. As USA Today reported, Dolly essentially paid their rent, doling out a $1,000 check per month for

---

27 "Check Out the Amazing Dalbury E—Electric Campervan," https://rvshare.com/blog/dolly-parton-wants-show-inside-tour-bus/d

28 "My 11 Minutes with Dolly Parton: How She's Helped Her Gay Mountain Family and Her Plan If She Were President," http://www.pridesource.com/article.html?article=77866

29 "Dolly Parton Gives Poignant Response to North Carolina 'Bathroom Bill,'" http://www.rollingstone.com/music/news/dolly-parton-gives-poignant-response-to-north-carolina-bathroom-bill-20160609

six months to more than eight hundred displaced residents.[30]

"She single-handedly keeps her hometown alive," Justin tells us.

After a long day at the park, I watch Justin ride the Drop Line, Dollywood's new 230-foot free-fall ride.[31] I watch him laugh as he plummets, then gather the courage to join him on the next go-round. We sit together at the top, spinning in our seats, looking out at the gently rolling Smokies under the fading daylight as we anticipate the drop. I love this strange unknowable man who came bounding into my life with the enthusiasm of a modern-day Johnny Appleseed.

Dolly once sang that "you choose your lovers, you pick your friends/ Not the family that you're in, nah." But with all due respect to Ms. Parton, queer people like me have lives in which friends and family aren't always so easy to differentiate. And sitting on top of the Drop Line, awaiting the pneumatic *Whoosh!* that will signal the start of our free fall, I don't feel like I picked Justin so much as fate picked him out for me. He feels as inevitable as the drop.

---

30 "Second Mississippi City Passes Major LGBTQ-Inclusive Non-discrimination Ordinance," https://www.usatoday.com/story/news/nation-now/2017/11/17/dolly-parton-gatlinburg-wildfire-relief-fund/873593001/

31 Dollywood, "Drop Line 101," https://blog.dollywood.com/index.php/2017/05/01/drop-line-101/

\*   \*   \*

I am lucky enough to have two families now: the family I chose *and* the family I didn't.

The last time I drove across the country before writing *Real Queer America* was in the spring of 2014, when Corey and I traveled from Atlanta to San Francisco so I could undergo sex-reassignment surgery. As we sped through the California desert in the evening, we fielded worried texts from my parents, who had caught wind of my surgery date. It was clear that they disapproved—and that they were hoping I would have second thoughts. I ignored them.

Up to that point, my relationship with my parents had been strained. They were still experiencing whiplash at the seeming suddenness with which I announced that I was transitioning back in 2012—and then just did it. From my perspective, I was making up for lost time; from theirs, I was moving at an alarming pace, changing my appearance—and now my genitals—as quickly as I could line up doctor appointments. I didn't have the patience to wait for them to play catch-up. And as much as they acted awkward around me, I have to admit that I cut myself off from them, too.

Hours after my surgery, Corey had to fly back to New York. She hadn't seen my vagina yet—hell, *I* hadn't even seen my vagina yet—because it was still wrapped in more gauze than an Egyptian mummy. But she had a degree to finish.

My convalescence was almost as challenging as the astronomy final she went home to take. I lived off Safeway sandwiches and split my abundant but lonely free time between doing surgical aftercare and lying on my back, waiting for life to resume. If I could make it through thirty days without any complications, I would be allowed to leave the Bay Area and return home.

I planned on driving back by myself. My mom had other plans.

She showed up at the San Francisco airport at the tail end of my recovery. I couldn't believe that she wanted to help me—but she did. We drove together for as long as I could comfortably sit up in the car, making it as far as Lake Tahoe the first day and Salt Lake City the next. There was no tearful moment of reconciliation—and, come to think of it, there never has been between us; the important thing was that we simply spent time in each other's presence. We were trapped in the same Honda Fit, with nothing but the salt flats to distract us from each other. That trip was a quiet turning point, the beginning of the resuscitation of a relationship we had both missed.

Corey and I had spent our first Christmas together as a couple by ourselves. After my surgery, though, we started flying to Seattle every December to be with my folks and my siblings. Everyone eventually got accustomed to my new name, my changing appearance, and my female pronouns. They started calling me their "daughter," their "sister," or their "sister-in-law," making my heart soar every time I overheard those recognition-laden syllables. And as the country collectively familiarized itself with the existence of transgender people, my impatience with educating others and answering their questions became less of an obstacle. I was allowed to be just me—just Samantha.

Over the years, my parents became close friends. Corey and my dad—both Scorpios—love to laugh, indulge their sweet tooths, and hold court at the dinner table. My mom and I—both Capricorns—roll our eyes and do our best to rein in our respective troublemakers. In the back of my mind, I know that Mormonism is still less than thrilled with transsexuals like me—and that my parents are still devout members of that faith. But I am just happy to have Mom and Dad back, and I would never expect them to do anything even close to contradicting their religion.

Which is why I wasn't anticipating what happened in the summer of 2016.

My parents came to visit us for a weekend trip in the Florida Keys. We rented adjacent bayside cottages—which, appropriately, already had Jimmy Buffett songs playing on their respective stereos when we opened the doors. Our days were spent driving up and down the Overseas Highway in their rental car, taking long lunches and going on boat tours. We rode out through the mangroves to the coral reef and watched the sunset near Islamorada. But Corey and I were harboring a secret: we had applied for our marriage license just before they arrived.

We had always wanted a wedding, but a ceremony was simply out of reach. There were so many other big expenses in our future—a down payment on a house, in vitro fertilization for the babies we would like to have—that we couldn't justify dropping big bucks on poufy dresses and a fancy party. In the same way I would never ask them to drink tequila or smoke a cigarette, it had never occurred to me to ask my well-off parents to help pay for a same-sex wedding.

But after that weekend, Dad called us and gravely intoned that he wanted to "talk to you about something."

"As you know, it's traditional for the parents of the bride to help finance a wedding," he told me. "We helped your sister with her wedding and we'd like to help you with yours, too."

Corey and I both cried.

Justin Mitchell was the first man ever to call me "sweetheart."

My dad was the first to call me a "bride."

On the last night Billy and I spend in Johnson City, we go to a pool party.

I swim around in my galaxy-patterned bathing suit, gathering all the foam pool noodles and submerging them beneath Jenn so I can pull her around the pool on a makeshift raft. She throws her head back and laughs. The setting sun lights up stray clouds in shades of pink and purple.

After dark we gather around the fire pit. The host of the party, Jeff, spins a story about a barrel of American whiskey purportedly in his possession that is filled with Pappy Van Winkle—a rare bourbon from Buffalo Trace distillery that has been aged for over a decade and retails for thousands of dollars a bottle. Jeff's tale is about as tall as it gets: a relative, he claims, met someone at an airport who was selling a barrel of the costly liquor. A mason jar filled with a caramel-colored liquid is currently working its way around the fire, supposedly containing the magical elixir itself.

The story is probably not true. Clever counterfeiters often try to pass off lesser whiskeys as Pappy.[32] But in 2015 authorities busted a syndicate that had been stealing bottles and barrels of the stuff, so there's a chance, however slim, that the mason jar contains the genuine article.[33]

Jenn's dad takes a sip and declares, "That is damn fine."

Jenn's mom, "Peppi," can't get enough of it, more than living up to her nickname as she gushes about the taste, smacking her lips together after each sip.

The mason jar reaches me and I initially decline, my old Mormon teetotaler side instinctively reasserting itself.

---

32 "Buffalo Trace Cracking Down on Counterfeit Pappy Van Winkle Bourbon Resellers," http://www.distillerytrail.com/blog/buffalo-trace-cracking-down-on-counterfeit-pappy-van-winkle-bourbon-resellers/
33 "At Last: Kentucky Authorities Bust Ring Behind Great Bourbon Heist," https://www.npr.org/sections/thesalt/2015/04/21/401318542/at-last-kentucky-authorities-bust-ring-behind-great-bourbon-heist

But persuaded by the shouts of my surrogate Tennessee family, I take a small shot of it with Jenn and feel the tingle of it spread from my mouth out through my nasal cavity and down my throat. The burn skips past my belly, sliding down my legs until I feel it tickle the arches of my feet. Jenn and I wriggle together as the alcohol works its magic.

I have no idea whether or not it's Pappy.

But drinking it with Jenn, I don't care.

# Chapter 6

# CROSSROADS

That's why I want to change things in Mississippi.
You don't run away from problems—you just face
them.

—*Fannie Lou Hamer*[1]

The last thing I want to do on the night of August 12, 2017, is go to WonderLust.

As amazing as Jackson, Mississippi's premier LGBT nightclub sounds,[2] I am tired, my thirst for travel finally giving way to homesickness. I have spent six hours of the slow-passing day driving through intermittent torrential downpours, caught in a cyclical purgatory of precipitation and sunshine. After five weeks on the road, and after having to say goodbye to my friends in Tennessee for who knows how long, I would rather hole up in a motel,

---

1 Kay Mills, *This Little Life of Mine: The Life of Fannie Lou Hamer* (Lexington: University of Kentucky Press, 2007).
2 "Inside the Hottest Gay Bar in the Most Homophobic State in the Nation,"https://www.washingtonpost.com/lifestyle/style/inside-the-hottest-gay-bar-in-the-most-homophobic-state-in-thenation/2016/07/19/70ad84ee4910-11e6bdb9-701687974517_story.html?utm_term=.2039b7797120

watch the Food Network with Billy, and digest the Pig and Pint barbecue we had for dinner.

Last night, dozens of tiki torch–bearing white supremacists and neo-Nazis stormed the University of Virginia campus in Charlottesville. (President Trump would go on to say that their number included "some very fine people."[3]) And as Billy and I worked our way down from Tennessee in the rain, a neo-Nazi drove his car into a crowd of Charlottesville counterprotesters,[4] killing thirty-two-year-old Heather Heyer, a progressive paralegal who, according to her boss, despised "any type of discrimination."[5] Sitting in our musty Mississippi motel room, catching up on the news, Billy and I are ready to give up on this day.

But then, at 11:30 p.m., I remember the motto Billy and I have lived by the entire trip: "Something gay every day." We came up with it in Utah to remind ourselves never to treat this trip like an extended vacation—and I recite it to myself every time I need motivation.

"Let's go," I tell Billy.

"Really?" he says, already pantsless, prepared for our Food Network binge.

---

3 "Trump Gives White Supremacists an Unequivocal Boost," https://www.nytimes.com/2017/08/15/us/politics/trump-charlottesvillewhite-nationalists.html

4 "James Fields Jr.: A Neo-Nazi's Violent, Rage-Fueled Journey to Charlottesville," http://www.chicagotribune.com/news/nationworld/ct-james-fields-jr-charlottesville-20170818-story.html

5 "Heather Heyer, Charlottesville Victim, Is Recalled as 'a Strong Woman,'" https://www.nytimes.com/2017/08/13/us/heather-heyer-charlottesville-victim.html

But I mean it. We drive up State Street through the Fondren district and turn onto the neglected side street that takes us to WonderLust. When we had passed by the nightclub after dinner, only a handful of cars were in the parking lot. Now, just after 12 a.m., the lot is full and the one across the street is filling up. We step out of the car into the Mississippi midnight, the air thick, wet, warm, and oddly inviting. It feels like we are walking into a Lynchian dream as we approach the club, the noise rising, the red-white-and-blue neon over the facade coming into focus through the haze as we approach.

From the outside, the bar is unassuming. You might drive by and not even notice it was there. But inside it feels like a palace: spotlessly clean with a large bar, a spacious dance floor, and a theater off to the side with a rainbow-tinsel backdrop draped across the stage.

Billy and I grab two high-top stools in the back of the theater and, as if on cue, the lights go down for the drag show. As the music rises, we look at each other and smile, glad that we got our asses out of that motel.

Bobby Flay will still be there when we get back.

The crowd in WonderLust is remarkably varied: white and black, gay and straight, transgender and cisgender, silver-haired and—because the club is open to anyone eighteen and over—young, too. I know that well-off white folks like me often dub a place "diverse" just because they see a couple of people who look different from them; believe me, that is *not* the case here. Along with the Back Door, it is one of the only LGBT nightlife spots I have been to where everyone seems to feel welcome. And as with my favorite Bloomington hangout, you can look around and see the care that has gone into making the club inviting: the bathrooms are sparklingly clean, the artwork is engaging but not hypersexualized, and the chairs—did I mention that there are *chairs*?—are cushy.

The show is splendid, full of gorgeous drag queens from New Orleans. The headliner is the Sensational Nicole Lynn Foxx, her three wardrobe changes alone worth ten times the club's cover.[6] When Miss Foxx needs some more time to don her next outfit, the emcee asks the crowd, "Y'all wanna get a little ghetto in here tonight?" We cheer—and when the DJ can't find a Cardi B. song, the emcee dances instead to Khia's "My Neck, My Back."

But before long, Miss Foxx reappears in a shimmering off-the-shoulder turquoise bodysuit to perform "I'm Every Woman" before closing out the evening with a surprise encore of "I Wanna Dance with Somebody (Who Loves Me)." It is a devastating Whitney Houston–themed one-two punch, delivered flawlessly.

The crowd dances and sings along as Foxx struts the runway collecting tips from her admirers, dabbing the sweat from her forehead with a spare dollar bill before

---

6 https://www.facebook.com/nicolelynn.foxx1

adding it to her thick stack. I survey the room, feeling the unrestrained joy in this space, and wonder: *Is* this a dream?

I had spent the day looking at the same horrifying images that everyone in the country had seen by then: photos of angry white people in polo shirts, their faces lit by the light of their torches, shouting the Nazi slogans "Blood and soil" [7] and *"Sieg Heil."* [8] Video of a gray Dodge Challenger ramming into the counterprotesters, sending bodies flying.

This hatred and violence have *always* been here in the United States; white supremacy is a constitutive value of America. But it's so much louder under Trump. The dog whistles are shouts now. The racist policies require fewer polite excuses to pass muster.

And yet somehow here in Mississippi (a state where a school district had to be ordered by the court system to desegregate *in 2016*[9]) there is this place: WonderLust, a vision of a future—or maybe even an alternate present—where people of all races, genders, and sexuali-

---

7 "'Blood and Soil': Protesters Chant Nazi Slogan in Charlottesville," http://www.cnn.com/2017/08/12/us/charlottesville-unite-the-right-rally/index.html

8 "Nazi Slogans and Violence at a Right-wing March in Charlottesville on Friday Night," https://www.vox.com/2017/8/12/16138132/charlottesville-rally-brawl-nazi

9 "Judge Orders Mississippi School District to Desegregate, 62 Years After Brown v. Board of Education," https://www.washingtonpost.com/news/education/wp/2016/05/16/judge-orders-mississippi-school-district-to-desegregate-62-years-after-brown-v-board-of-education/?utm_term=.835f1f218b4b

ties joyfully share space. As Billy and I walk back into the hot mist of the Mississippi night, I feel not a naive hope for the future, but a scrap of comfort in an uncertain present.

I may not live to see a day when the whole country feels as welcoming as this nightclub in the Deep South. But if America can prove itself to be better than Trump and half as good as WonderLust, perhaps one day someone will.

"Why do I still love Mississippi?"

That was the question my friend Kayley Scruggs asked herself in a 2014 op-ed in the Emory University student newspaper the *Emory Wheel* when her home state passed a Religious Freedom Restoration Act (RFRA) allowing business owners to deny service based on "religious beliefs"[10]—a law not unlike the Indiana RFRA that would inspire so much outrage the following year.

"Why am I proud to be from a state that continuously invalidates my identity?" she went on.

I wondered the same thing about Kayley when I first met her, back when we worked together as student employees in the Office of LGBT Life at Emory. Here was this incredible bisexual reproductive-justice activist who, I thought, should have been glad to have escaped to Atlanta, yet she waxed lyrical about Mississippi in her gentle Southern accent whenever she got the chance. She

---

10 "LGBT Southerners Must Lead Fight," http://emorywheel.com/lgbt
-southerners-must-lead-fight/

was—and still is—the sort of person who *never* lets you forget where they're from.

My skepticism about queer life in Mississippi was not without basis. When it comes to LGBT rights, the Hospitality State has been dragged kicking and screaming into the twenty-first century. It took major court rulings to force Mississippi to legalize same-sex sexual behavior in 2003, same-sex marriage in 2015, and same-sex adoption in 2016.

All of that foot-dragging has earned the state a permanent place on the queer shit list. In 2014 *Rolling Stone* placed Mississippi atop its roster of "The 5 Worst States for LGBT People," citing the RFRA as well as the state's bans at the time on same-sex marriage and adoption.[11] The state also fell at the bottom of similar rankings by MSNBC[12] and *Out*.[13] The Mississippi city of Southaven even earned the dubious honor of being declared "the worst city for LGBT rights" by *USA Today*.[14]

But there's only so much a national newspaper or an online magazine can tell you about a place, and unlike many of the reporters who wrote those "worst of" lists, Kayley had grown up in Mississippi. I met her when she

---

11 "The 5 Worst States for LGBT People," http://www.rollingstone .com/politics/news/the-5-worst-states-for-lgbt-people-20141124

12 "The Best and Worst States for LGBT Equality," http://www.msnbc .com/msnbc/the-best-and-worst-states-lgbt-equality

13 "And the Worst States for LGBTs Are...," https://www.outtraveler .com/features/2014/11/28/and-worst -states-lgbts-are

14 "Worst Cities for LGBT Rights," https://www.usatoday.com/story/ money/business/2014/11/22/247-wall-st-lgbt-cities/19354553/

was a freshman and I was finishing up graduate school but despite our age gap *she* was the one who taught *me:* about feminism, about queerness, about womanhood.

I had transitioned already, but just barely, by the time we became friends. She still sticks out in my memory as one of the first cisgender women to treat me no differently because I was transgender. We had a sleepover one night—the kind of sleepovers I never had growing up, for obvious reasons. At the terrible sleepovers I had been invited to in high school, my guy friends introduced each other to pornography and went to masturbate in the basement while I awkwardly stayed upstairs; I never got the nail painting and the movies—until Kayley.

I went to Jackson the following year almost entirely to learn more about her place of origin. My nominal reason for visiting, though, was to write an article about the Pink House, Mississippi's only remaining abortion clinic, where Kayley worked as a volunteer. Before she came to Emory—and then whenever she found herself back home—Kayley helped escort women from their cars past the antichoice protesters on the edge of the property into the clinic itself.[15]

It was there that I saw Kayley, at age twenty, listen to a sobbing young woman who was considering terminat-

---

15 "Working at Pink House, Mississippi's Last Abortion Clinic," https://www.thedailybeast.com/working-at-pink-house-mississippis-last-abortion-clinic

ing her pregnancy and then inform her of her choices with a level of compassion that seemed almost impossibly beyond her years. It is that single interaction that I remember more than the cluster of conservative pamphlet holders camped out on the sidewalk.

And ever since then, whenever I think about Mississippi, I don't think about its anti-LGBT backwardness; I think about sharing tacos with Kayley at a tapas place called Babalu, watching her beam with pride as thanks to her I fell in love with her home state. That was when I first experienced Mississippi as a place instead of a headline. The sort of person who never lets you forget where they're from often won't rest until they make you wish you were from there, too.

Kayley, who became a labor-and-delivery nurse in Atlanta after graduating in 2017, remains my most outspoken ally within the queer community. She met her boyfriend on OKCupid, where they were a 99 percent match, but his interest was first piqued by her characteristically Kayley answer to a question about anti-transgender laws: "I would rather pee with a transgender woman sitting on my lap than share a bathroom with a bigot."

I have not sat on Kayley's lap while she uses the bathroom, but I like to think our bonds run deeper: we have worked together, marched in Pride together, conked out on the same Atlanta airport bench together after a canceled flight. There is no one I trust more to have my back.

What I realize now is that Kayley didn't become a

queer powerhouse in spite of her home state, but because of it.

"Mississippi's progressive activists are unique," she wrote in her *Emory Wheel* op-ed. "We are often found in small numbers in pockets around the largely rural, conservative state. We are angry and raw. We have not lost our culture in our frustration with our state."

Mississippi *made* Kayley Scruggs. Nietzsche's famous claim—"That which does not kill us makes us stronger"—is bullshit, statistically speaking. Young bisexual women are at particularly high risk for depression and suicide.[16] A 2016 study of youth between the ages of fourteen and twenty-four published in the *Journal of Adolescent Health,* for example, found that bisexual women had the highest rate of suicidal ideation of all female respondents.[17] And as the Trevor Project notes, every "episode of LGBT victimization" increases the likelihood that an LGBT person will self-harm "by 2.5 times on average."[18] For queer people, that which does not kill us often makes us more likely to hurt ourselves.

But perhaps it's safe to say that those who survive are

16 "Bisexual Women Are at Higher Risk for Depression and Suicide," https://www.thedailybeast.com/bisexual-women-are-at-higher-risk-for-depression-and-suicide

17 "Bisexual and Questioning Young Women More Susceptible to Depression, Drexel Study Finds," http://drexel.edu/now/archive/2016/May/LGBQ_Mental_Health_Symptoms/

18 The Trevor Project, "Preventing Suicide," https://www.thetrevorproject.org/resources/preventing-suicide/facts-about-suicide/

sometimes strong out of necessity—and Kayley not only endured Mississippi, she came out of it swinging.

"Because I love my state and I believe in its ability to improve, I want to be part of the reason why it changes," she wrote in her op-ed. "I want my voice to be heard because I have lived and witnessed what we activists are working to change."

I'm back in Jackson three years later to check up on those same activists and take the pulse of that change. But more important, I'm here to deepen my own love for this misunderstood state.

I want to see what Kayley sees.

Tyler Edwards always wanted to leave Mississippi—until he got the opportunity to leave it.

The twenty-seven-year-old man grew up closeted and Baptist in a quintessential Fox News household—the sort of white conservative family in which Rush Limbaugh's and Sean Hannity's radio shows carried as much weight as the weekly sermon. He tells me that he "never attempted suicide but I thought about it," going on antidepressants and taking sleeping pills at age seventeen. He started coming out as gay only six years later, when his mother found some incriminating text messages on an old cell phone of his. Her first, tearful response: "Are you even still a Christian?"

When Tyler got accepted to a PhD program in Washington, D.C., he thought he had bought himself a one-way ticket to homosexual freedom. ("I had a solid thing lined up," he remembers. "I was leaving. I was getting out.") By the summer of 2016 he had registered for classes, put down money for a new apartment, packed his car, sold his house, and quit his job.

But after packing his trailer, Tyler broke down.

"I started thinking about it harder and I just started crying," he recalls. "I was like, 'I can't leave. I can't leave Mississippi...I'm running away. I've been complaining this whole time about what's going on in politics and how Mississippi is backward, and I'm about to go spend four years getting a PhD when I should be doing something to try to make a difference *here*.'"

Tyler unpacked. He moved to the hip and relatively progressive downtown Fondren district. And then he got a new job with the alt weekly *Jackson Free Press*. That's how I found him: Tyler penned an essay for Pride 2017 in which he shared that the "immediate reaction" he gets from out-of-staters who learn he's from Mississippi is "a facial-expression cocktail that's two parts shock with a shot of pity."[19]

Exactly one month after Tyler wrote that memorable line, Billy and I are sitting across from him at Cups, a glass-fronted coffee shop in Fondren. The neighborhood itself is a beautifully contrasting combination of retro architecture and forward-thinking people, pastel store-

---

19 "Pride Month Is Over, but the Fight Isn't," http://www.jacksonfreepress .com/news/2017/jul/12/pride-month-over-fight-isnt/

fronts that seem lifted out of 1955 and progressive politics that are straight out of 2017. My favorite example: the Pink House sits across the street from a classic Southern diner festooned with a Space Age–style silver sign that says FONDREN in looping, cursive font. The rain has returned, stopping and starting outside the windows, interrupting Tyler's train of thought, seeming to remind us that we are still subject to the whims of the state in this zone of relative safety.

Even here in Fondren, Tyler doesn't feel completely at ease being out with his boyfriend.

"Just existing as a gay person, I am very fortunate to be white and male being here," he tells me. "But it's still—I don't hold hands in public and I would like to be able to do that."

The Mississippi of 2017 is still a hard place for queer people to love thanks to a new anti-LGBT legislative atrocity. House Bill 1523, or the Religious Liberty Accommodations Act, was signed by Governor Phil Bryant in the spring of 2016 and has been the subject of judicial tangling ever since.[20] Reporters, myself included, have called it "America's Most Anti-LGBT Law": not only does it allow discrimination in the name of religion, it enumerates three "sincerely held religious beliefs" that can be cited by business owners, including the belief that

---

20 "Real Talk: Charter Schools in the Mississippi Delta," https://mississippi today.org/2017/10/10/hb-1523-how-did-we-get-here/

marriage is "the union of one man and one woman" and the belief that biological sex is "immutable," "objectively determined by anatomy and genetics at time of birth."[21] It is a vicious law, designed to hurt some of the state's most vulnerable people.

But even though HB 1523 is the definition of political evil, there is good happening in Mississippi that is too easily elided in a Trump-driven media economy. For national reporters like myself, it is simple to cite the text of an awful bill, get two predictable comments from either side of the issue, and file your story.

"That's the easy way to cover anything…and that's the obvious thing," Tyler agrees, adding that it's "even harder" these days, when Trump seems to tweet out a new pile of textual vomit every morning, for reporters to "dig deeper and look beyond the negative of what's happening."

Capturing the positive cultural shifts that are under way in this part of the country requires resources that too few news organizations are willing to invest.

In 2016 UCLA's Williams Institute reported that 35 percent of the LGBT population in the country lives in the South—and that "attitudes about marriage for same-sex couples have been improving across the

---

21 "Mississippi Is Close to Enacting America's Most Anti-LGBT Law," https://www.thedailybeast.com/mississippi-is-close-to-enacting-americas-most-anti-lgbt-law

Southern states."[22] But to capture those shifting social attitudes, reporters would have to *come* to Jackson—and they rarely do.

People here still talk about the time a *Washington Post* reporter came to see WonderLust in 2016 because it was so rare.[23] Indeed, in the clarifying aftermath of the Trump election, national news organizations collectively realized—at least for a moment—that requiring most of their reporters to live in New York or D.C. had limited their ability to understand the country. The *Post*,[24] NBC News,[25] and *The Guardian*,[26] among others, all made plans to invest in more reporting between the coasts—in part, it seemed, to figure out how Trump had happened.

But the media also need to document the red-state forces coming to a head that could one day dethrone Trumpism. In February 2017 the Jackson City Council

22 "LGBT in the South," https://williamsinstitute.law.ucla.edu/research/census-lgbt-demographics-studies/lgbt-in-the-south/

23 "Inside the Hottest Gay Bar in the Most Homophobic State in the Nation," https://www.washingtonpost.com/lifestyle/style/inside-the-hottest-gay-bar-in-the-most-homophobic-state-in-the-nation/2016/07/19/70ad84ee-4910-11e6-bdb9-701687974517_story.html?utm_term=.0c84801f4e42

24 "Job Posting: America Editor," http://washpostpr.tumblr.com/post/152423909107/job-posting-america-editor

25 "Chuck Todd: Media Must Improve Reporting on Rural America," https://www.washingtonpost.com/blogs/erik-wemple/wp/2017/03/14/chuck-todd-media-must-improve-reporting-on-rural-america/

26 "Beyond the Bubble: Write for Guardian US About the Places That Others Ignore," https://www.theguardian.com/media/2017/mar/17/how-to-write-for-guardian-us-pitch-guide

added LGBT protections to the city's nondiscrimination ordinance;[27] the move was challenged in court but ultimately stuck.[28] The twenty-four-hundred-person town of Magnolia in South Mississippi followed suit in March.[29] It may be, as Tyler notes, "very, very *slow* municipal progress," but it's progress nonetheless.

And as slowly as things move here, there is magic to be witnessed in the meantime. Magic like WonderLust. Mississippi's hostile climate doesn't attract a lot of potential gay-bar owners, so the community's reliance on a single nightclub has created something special: an LGBT gathering spot where it is impossible to silo yourself off from people who don't look like you.

"That's something kind of nice about having only that one space," Tyler tells me. "It's not...*segregated* isn't the right word, but there's not a separation where 'This is the bar where African Americans go' or 'This is the spot where lesbians go.' It's just *the* spot, so we all go."

And what's happening even faster than progress on paper is change within families like Tyler's.

After his mom found those incriminating text mes-

---

27 "It Passed: Jackson City Council Approves Non-discrimination Ordinance 5–2," http://www.mlive.com/news/jackson/index.ssf/2017/02/it_passed_jackson_city_council.html

28 "NDO Efforts Earn Pair of Jackson Leaders Change Maker Award," http://www.mlive.com/news/jackson/index.ssf/2017/10/pair_of_jackson_leaders_win_ch.html

29 "Second Mississippi City Passes Major LGBTQ-Inclusive Non-discrimination Ordinance," https://www.hrc.org/press/second-mississippi-city-passes-major-lgbtq-inclusive-non-discrimination-ord

sages, Tyler "basically.didn't talk about it with my parents for at least a year." His sexual orientation, he tells me, was "completely swept under the rug" for the sake of their relationship. Then his mom started sending him random pro-LGBT articles and giving other "hints that she [was] kind of coming around." Finally, shortly after Christmas 2016, when Tyler had been dating his boyfriend, Zach, for three months, something shocking happened: the young couple was sitting in a Chick-fil-A together when Tyler's parents asked them both to come by. They now "love" Zach, Tyler reports. And neither of his parents, for the record, ended up voting for Trump.

"It was absolutely a gradual process—and there were fights and tears along the way—but it happened," Tyler says. "I knew deep down, especially how close me and my mom were, that there was no way she was going to hate me or disown me."

Nor is Tyler going to disown Mississippi. Like Kayley, he loves this storied place, the birthplace of the blues, with its rich history and its water views. He knows that it can be "backward" but he "[doesn't] like people talking bad about it either," finding it deeply unfair to reduce this state to its depressing statistics—or to automatically abandon it because of them.[30]

---

30 "Study Finds Mississippi Is the Worst State in Which to Live," http://blog .gulflive.com/mississippi-press-news/2015/11/study_finds_mississi ppi_is_the.html

As of 2017, *U.S. News & World Report* ranks Mississippi forty-sixth out of the fifty states for education, forty-eighth for its economy, forty-ninth in infrastructure, and dead last in health care.[31] It currently has the highest infant-mortality rate in a country where that rate already exceeds most other developed nations'.[32] Those statistics don't get better if the people who care about education and economic justice and health care all decide to leave.

"Mississippi is my home and I don't know if I'll stay here forever," Tyler says, "but for now I want to try to see things change."

Even if he does move away one day, Tyler will always be happy he grew up gay here. Looking at him across the coffee-shop table—and seeing a well-groomed, brown-haired Southern young man but not a visibly gay one—I could picture someone who looks a lot like him marching at an alt-right rally like Charlottesville or defending a Confederate monument instead of witnessing racism in the South and asking himself, as he does, "Why are we doing this to ourselves?"

"I tell people all the time I'm so glad I am gay," Tyler says. "I would be the most obnoxious conservative straight white male had I not had something that made

---

31 "Overall of Mississippi," https://www.usnews.com/news/best-states/mississippi

32 "Mississippi Holds Title for Highest Infant Mortality Rate in U.S.," http://www.msnewsnow.com/story/37230413/mississippi-holds-title-for-highest-infant-mortality-rate-in-us

me realize there are people who are marginalized, there are people who do not benefit from cuts to every program imaginable."

As the sky clears, I ask Tyler when he thinks change will happen—when the obnoxious conservative straight white people here are going to care about the marginalized. When will Tyler no longer think twice about grabbing Zach's hand as they walk through Fondren?

"I will be an optimist and say I think it will be in twenty years," he guesses.

I hope he's right. I worry that it will take longer, but I'm heartened by the fact that change here is unmistakably happening. After talking to Tyler, the rain doesn't remind me of anti-LGBT legislation anymore. People might leave Mississippi, but progress is a lot like the summer rain: it comes in bursts, eroding sedimented hatred bit by bit and bringing the sun behind it.

When I ask Temica Morton to pick out her favorite local spot for lunch, she texts back: "CRACKER BARREL LOL."

But she's serious—and I'm serious when I enthusiastically agree to eat there. When I was a kid, I was obsessed with the rocking chairs and the tabletop peg puzzle at this ubiquitous roadside eatery; now, as a carbohydrate-deprived adult, I am Oprah-level obsessed with their bread basket. Being able to buy some cotton candy–flavored Peeps for my Emory mentor, Michael Shutt, in the gift shop only sweetens the deal.

Temica appears in a blue T-shirt with an American-flag pattern on the front. She doesn't carry herself with the bearing of someone who knows they have made history, but she did: As Jackson's *Clarion-Ledger* reported, she organized Jackson's first (and long-overdue) Pride parade, which marched down State Street in Fondren in the heart of the summer.[33] New York and Los Angeles held their first Pride parades in 1970; Jackson's didn't happen until 2016.[34]

"I decided to start it because of the hate in our state," Temica tells me, as we take our seats and begin browsing the book-length menu, settling on baked chicken and dressing for her and Billy, grilled chicken tenders with honey-mustard dipping sauce for me—and, most important, a basket of biscuits and corn muffins for the table.

The Pride parade was, as the *Clarion-Ledger* noted, an offshoot of Temica's long-running Metro Reunion Weekend,[35] a Jackson-area picnic that she has hosted for people in the LGBT pageant-and-ball world for the last eleven years. MRW, as Temica calls it, provides an informal setting "out of the club scene" for these performers to socialize and eat.

---

33 "Jackson Holds 1st LGBT Pride Parade," http://www.clarionledger.com/story/news/local/2016/06/11/participants-enjoy-jacksons-1st-lgbt-pride-parade/85755482/

34 "Some Memorable Moments of the L.A. Pride Parade Through the Years," http://www.latimes.com/local/lanow/la-me-la-pride-history-2017-htmlstory.html

35 "Jackson Holds 1st LGBT Pride Parade," http://www.clarionledger.com/story/news/local/2016/06/11/participants-enjoy-jacksons-1st-lgbt-pride-parade/85755482/

Temica, who grew up in Jackson, explains the ethos of the weekend as follows: "We have free food, I pay the guy, he barbecues for us. Y'all don't have to pay nothing. Just come out."

Going from picnic to parade was a natural progression. Temica hoped that the more visible march down the main drag of the capital city would help the state legislature realize that LGBT people are *people* first and foremost—a simple but essential form of queer visibility in a state that sorely needs more of it. Indeed, before Pride parades in big cities were corporatized,[36] this is the purpose they served: simply to prove that queer people are here, living among you.

"I also decided to start it because I said that it's funny that people can sit there in an office—I mean the legislature—and judge you for something that they know nothing [about]," Temica explains. "I wanted them to see that there's more to life than us just saying, 'Oh, we're gay.' We actually are business owners, homeowners. We have a lot of other things going on."

I ask Temica if Mississippi is the worst state for LGBT people—if its low ranking on all those online lists I have read is earned.

"Not to me," she says. "Because anything I do in

---

36 "Why LGBT Pride Festivals Have Become Increasingly Corporate," https://www.marketwatch.com/story/why-lgbt-pride-festivals-have-become-increasingly-corporate-2017-06-23

the community, I get support....Most of the people we invite here—that I invite here—love it. They actually love it: the atmosphere, everyone's so inviting. So I think it's not so much the people; it's just the government itself."

Temica's work as a pageant promoter has taken her all around the country. She has of course been told that she should relocate to Houston or Atlanta, both to seek out professional success and to ensure her personal security. And Temica is willing to admit that life in Atlanta might be easier—there would be more support from the local government, for one—but she couldn't go.

"I was like, 'I can't do that,'" she says, "because this is where I started everything at, so it would be crazy. If I go somewhere else, I have to start all over."

In Temica's experience, the lack of official support here binds the LGBT community together—and like so many people I meet in Jackson, she cites WonderLust as the primary example of that phenomenon because it's "a mixture of everybody."

"When you go other places, it's the same: you got men over here, black men over here, white men over there, black girls over here, white girls over there," she says. "Everybody ain't *right here*. And I think it should be like that. It's fun because it gives you different things to look at."

Indeed, whereas the national media continue to humor bad-faith arguments about whether LGBT should drop the $T$[37, 38]—and although racial divisions within the LGBT community stubbornly persist—WonderLust is simply, as Temica beautifully puts it, "right here," providing a space where those debates seem both literally and figuratively far away. In fact, a lot of outside noise seems far away in Jackson. *Slow* and *relaxing* is how Temica describes it—a "place where you can come home and sit on the porch and say, 'Oh, okay, okay.'"

"This is the life," she tells me. "It's really, really nice. It ain't all mean and cracked up like they [say it is]. It's really not.... We have our ups and downs but, overall, it's homey."

And Temica doesn't want to give up on home. Something vital would be missing if she left. In the metaphorical house that is Jackson's LGBT community, she is a load-bearing beam. When the bar that was once in WonderLust's space closed, there simply was no gay bar in Jackson for a year or two. If Temica left, who knows what would happen to Metro Reunion Weekend—or when the next Pride parade would happen? Often on this trip I have met people who stay where they are because they can't leave; Temica stays because she can't quit.

37 "Gay, Transgender Movements Need a Divorce," https://www.usatoday .com/story/opinion/2016/02/28/gay-rights-trans-rights-south-dakota-bathroom-legislation-column/80710176/

38 "LGBT Groups Respond to Petition Asking to 'Drop the T,'" https:// www.advocate.com/transgender/2015/11/06/lgbt-groups-respond-petition-asking-drop-t

"I think others have tried it and it didn't work so they gave up," she says, before launching into a speech that makes me want to push back my chair and roll up my sleeves: "Me, I'm the type of person, I don't give up, you know. If I'm gonna do something, I'ma put my all into it and move forward: win, lose, or draw. Even with the parade, we could have had ten people versus a hundred, and I'm still gonna go for it. I'm gonna make it bigger and better. Some people get discouraged and just give up. 'Oh, it didn't work out, I ain't gonna worry about it.' But when you start something like that, you just can't give up. You gotta continue on."

But that kind of work ethic requires energy, and energy requires carbs. I grab the last biscuit out of the basket and take a big bite.

The rain on the day we meet WonderLust owner Jesse Pandolfo for lunch is so intense that she has to pull over on I-55 and wait for it to quit. She sends a flurry of unnecessarily apologetic texts to let me know she'll be at Babalu as soon as the weather allows.

When we finally meet at the tapas restaurant and grab a table under the patio's clear plastic covering, Jesse looks radiant, fresh out of the rain, bustling with energy and ready to entertain her new friends. If Troy Williams was the "gay mayor" of Salt Lake City, Jesse just might be the lesbian mayor of Jackson. The waitress overhears her telling me about the start of the club—back in 2015 when "random people and friends," she says, painted and sanded the previously closed space into shape—and asks if Jesse is talking about WonderLust.

"Yeah, that's my club," Jesse says, proudly. "I own it."

"Oh, I love WonderLust!" the waitress says, setting down our guacamole.

Jesse fishes around in her purse for a drink card and hands it to her.

"That happens every day," Jesse tells us.

She has become an instantly recognizable figure in the Jackson LGBT scene since moving here from Boston. An absentee business owner she is not. On the night when Billy and I went to the drag show, Jesse was patrolling the floor of the club, ensuring the performances were running on schedule and greeting customers at the bar, darting back and forth like a blond Ping-Pong ball.

"I'm like always there," Jesse admits. "I live there."

So much of what makes WonderLust great can be attributed to her vision for the space. The previous club in the same building—Bottoms Up—was, Jesse tells us, "more geared toward males," with "really provocative pictures on the wall" and a mirror over the row of urinals in the bathroom; Jesse has made it into a club where everyone—including Jackson's burgeoning transgender community—feels welcome. And she has made the bathrooms not only inclusive but female-friendly, too.

"We made sure the bathrooms are up to standards for women," Jesse says. "My whole goal was that I need a bathroom where a girl can sit down and pee and be okay with it."

To a vagina owner who has been to a lot of LGBT bars around the country, that is no small detail. It can be challenging to go to establishments built around drinking that have dirty toilet seats—so Jesse, as she tells us, will go into the bathroom a couple of times a night to "wipe everything down." It's hard to imagine how she could be *more* hands-on.

But if Jesse seems zealously committed to her business, it's because she knows what it means to Jackson. WonderLust is proof that LGBT people in some parts of the country still need nightlife in order to live authentically.

"There are some people who feel like they can't breathe without it," she says, telling us about the view she has of the dance floor from the DJ booth. "You can see a guy reach over and grab his boyfriend or partner or whoever and pull him into him and [they] just look at each other and snuggle and dance—and you can tell that they don't feel like they can do that somewhere else."

Jesse certainly did not keep WonderLust open because it was easy. As her shrimp and grits arrive, she tells us that the business was "barely breaking even" the first year they opened, that she was using "quarters for groceries," and that her relationship with her wife, Hayley—then her girlfriend—was, to put it bluntly, "shitty" due to the stress.

"But at the same time," she says, "every week would roll around and I'm like, 'I have to open. I have to. There are people who can't go somewhere else. What are they going to do?'"

Even making the club eighteen-and-over was a losing proposition at the start. As Jesse explains, "You're not making money on them [the under-twenty-one set] because they are not drinking and it opens you up to getting in trouble if they *do* drink." (They don't—WonderLust has a very strict no-drinking policy for patrons under age twenty-one.) But Jesse didn't feel like she could turn the youth away.

"That age group—eighteen to twenty-one—is *so* important," Jesse says. "That's when a lot of people are coming out—and that's when a lot of these kids [don't know] what the community is like, what it's like to really be *like that*. Maybe they walk in and that is the first time they see another gay person."

Finally, though, the bar began turning a profit in its second year. She married Hayley—who was born and raised in Mississippi—and now the lesbian couple holds hands whenever they're out together because, as Jesse says, "I literally have that 'Fuck 'em' mentality, I'm gonna hold hands with whoever I want." They are raising a daughter together—a daughter whom Jesse wants to shield from the hate that sometimes gets launched her way because of her mother's prominent place within the city's LGBT community.

Protesters have picketed the bar. Two nights before we met, Jesse says, she got a "hate call" on her private line. And when she went to a Human Rights Campaign rally at the governor's mansion with her wife and daughter, anticipating a "happy atmosphere" at the protest itself, they ran into anti-gay counterprotesters with a bullhorn who, she said, "started screaming the most hateful things right to me, my wife, and my little girl, who was about six at the time."

"That was probably the lowest point of being gay [in Jackson]," Jesse tells me. "Having my daughter screamed at through a megaphone by a grown man."

Jesse doesn't sugarcoat her feelings about Mississippi, unfavorably comparing the experience of being LGBT here with being LGBT in Boston, which she has just returned from visiting. And she is still flattered by comparisons of WonderLust to LGBT nightlife on the coasts. When I tell her that I'd rather go to her club than anywhere in New York City, for example, Jesse leans over my voice recorder and says, "Let's bookmark that—she'd rather be at WonderLust than a New York City gay bar."

She is not a Tyler or a Temica; she's like me, a relative newcomer to red-state America.

"I don't want to sound like I completely hate everything about here because I don't," Jesse says. "But I think I'm still riding a high from being home [in Boston] last month. It's really hard to say that Mississippi has a one-up on Boston or anything like that because it doesn't."

The silver lining is that someone like Jesse, with a little bit of capital and a lot of hard work, can create something necessary.

"You can make a bigger impact much faster, and much easier—and you can see the impact immediately," Jesse says.

But the thing that keeps Jesse in Jackson is even more tangible than that. She has spent a third of the meal talking about WonderLust, a third of the meal eating, and a third of the meal *talking* about eating: "How good is this guacamole?" she raves, before declaring herself "a sucker for shrimp and grits, even being my Northern self." She describes the food in this town as "unreal"—an adjective that, having devoured my carnitas, I can vigorously endorse.

Jesse ventures a more serious answer about how people "stick together" down here—about how she and her friends "roll in a much larger, tight-knit group" down here in the South than up north. That makes her think about all the times she has gone out to eat with her friends.

"Did I mention the food?" she asks.

On the morning of August 15, 2017, I do what too many young people do: I leave Mississippi.

As Governing.com reported, Mississippi lost almost 4 percent of its millennial population between 2010 and 2017.[39] In fact, the state is one of only a handful in the

---

39 "States Where Each Generation of Americans Is Growing, Declining," http://www.governing.com/topics/urban/gov-state-population-changes-by-generation-census.html?utm_content=buffer51af9&utm_medium=social&utm_source=twitter.com&utm_campaign=buffer

country witnessing an overall population decline, and it's easy to see why.[40] Why would you stay in a largely rural state with an aging population that consistently lands at the bottom of economic rankings?[41] Drive six hours in any direction from Jackson and you could be in Houston, Nashville, or the place where Billy and I are headed next in the bright, post-storm sunshine: Atlanta.

Atlanta is where Kayley Scruggs has ended up for now. She may have left her home state, but she's still fiercely loyal to the region. When she was a sophomore, she told Emory's LGBT school alumni association that she decided to stay in the South for college because she was "immensely proud" of her roots and because she had "witnessed profound acts of compassion that constitute my faith in the South's aptitude for progress."[42] But she is still apologetic about having left Mississippi behind—and taking a full-time job in Atlanta.

"Sometimes I feel guilty when I think about Mississippi and the fact that I did escape it," my friend tells me, when I call her with my full report on her home state. "The amount of love I have for it hasn't changed and my frus-

---

40 "What's Driving Population Declines in Mississippi, More States," http://www.sunherald.com/latest-news/article131236654.html

41 "2018's Best and Worst State Economies," https://wallethub.com/edu/states-with-the-best-economies/21697/

42 "Out on Campus: Kayley Scruggs," https://emorygala.wordpress.com/2015/06/03/out-on-campus-kayley-scruggs/comment-page-1/

trations with it haven't changed. But I don't have to deal with them on a day-to-day basis—and sometimes I feel guilty for that."

But with a résumé that includes the Emory University Office of LGBT Life as well as the only abortion clinic in Mississippi, Kayley would have had a hard time anyway landing a nursing job at one of Jackson's religiously affiliated hospitals. And now that she's kicking off her career as a nurse in Atlanta, she has fewer opportunities to go back and volunteer at the Pink House, the state's sole abortion clinic.

Kayley tells me that she has "ideas of going back and working with Mississippians again and making an impact in communities," but "the unfortunate reality is that most of the people who leave Mississippi do not come back."

On one hand, I would understand if Kayley wanted to disavow her home state entirely.

She grew up in a hostile school environment, overhearing anti-gay slurs "all the time." Indeed, the advocacy group GLSEN found in 2011 that students attending schools in the South were more likely to report "frequently" overhearing remarks like "That's so gay" and "No homo" than students in any other region.[43] Kayley

---

43 "2011 National School Climate Survey," https://www.glsen.org/sites/default/files/2011%20National%20School%20Climate%20Survey%20Full%20Report.pdf

watched the rumor mill force her fellow students out of the closet before they could come out themselves. She tried to start a Gay-Straight Alliance at her high school with a friend but couldn't secure a faculty sponsor, even though there were several Christian organizations at her school.

"Nobody was willing to put their reputation and their job on the line to have that space for students," she remembers. "Even under the guise of the respectable GSA."

Kayley herself, of course, was neither gay nor straight but bisexual—a concept that was difficult to communicate to people who had certain preconceived notions of what queer women should look like and how they should act.

"Even when I was doing the GSA and people started hearing about it, people assumed that I was straight because people knew I dated boys and I presented a certain way," she tells me, explaining why she wasn't on the receiving end of much bullying at school.

To this day, Kayley is vocal about her queerness among friends but is out to only some of her family members. Pew Research Center polling has shown that bisexual people are considerably less likely than gay men or lesbians to be out to "all or most of the important people in their life."[44] When you're bisexual, coming out often

---

44 "A Survey of LGBT Americans," http://www.pewsocialtrends.org/2013/06/13/a-survey-of-lgbt-americans/

means subjecting yourself to a constant parade of people trying to define your sexuality for you—or question its validity altogether.[45] The closet may not be comfortable, but at least it's quiet.

"I'm not even from a particularly religious family, but I still have that fear that I always had," Kayley tells me. "Being bisexual complicates that because, one, you have to explain what bisexuality or pansexuality or queerness is in the first place, which is emotionally taxing enough on its own, and two, you have to defend the fact that you've been dating people who would place you in the category of being in a heterosexual relationship."

Somehow, in 2017, attraction to more than one gender still boggles people's minds.

So why should Kayley remain attached to a state where she would have to worry about being outed at work? Why go back to visit a place that never understood her, that resisted—and continues to resist—her many efforts to change it? What does she miss about Mississippi?

"Warmth," Kayley says. "It's just like a familiar warmth. I think Mississippians have a certain type of generosity that you can't find anywhere."

I feel called out when Kayley explains that "folks in big cities" are often "just being kind so that they can

---

45 "Why Bisexual Men Are Still Fighting to Convince Us They Exist," https://splinternews.com/why-bisexual-men-are-still-fighting-to-convince-us-they-1793857998

prove that they're kind to people" but that Mississippians are generally more "genuine in their kindness." I express kindness by picking up the bill for a meal; the Mississippians I have met express kindness by actually being kind, in manner and in deed. It would be impossible to quantify that observation with anything other than anecdotes, but that kind of hospitality is what Kayley grew accustomed to in Jackson—especially within the queer community.

She went to the club that was once called Bottoms Up and is now WonderLust for her eighteenth birthday. She remembers how welcoming it felt to walk through those doors compared with, say, a big-city LGBT bar where "everyone is trying to figure out everyone else's identity" in order to find someone they could potentially take home to bed. "Meat market" is the parlance for that kind of club, which undoubtedly has its place in the LGBT universe but shouldn't be the only nightlife option. It's a relief, sometimes, to feel free from being categorized and sized up.

"I've never had that feeling at WonderLust or Bottoms Up," Kayley tells me. "It was just like: we're all a part of this blanket [LGBT] identity and this is basically the only place that we can be ourselves outwardly, so it doesn't really matter which section of our big blanket identity you belong to."

Kayley is the first to acknowledge that Mississippi isn't perfect; she wouldn't have had to protest the state government so fiercely if it were. But she initially had a hard time adjusting to life in Atlanta, where it seemed that people wanted not only to criticize her home state but dismiss it altogether. Kayley responded to that attitude with characteristic tenacity "by making [Mississippi] a very salient part of my own identity and rubbing it in everybody's faces." She remembers that she was "automatically on the defensive" with her undergraduate classmates at Emory, many of whom came from the Northeast and "look[ed] down on the South," unwilling to see the good that Kayley experienced here. Above all, she wanted to prove to them that "a queer little feminist activist like me existed in Mississippi.

"People who come from unique places—or places where people have struggled, especially—they're just proud of their homes," Kayley tells me. "They're so excited to show them off. And especially when I met you, I hadn't been away from home really for a substantial amount of time. It was so different. Where I was was so different than my home."

And just like Michael Shutt wouldn't be who he is without having grown up in Angola, Indiana, Kayley Scruggs wouldn't be herself without Jackson, Mississippi. She remembers being the token feminist at her high school, studying political issues thoroughly enough that she could expertly counter the antagonistic questions her conservative Christian classmates threw at her. She remembers working at women's shelters, listening to the stories of impoverished black women, and later meeting even more of the Jackson community at the Pink House.

There is an alternate-universe version of Michael Shutt who is still climbing the ladder in D.C. and there is an alternate version of Kayley—one who grew up somewhere other than Jackson—who came to Emory half a decade less wise than she was. I'm glad that I live in *this* universe.

Kayley knows that her Mississippi activism shaped her: "To do that work in a place like Mississippi, you have to be vocal, you have to be assertive, you have to be honestly fearless in a way—and I think I carry that with me no matter where I go.

"I think that's always who I'm going to be," she adds, "and I don't want to change that."

Kayley can leave Mississippi, but Mississippi will never leave her. When you're in her company, no matter where you are in the country, you feel like you're settling into a cozy chair at WonderLust or sitting on the patio at Babalu watching the rain. And now I too carry a piece of Mississippi with me, rough and imperfect but precious nonetheless. The most hopeful vision for America's future that I have seen to date is here, in a place that too many people will never see.

# Chapter 7

# GOING HOME

My dear, here we must run as fast as we can, just to stay in place. And if you wish to go anywhere, you must run twice as fast as that.

— *The Red Queen,* Alice's Adventures in Wonderland

**B**efore Atlanta was Atlanta, it went by the nickname Terminus because it fell at the end of the railroad line.[1] For me, this city is still a place of endings.

This is where I left Michelle. This is where I laid my life before transition to rest. It is where I heard my former name for the last time, got called "sir" for the last time, wore boxer shorts for the last time. And then, like so many people who move to this Southern capital, I moved away as soon as my obligations here were over. In 2007, a *New York Times* travel writer called the ATL (to use its airport code) "a city so transient it barely recognizes itself,"[2]

---

1 City of Atlanta, Ga., "History," https://www.atlantaga.gov/visitors/history

2 "36 Hours in Atlanta," http://www.nytimes.com/2007/01/07/travel/07hours.html

and although there is an increasing sense today that Atlanta is establishing its own identity, it is still full of people who are just passing through.

Yet Atlanta remains, somehow, my best answer at the moment to the impossible question: "Where are you from?"

Born in California, raised in New Jersey, educated in Utah and Georgia, living in Florida, I have no concise way of responding to that frequent small-talk question. I'm no army brat, but I haven't stayed anywhere long enough to put down the kind of roots that truly tie you down. So, for lack of a better answer, I just say that I'm from Atlanta and deal with the fact that it feels like a lie.

I think I covet permanence.

This entire time that I have been gathering the stories of the people who stayed in the places I left behind, I have been trying to answer a personal question, too: Why didn't I stay? Why *don't* I stay now? For six weeks I have traveled the country meeting queer people who pour their whole lives into a place, be it Provo or Houston, Bloomington or Jackson. I have felt almost parasitic, like a transsexual vampire feeding off attachments to homes that I wish were my own. At many points along the way I have wanted to unpack my suitcase and integrate myself into their routines. But that wouldn't feel right, either. None of those places are mine.

Atlanta's not really mine, either, but Atlanta isn't picky: it allows almost anyone to adopt it.

I still remember the first time I checked out of a grocery store after moving to the South from New Jersey. The cashier asked me, "How are you doing tonight?"— and it sounded like she actually wanted to know. After years of Northeastern brusqueness, I was instantly suspicious. Why did it matter how I was doing? What did she want from me? But within a few weeks, "y'all" had become part of my vocabulary, I had adapted to the niceness, and I never looked back.

On the evening of August 15, one month and five days after I first picked Billy up in Salt Lake City, we drive over a crest on I-20 East and see the ever-expanding Atlanta skyline in the distance. I feel less like I'm driving home and more like I'm rushing to meet an old friend—an old friend made out of concrete and megachurches and river birch trees. Our first stop is a Publix supermarket, where we pick up a couple of the legendary chicken-finger subs for dinner along with an obligatory case of Diet Coke—or, as it probably ought to be called in Georgia, "water."

I can say I'm "from" Atlanta only in the sense that I am deeply familiar with and fond of its cultural amenities: the indulgent food, the slower pace of life, the unseasonable warmth. This city is a gateway drug that will get you addicted to the South. The longer you stay here, the more you want to flip the map of the United States upside down—half out of love for Georgia, half out of spite for New York. But although I have deep affection for Atlanta,

I could never call it home. Set aside the fact that my childhood was spent elsewhere; when you're transgender, the city or town in which you transitioned can feel strangely impermanent.

When I lived here I was a transient person in a transient city, leading a Gaussian blur of a life. But if there's one part of this city that feels permanent to me, it is a person, not a place.

With Publix subs in hand, Billy and I show up in Michael Shutt's driveway, ready for a sound night's sleep in his immaculate guest rooms. We step inside, I embrace my bighearted mentor, and then my feet promptly get eaten alive by his two new puppies, Bea and Arthur, who, yes, are named after the *Golden Girls* actress.

Back in July, when I informed Michael which nights we would be in town, he sent me a formal email that began, "We would like to confirm your reservations for two rooms. Each room comes with a queen-size bed and luxurious linens." The missive went on to describe said rooms in marketing copy more vibrant than you'd find in most travel brochures. That ridiculous attention to detail is part of why I love this man—and why I jumped at the opportunity to stay with him at the end of the trip.

Our accommodations are as promised: luxurious. There are bathrobes for both of us hanging in our closets. The sheets have a thread count beyond human comprehension. The hot tub embedded in the back deck is carefully chlorinated by Brian—and enjoyed by Michael—every night. Their home is like our own personal LGBT-friendly five-star hotel, complete with a picture of Betty White in the foyer.

Everything feels homey—but it's still not quite home.

Dohyun Ahn has made Atlanta home. Over a tray full of Chinese pastries at a notoriously yummy bakery called Sweet Hut on Buford Highway—a stretch of road in northeast Atlanta renowned for its nondescript strip malls full of affordable international cuisine—my old friend from Emory tells me that he thinks of himself as part of a "New South," a region "that's younger, that's more queer, [and] has more people of color."

"I'm an immigrant and so my heritage, my roots are in a different country, but I've really adopted Atlanta and the South as my home," he tells me, as I take a bite out of the savory green onion roll I have been waiting this entire trip to eat. "And I have taken up that kind of different heritage: I absolutely identify as a Southerner, I love being a Southerner, and I love the South."

If you were openly LGBT at Emory between the years of 2010 and 2014, you knew Dohyun Ahn's name. As an undergraduate, he had a résumé that made a schlubby graduate student like me feel even schlubbier. A Korean immigrant, Dohyun has been doing LGBT-related work since at least 2009, when he created a Gay-Straight Alliance at his high school in nearby Marietta despite pushback from the administration.[3] When he came to Emory, he founded the Queer and Asian discussion group—a group that placed heavy emphasis on confidentiality so that participants could keep their families from discovering their queerness.

As Dohyun tells me now over our pastries, he created the group to address the specificity of queer Asian experience: "There's just so few of us out there and we are all sort of scattered, and half of us are in the closet and we come from a culture that is very homophobic."

I thought of Dohyun as "Michael Shutt Jr." back at Emory because of his burgeoning interest in student affairs and his long track record of LGBT advocacy. He even got invited to meet Vice President Joe Biden once—and I am still jealous of the resulting photo opp.[4]

Now, post-college and post-graduate school, Dohyun works as a bakery clerk at a Publix while volunteering with the small but fierce LGBT activist organization Southerners on New Ground. To put the size of SONG into perspective, consider that the Human Rights Campaign—the most widely known national LGBT advocacy organization—reported a revenue of over $36

---

3 "What It's Like to Start a Gay-Straight Alliance in the South," https://www.buzzfeed.com/annanorth/what-its-like-to-start-a-gay-straight-alliance-in?utm_term=.eyrznK1P3#.yvdXvWpRy

4 "Emory Student Attends White House LGBT Summit," http://news.emory.edu/stories/2012/10/er_LGBT_student_whitehouse/campus.html

million on its Form 1990 in 2015.[5] SONG reported a total revenue of less than $750,000 that same year.

In the absence of abundant resources, Dohyun believes, legwork is what really matters.

"Southerners need to band together," he says. "People who see themselves as part of this New South need to band together, and pool our money, and put it to [use] where we are—put it to use in the South. That's where the grassroots has to come in because we are not really getting help from people in Washington, D.C., and New York and San Francisco. We have to do the work ourselves."

And Georgia still needs a lot of help. With no statewide nondiscrimination protections for LGBT people, and huge hurdles standing in the way of transgender people who wish to update their ID documents, the LGBT population here has a target on its back. Every year, it seems, the Republican-dominated legislature threatens to pass an anti-LGBT law and then, like clockwork, they fail to pass it—presumably because they don't want to risk losing revenue from sporting events, or from the state's exponentially growing film industry.[6]

Dohyun grew up under those constant threats—and he not only faced them, he had fun doing it. My favorite memories of Dohyun from our days together at Emory

---

5 https://assets2.hrc.org/files/assets/resources/FY17-HRC-990.pdf
6 "Hollywood Hits Back at Georgia Anti-LGBT Adoption Bill," http://variety.com/2018/film/news/georgia-anti-lgbtq-adoption-bill-hollywood-response-1202712455/

are us hanging out in hotel rooms at LGBT conferences, where I would make him turn on Grindr and we would watch his phone explode. At the time he was living the kind of activist life that could very easily have taken him to D.C. after graduation. His Joe Biden visit, for instance, came about because he had received a prestigious invite for a group of "LGBT Emerging Leaders" that, as Emory's news website boasted, connected him with "major national LGBT organizations."[7]

The Dohyun of 2017 has zero interest in moving north. He describes D.C. as a place where "everyone is a politician, even if you're not in politics"—and I almost spit out my onion roll laughing as his rant continues: "People just use their jobs or the people they meet as stepping-stones to get further in their career....Everyone you meet, no matter where. You can be at a gay bar and hook up with someone and it's a networking opportunity....You suck their dick and then the next morning, you're like, 'Here's my business card!'"

Dohyun finds New York more tolerable, but even there he would miss exactly what I have been trying to capture in this book: the ways in which, as Adam Sims memorably put it to me back in Utah, "oppression and opposition can build the most beautiful connections."

---

7 "Emory Student Attends White House LGBT Summit," http://news.emory.edu/stories/2012/10/er_LGBT_student_whitehouse/campus.html

In places like New York, "Maybe you can go outside and run into a queer person constantly, but how much of a community of support is there?" Dohyun asks, adding that "another reason I love the South" is because "our communities are so tight," with especially "few degrees of separation for queer people in Atlanta."

According to a 2015 estimate, about 4.2 percent of metro Atlanta's population is LGBT[8]—and if you befriend one of the people in that 4.2 percent, you will soon meet seemingly all of them. I can't count the number of conversations I have had with LGBT people in Atlanta that eventually end in all parties discovering their list of mutual friends. Queerness turns the ninth-largest metropolitan area in the country into a small town. And Dohyun is seeing little signs that more people are deciding to stick around.

He remembers hearing his high school friends promise that they were "getting out of Georgia as fast as we can and going as far away as possible for college."

"I see kind of less of that now," he says. "Lately Atlantans just want to stay in Atlanta and put down roots here."

A surprising number of the people I knew in graduate school decided to plant roots here, too. They stopped running and made Atlanta their home. One woman in

---

8 "Gallup: Percentagewise, Metro Atlanta Has a Larger LGBT Population than New York," http://politics.blog.ajc.com/2015/03/20/gallup-percentagewise-metro-atlanta-has-a-larger-lgbt-population-than-new-york/

my cohort bought a house here. Another got a teaching job nearby. A third found a job at Emory instead of going back to Canada. So why didn't I stay?

The Atlanta of 2017 is—to quote Janis from *Mean Girls*— "almost too gay to function."

The thought occurs to me as Billy and I walk over the crosswalk at 10th and Piedmont, which has been painted in the colors of the Rainbow Pride flag since I moved away. The orange stripe on the asphalt matches the color of Billy's shirt to a T. Understandably the intersection has become an Instagram sensation. The secret has gotten out, it seems, that Atlanta is super queer. (Now if only people would stop calling it "Hotlanta.")

In the days that Billy and I spend here, eating breakfast with Bea and Arthur in the morning and then braving the infamously bad traffic to meet LGBT people, I can almost picture coming back on a more permanent basis. It doesn't hurt that I'm experiencing the greatest-hits version of the city, seeing only people I cherish. I visit Faughn Adams, the therapist who helped me through transition in 2012—and she hugs me before telling me all about her motorcycle adventures through the South. I have brunch with Kayley Scruggs at a Creole-Vietnamese fusion restaurant—a combination that can be found only in an international Southern city like this one.

But my favorite Atlanta meal is a trip to the Marietta Diner with Monica Helms, the charming navy veteran who created the Transgender Pride flag in 1999.[9] After weeks of watching the Food Network, I take comfort in knowing that we are eating at a Guy Fieri–approved restaurant, complete with chrome-colored exterior, neon sign, and plush booths that instantly transport me back to New Jersey. Over sandwiches and chicken fingers, sweet tea and Diet Coke, she tells us tales from her time in the military, about flying kites from the top of submarines in the Bahamas and reading the *Lord of the Rings* trilogy on her long tours of duty.

Monica Helms's house, which we visit after lunch, bears a sign that says HELM'S DEEP—a joke extremely relevant to my interests. The original version of her famous flag is nowhere to be found inside her modest living space because it currently resides in the Smithsonian. But Monica does have model submarines on display in the living room and, in the basement, a large collection of miniature rockets that she likes to launch with her wife, Darlene, on weekends.

I knew that I was hopelessly in love with this woman when I called her once to interview her for an article[10] and we ended up talking about how much cohesion there is among LGBT people in the South compared with coastal LGBT-friendly metropolises.

---

9 "'Divine Intervention' Helped Monica Helms Create the Transgender Pride Flag," https://www.thedailybeast.com/divine-intervention-helped-monica-helms-create-the-transgender-pride-flag

10 Ibid.

"A lot of these places like New York and L.A. and San Francisco and Chicago—in these places, when the community came up, they came up a lot earlier than here in the South, in Atlanta," she told me, referring to the historic trend of gay men and lesbians getting acceptance first while leaving transgender people behind—or, worse, throwing them under the bus.

"When the community started becoming visible here in Atlanta," Monica went on, "everybody came out together. Trans people were included right off the bat."

Queer life in Atlanta is still as amazing as ever thanks to that unity. But I also recognize the dangers inherent in becoming a nationally renowned LGBT metropolis. To progressive advocates living in other parts of the South, Atlanta is starting to develop some of the same problems that I complain about in New York or San Francisco: a rapidly rising cost of living,[11] a certain complacency creeping in at the edges. Back in Austin, my friend Michelle Colon—a veteran reproductive-justice activist and LGBT ally who has since returned to her home in Mississippi—had reminded me, "Not everybody can move to Atlanta."

Michelle Colon has spent years defending Mississippi's only remaining abortion clinic: the Pink House in Jackson's Fondren district, where Kayley Scruggs volunteers.

---

11 "Cost of Living Is Surging in These Major Cities and What It Could Mean for 2018," https://www.forbes.com/sites/andrewdepietro/2017/12/28/cost-of-living-is-surging-in-these-major-cities-and-what-it-could-mean-for-2018/#105d477671c6

Michelle's job description at the Pink House is expansive, but one of her most important tasks is ensuring that the antichoice protesters stay on their side of the property line. She lives for the fight—and to her, Atlanta would almost be too easy.

"Why would I want to be somewhere where I know I'm going to win?" she asked me. "That doesn't make one a warrior."

That's not to say there are no progressive causes left to champion in Atlanta. There are still so many battles to be fought in this city—battles that require you to look beneath the city's increasingly glossy, LGBT-friendly surface.

Indeed, the glossy surface is part of the problem. The city is gentrifying—and *fast*—displacing black residents, making it harder for queer people of color and low-income queer people to get a foothold here.[12] An estimated 28.2 percent of the homeless youth in the Atlanta metro area, as the *Georgia Voice* reported, are LGBT.[13]

"They are discriminated against in other shelters," Brittany Garner, a social worker with the LGBT youth homeless organization Lost-n-Found Youth, explains to me at their drop-in center one afternoon. Before Lost-n-Found

---

12 "Atlanta's 'Runaway Gentrification' Chronicled by National, International Media," https://atlanta.curbed.com/2017/11/14/16640524/atlanta-gentrification-article-citylab-gaurdian
13 "Georgia State Study: Atlanta Homeless LGBT Youth Numbers Higher Than Previously Reported," https://thegavoice.com/georgia-state-study-number-atlantas-homeless-lgbt-youth-higher-previously-reported/

began serving them five years ago, she notes, there was no shelter in the city where openly transgender people could get beds.

If this description sounds eerily familiar—a gentrifying city whose cosmopolitan and gay-friendly Midtown papers over problems such as poverty and homelessness—that's because so many major LGBT-friendly metropolises in this country fit the same bill. And Atlanta, despite its many pleasures—perhaps even *because* of them—risks becoming too much like them. I can joke that Atlanta is now "too gay to function," but the hard reality is that it could one day be a Southern San Francisco, with skyrocketing income inequality and all its attendant problems.[14]

I hope that Atlanta can dodge that outcome. That it can hang on to the spirit of unity that allowed the LGBT community here to rise up together. That it will remain a city of warriors. That it won't stop working on issues affecting transgender women and queer people of color just because there are now gay-friendly brunch spots all over Midtown—and a rainbow crosswalk connecting them.

I love Atlanta, but I worry about Atlanta. I worry about it for the sake of the people who don't just drop in like me to see friends, but who are living here, watching it grow around them, and hoping that it doesn't lose itself.

---

14 "City and Metropolitan Inequality on the Rise, Driven by Declining Incomes," https://www.brookings.edu/research/city-and
-metropolitan-inequality-on-the-rise-driven-by-declining-incomes/

★　　★　　★

"I don't think I ever identified as being a Southerner from Atlanta as much as I did when I had my brief stint in New York City," Charles Stephens tells me, in a featureless conference room at the Phillip Rush Center, just east of the hip Little Five Points neighborhood on DeKalb Avenue.

His presence is more than striking enough to make up for our nondescript surroundings. He is wearing a dark T-shirt with stylized white lettering that says MARLON & ESSEX & JOSEPH & ASSOTTO, all notable late-twentieth-century black gay writers and poets whom Charles admires: Marlon Riggs, Essex Hemphill, Joseph F. Beam, Assoto Saint. All of them died from AIDS-related complications between 1988 and 1995, their powerful voices suddenly gone from the world at a time when the stigma around black male homosexuality was especially strong.

Charles has always looked after his history. He regularly invokes artists, intellectuals, and civil rights leaders who have influenced him, though he is not at all showy about it; speaking to him, you get the sense that he feels a genuine debt to titans such as Audre Lorde and Congressman John Lewis more than he wants to impress you with his encyclopedic knowledge.

"Part of why I'm so committed to the city," he tells me, "is the city has given so much to me."

Apart from his "brief stint" in New York—a time that made Charles miss Southern politeness, even if it sometimes feels disingenuous—he has learned to call Atlanta home since his 1980 birth.

"I think it's something that I've arrived to over time," he says of that permanent designation.

Charles is now the founder and executive director of the Counter Narrative Project, an Atlanta-based organization that advocates for black gay men.[15] The name he chose for the advocacy group is a direct challenge to popular conceptions of what it means to live at the intersection of those identities; as he wrote in a 2015 blog post, "The most pervasive articulation of 'black gay man' is through HIV statistics or in popular culture as uncomplicated accessories for privileged straight women."[16] Charles wanted to, as he explained it, "snatch our stories back from these narrow, superficial representations of our experiences" to help people see "a far more complex and ultimately far more human picture" of black gay male experience.

The Counter Narrative Project, as Charles wrote, is focused on "amplifying the voices of our brothers" so that black gay men can break free from the harmful stereotypes through which the mainstream sees them.[17] That mission is one that the men listed on Charles's shirt would surely approve of: author Joseph F. Beam believed

---

15 https://www.thecounternarrative.org/
16 "Guest Post: 'Because Our Stories Are Also Our Weapons,'" https://www.glaad.org/blog/guest-post-because-our-stories-are-also-our-weapons
17 Ibid.

that "survival is visibility."[18] Filmmaker Marlon Riggs wrote that "silence kills the soul" and "diminishes its possibilities to rise and fly and explore."

"Silence withers what makes you human," Riggs said. "The soul shrinks, until it's nothing."

The generation of black gay male writers sharing space with us now by way of Charles's T-shirt knew that the silence around their experiences was made to be broken. As poet Essex Hemphill said, "The sacred constructions of silence are futile exercises in denial."

"We will not go away with our issues of sexuality," Hemphill insisted. "We are coming home."[19]

Charles was born just eight years before these men, his intellectual ancestors, began to die in the AIDS crisis. But his work is a direct continuation of theirs in a city that has become a hub for the community they were taken from too soon.

I have learned much from keeping up with Charles online, ever since he gave a guest lecture to an Emory class in which I was a TA. As proud as I am to have gotten my doctorate at that university, it is an ivory tower with an

---

18 Guy Davidson, "The Time of AIDS and the Rise of 'Post-Gay,'" in *The Cambridge Companion to American Gay and Lesbian Literature*, edited by Scott Herring (New York: Cambridge University Press, 2015), 139–56.

19 Dwight A. McBride, "Straight Black Studies: On African American Studies, James Baldwin, and Black Queer Studies," in *Black Queer Studies: A Critical Anthology*, edited by E. Patrick Johnson and Mae G. Henderson (Durham, NC: Duke University Press, 2005), 68–89.

emphasis on ivory. As of the 2010 census, the population of the city of Atlanta was 54 percent black; the incoming class of Emory undergraduates in the fall of 2017, by comparison, was just 9.5 percent black.[20] I worked in a white bubble, full of academics more comfortable theorizing about marginalized experiences than sharing space with the people who lived them.

And to my shame, during my five years in Atlanta, I was a bubble dweller, too. I lived in a city that was the black LGBT capital of the country—and spent most of my time either at class, where I was mainly surrounded by well-off white folks like myself, or at home, watching TV.

That insular life is a failing I have been trying to correct as I get further away from academia and more enmeshed in what grown adults who come out of PhD programs still refer to as the "real world." So if Atlanta feels fleeting and transient to me, perhaps I have only myself to blame, as Charles's rich sense of legacy proves.

He jokes that he was "socially engineered by the queer community here," coming of age at Morehouse, a historically black men's college in west Atlanta, where he connected with local black leaders such as HIV public health expert Dr. Edith Biggers, activist Imani Evans, and Georgia state representative Simone Bell—all while learning from veteran organizers of the HIV/AIDS crisis. In 2002

20 "Fast Facts: Admission Profile," http://apply.emory.edu/discover/fastfacts.php

Charles cofounded the black LGBT student organization Blackout at Georgia State University with a group of students that included a woman who would later perform alongside me in a local production of *The Vagina Monologues*—such is the beautiful smallness of queer worlds.

"I just felt so held and supported in this city," Charles tells me, noting that he yearned for Atlanta's "civil rights heritage" during his sojourn in the Big Apple. (And New York, for the record, is actually "hotter than any place I've ever been," including so-called Hotlanta.)

Charles feels lucky to have built something lasting here. If he had been "born ten years later"—in 1990 rather than 1980—his family would "never have been able to afford living in Atlanta," because of rising costs and the local unemployment rate for black people. It is in large part *because* he can stay—and because so many people helped him find a place here—that he does.

"There are still moments of despair and disappointment but ultimately, I think those early experiences of being loved and nurtured and shaped—I still draw from those experiences for inspiration," he says, adding, "I have to bear witness because I owe it to the folks before me."

This city can still be a vexing place. Charles tells me that, given Atlanta's LGBT friendliness relative to other major Southern cities, people expect it to "be a place where all of their dreams can come true"—something comparable to what San Francisco came to represent "in the seventies for white gay men." But he knows how much work is still to be done here, whether it's caring for victims of anti-LGBT violence or pushing back on public health narratives that reduce the lives of black gay men living with HIV to cold statistics. Where other people might throw their hands up, Charles just sees room to grow: "There's so much potential here, there's still so many things that can be done and shaped and moved.

"Atlanta is home," he says. "Home isn't always perfect and it isn't always totally comfortable. Sometimes it can be a bit uncomfortable, it can be a bit frustrating. But it's just a feeling."

If home is a feeling, I don't have that feeling about Atlanta. Perhaps I could have cultivated it—but I didn't. I'm glad Charles did.

Transitioning from one gender to another is not a thing that happens all at once.

There was a time in the fall of 2012, shortly after I came out, when everyone but my Emory students knew my secret. I told myself that I should wait until the start of the next semester, when I would get a fresh crop of kids who had never laid eyes on me before, to come out of the closet professionally.

For an agonizing month, I lived a double life: when I finished teaching, I rushed off to a single-stall unisex bathroom in the corner of Candler Library—and, like some transgender version of Clark Kent ripping off his clothes in a phone booth, I would emerge half an hour later as myself.

On August 21, 2017—the day of the total solar eclipse—I find myself back in that same bathroom, for old times' sake. I couldn't even begin to estimate how many hours I spent here, my backpack full of supplies on the windowsill, as I carefully adjusted the lace front of my wig, wishing I could ingest some sort of illegal supplement to make my hair grow down to my shoulders overnight. Most of all, I remember the gripping fear that has now all but subsided—the fear of simply being in the world in this awkward state.

In hindsight I realize the irony of teaching an undergraduate course called "Introduction to Women's, Gender, and Sexuality Studies" while hesitating to reintroduce myself to my class as a queer transgender woman. Readings about my various and sundry identities were all over the syllabus, so it's not like my students didn't know what it meant to be transgender.

But I was terrified of them—these bright, energetic young adults with their unimaginably large friend groups and their keg parties and their constantly texting fingers. Meanwhile my male-gender presentation suffered, growing more disheveled by the day, but I still dutifully whipped out the cargo shorts and oversize T-shirts for the three days a week I had to teach.

As it turns out, my terror was baseless. When I decided to consolidate my dual identities earlier than originally planned, my students barely batted an eye. I told them at the end of class one Friday that I would look much different the next time they saw me and explained why.

"I knew it," said one, a little too loudly.

"I thought you just didn't care about your appearance before," another admitted to me later—a bold comment that I still laugh about today.

My students, all born in the early- to mid-nineties, were happy for me. And why wouldn't they be? They were—and still are—at the vanguard of the most LGBT-friendly generation in American history. Seventy-four percent of U.S. millennials now support same-sex marriage, compared with a little over half of boomers.[21] And as Reuters reported, eighteen- to twenty-nine-year-olds support transgender restroom rights "by a 2-to-1 ratio," with the reverse being true for people over sixty.[22]

This generation is also the most likely to be openly LGBT themselves: in 2016 Gallup found that 7.3 percent of millennials identified as LGBT.[23] And initial indications suggest that Generation Z is going to be even queerer, especially when it comes to gender: one

21 "Changing Attitudes on Gay Marriage," http://www.pewforum.org/fact-sheet/changing-attitudes-on-gay-marriage/

22 "Exclusive: Women, Young More Open on Transgender Issue in U.S.–Reuters/Ipsos Poll," https://www.reuters.com/article/us-usa-lgbt-poll/exclusive-women-young-more-open-on-transgender-issue-in-u-s-reuters-ipsos-poll-idUSKCN0XI11M

23 "In U.S., More Adults Identifying as LGBT," http://news.gallup.com/poll/201731/lgbt-identification-rises.aspx

2016 report from a forecasting agency found that only 48 percent of people in this teenage bracket said they are "exclusively heterosexual," while just 44 percent said they bought clothes based exclusively on the gender they were assigned at birth.[24] The kids, as they say, are all right.

When I'm done feeling nostalgic in the bathroom, I rejoin Billy outside on the tree-dotted quad.

The incoming class of 2021 has gathered here to watch the moon obscure 98 percent of the sun.

They are entering higher education at a time when both conservative and liberal commentators in the press seem to be redoubling their efforts to chastise them for being "politically correct," what with their gender-neutral pronouns and their protests against campus speakers with whom they vigorously disagree. Oh, the humanity![25] "Snowflakes" has now become a fashionable all-purpose insult to hurl at these mostly progressive millennials and Gen Zers.[26]

But having taught rooms full of these kids relatively recently, I don't see precious, delicate little flowers when I

---

24 "Teens These Days Are Queer AF, New Study Says," https://broadly.vice.com/en_us/article/kb4dvz/teens-these-days-are-queer-af-new-study-says

25 "The Phony Debate About Political Correctness," https://thinkprogress.org/the-phony-debate-about-political-correctness-f81da03b3bdb/

26 "The Surprising History of 'Snowflake' as a Political Insult," https://thinkprogress.org/all-the-special-snowflakes-aaf1a922f37b/

look around at them now sitting on the grass and the white granite steps of Emory's historic buildings. I see a generation brave enough to settle for nothing less than full equality, irrespective of sexual orientation or gender identity. I see people for whom a secret I carried in my gut for twenty-five years is nothing but an interesting footnote.

In twenty years, maybe sooner, it will matter even less which parts of the country queer people choose to inhabit because this is the generation that will be in power—a generation that believes in facts, that sees anti-LGBT discrimination as an archaic holdover from the past, that refuses to erase their lived authenticity to satisfy their elders. Queer kids in the future won't think twice about going to school in Georgia because acceptance will be the new nationwide status quo. Like transitioning, change is not a thing that happens all at once. But these kids will make it happen faster than anyone sees coming.

They will make this book seem outdated and quaint—and I can't wait.

The bugs begin to emerge from the trees and bushes in droves, fooled by the dimming light into believing that dusk is coming soon. As we glance around the crowded quad, I see a few people I know milling around—friends from graduate school, former professors—but I don't want to say hello to them; I just want to be in this final, cosmic moment of anticipation. The light takes on a muted, almost amber quality and I look up through my safety glasses to watch the moon slide into position: 96 percent, 97 percent, *98 percent*. The shadows that form on the ground through the tree branches above us look like hundreds of little smiley faces, little slivers on the sidewalk.

I have no grand revelations about the trip, but I know that it is over. I have finished finding what I was looking for. And somewhere along the way, I closed a chapter of my own life, too—a life that not too long ago seemed impossible. A life that began in Utah but took fuller shape in Atlanta—and that could have stayed here, but ultimately can't rest in one spot very long.

I know I will always be a wanderer, but I think I understand a bit better now why I roam.

I take off my safety glasses, give them to a freshman who doesn't have any, and we walk away.

"I never had a real house to grow up in," my favorite fictional detective—Sarah Linden of *The Killing*—tells her partner in the series finale, as she realizes that she is in love with him. "You know—home. I never belonged anywhere."

Linden tells him that she has been "looking for that *thing*" her entire life, "thinking that it was out there somewhere, that all I had to do was find it."

"But I think...," she concludes, "maybe that home was us. It was you and me together in that stupid car, riding around, smoking cigarettes."

I think I covet permanence—but I wouldn't know what to do with it if I had it.

For the first two and a half decades of my life, I didn't feel at home in my own skin. I was raised in a religion that taught me everything I was feeling was wrong—that I should never become the queer woman I am today. So never mind the cross-country move at age eleven or my back-and-forth between New Jersey and Utah as a young adult; being inside my own head was alienating enough. Testosterone, as transgender women are wont to say, is a hell of a drug.

In the illusory invincibility of my youth, I always believed that womanhood would just happen to me one day and everything would be fine. Constrained by circumstance, closeted transgender kids like the one I used to be tend to indulge in magical thinking, telling ourselves that maybe one day we will simply wake up in our desired bodies, with our desired brain chemistry.

But in actuality, getting here—becoming a married queer woman—required a soul-wrenching and often excruciating reorientation of everything I knew to be true, not to mention the careful resculpting of mind and body through hormones and surgery. Coming out of Mormonism and the male gender within a few years of each other was an epistemological and ontological double whammy from which—I am now old and scarred enough to admit—I will never fully recover.

So even as I envy all these queer people I met who stayed, I know that the part of me that envies them is wounded—that I have trouble feeling settled because movement was always my escape, whether it was driving up Provo Canyon late at night or leaving Atlanta behind for a healing sojourn in Florida as I did in 2015.

In truth, I know I will never buy property on Corey Drive in Johnson City, unless y'all buy enough copies of this book that I can start collecting houses. I will never move to Bloomington and show up at the Back Door every night. Jess Herbst has not yet offered me a position as her and Debbie's maid (though if you're reading this, Jess, please know I'm available). And I won't return to Atlanta on a permanent basis, as much as I would love to spend summer weekends tubing the Chattahoochee River—or "shooting the 'Hooch," as the locals call it.

But maybe, as Detective Linden might say, my perpetual motion can be a sort of home in itself. Maybe home is Billy and I in that seven-seat SUV, eating ungodly amounts of Chick-fil-A and making up songs about how badly we have to pee. Maybe home is Corey and I cuddling in a dozen different states, taking goofy pictures of our naked butts in floor-length hotel mirrors.

Atlanta was never my home because it couldn't be. The queer people who stay in one red state forever are doing work that I could never do; it wouldn't be long before I got the urge to get up and run. Perhaps my place in this great big queer American movement is the supporting one of simply showcasing their efforts in a book like this—to be a sort of queer Vanna White for the beautiful worlds they are building, and which I have been privileged enough to glimpse.

On the morning of August 23, 2017, I drop Billy off at the Atlanta airport, hugging him close and telling him that I love him. And then I am in the familiar position of driving alone, down toward Tampa through the thunderstorms that define the humid Florida summer. Exactly ten years ago this month I was driving around Utah late at night, feeling like life itself was barely possible. Now I have traveled the whole damn country—out, loud, and proud.

Late that same night, I return my rental car at the Tampa airport after snapping a picture of the odometer: forty-three hundred miles since I reset it in Texas. More than ninety-eight hours spent driving since saying goodbye to Jess Herbst.

I hope that I have accomplished what I set out to do: prove that America is a queer country. Looking back, I spent almost two months driving the breadth of it and can count on one hand the number of straight cisgender people with whom I spent more than five minutes. But in testing the hypothesis of this book, I've also learned that my place in "real America" is not to inhabit any particular corner, but to traverse it—remembering always Eve Sedgwick's reminder that *queer* literally means *across*.

And I think I'm finally not just content, but actually happy being the semi-broken queer transgender nomad my circumstances have shaped me into. I belong. Just not to a place.

I used to wince when I remembered the hours I spent in my hand-me-down Honda Accord in 2007, my eyeliner smudged, my religious mind reeling. I used to focus on the pain I felt as I hurtled up those canyon roads. But now, at the end of this journey, I remember those illicit hours differently—as being full of delicious potential. They were the first hours of my life in which I looked in front of me and saw a bright road ahead, however precipitous, instead of a dead end.

I was reborn in a car. And if home is where you're born, maybe I've been there the whole time.

# Epilogue

# THE BRIGHT ROAD AHEAD

It was all very queer, but queerer things were yet to
come.

—*Joe Gillis,* Sunset Boulevard

If you had told me when I came out as transgender
five years ago that I would one day sit inside a Baptist
church in Waco, Texas, I would ask you who had kid-
napped me.

But that's exactly where I found myself near the start
of my *Real Queer America* trip—which, at the time I'm
writing this epilogue, shortly before Christmas 2017, already feels far away.

I chose Waco for a pit stop between Dallas and Austin
so I could meet Kyndall Rothaus, senior pastor of Lake
Shore Baptist Church, who graciously invited me into her
office on just a few hours' notice. In December 2016 her
congregation had overwhelmingly voted to accept LGBT
people, with 118 out of 140 attending members approv-

ing the formal change.[1] But that inclusiveness came at a cost:[2] Lake Shore was ejected from the Baptist General Convention of Texas the following February.[3] Students from the Lake Shore congregation lost their seminary scholarships as a result, so the other members had to help them pay their way.

Pastor Rothaus had a small voice, a big heart, and a towering intellect. On her desk was a photo of the first same-sex couple to wed at Lake Shore—and the sight of it instantly made me feel at ease. Waco, after all, is a city where billboards recently advertised the discredited practice of conversion therapy.[4] And Southern Baptist churches carry their own anti-LGBT baggage, as Pastor Rothaus readily acknowledges.[5]

"If you're a Baptist church in the middle of Texas," she admitted, "the assumption is not, 'I'm gonna walk in here and be welcomed.'"

1 "Lake Shore Baptist Church Welcomes LGBT Community," http://www.wacotrib.com/news/religion/lake-shore-baptist-church-welcomes-lgbt-community/article_6697b7f6-b7c3-5146-9be6-935e5e23c17e.html

2 Ibid.

3 "Lake Shore Baptist Among 3 Churches Removed by BGCT Board," http://www.wacotrib.com/news/religion/lake-shore-baptist-among-churches-removed-by-bgct-board/article_59c795fa-cacf-5923-a1cd-cfa6ce78a28a.html

4 "'Ex-Gay' Billboards Have Popped Up in Waco and People Aren't Happy About It," https://www.dallasnews.com/news/texas/2016/09/08/exgay-billboards-in-waco

5 "Most U.S. Christian Groups Grow More Accepting of Homosexuality," http://www.pewresearch.org/fact-tank/2015/12/18/most-u-s christian-groupsgrow-moreaccepting-of-homosexuality/

And yet I was there, welcomed. I wanted to know how Pastor Rothaus had become an LGBT ally. How had this issue become personal for her? Because if a devout Baptist pastor could go out on a limb to include LGBT people, I thought, everyone in this country could do the same.

She told me that her process began with private study. As a seminary student, it was "pretty obvious" that the Church had been "hateful and demeaning toward the LGBTQ community," but she continued "wrestling with that," scrutinizing Bible passages to try to understand the situation. Then she befriended a fellow female student who one day, with tears in her eyes, admitted to Pastor Rothaus that she was not straight. That's when it clicked.

"That was the complete turning point for me, because here I was sitting across from a human being telling me their story and I was like, 'Well, of course I support you!'" the pastor told me. "What else would I do? It took me out of the whole academic, theological thing I was stuck trying to sort out—and it was just so obvious."

*Obvious.* It should be obvious, shouldn't it, that LGBT people are, well, people? But prejudice, religiously motivated or not, can cloud that simple fact. Sometimes we need to break bread with a stranger before we can call them a friend. It is not a coincidence that, over the past decade, the percentage of Americans who support LGBT people and the percentage of Americans who report personally knowing an LGBT person have risen in tandem.[6] According to Pew, 87 percent of adults know a gay or lesbian person and 30 percent now know a transgender person.[7] Those numbers are going to go the same direction as my odometer did on this trip: up.

And if you've read this book, I think it's safe to say you know one transgender person: me.

In my travels across the country, I heard some version of Pastor Rothaus's story countless times. You might have one, too: a tale about your lesbian aunt, your gay uncle, your bisexual best friend, or your nonbinary "nibling," which is a gender-neutral alternative to "niece" or "nephew."[8] LGBT people may have survived in the twentieth century by flocking to big cities, but we will continue to change this country in the twenty-first inside our homes.

It has been a challenge for me, since writing this book, to reintegrate myself into the 24/7 news cycle in my day job as a journalist. There's nothing like a road trip across the country to make you realize how narrow the view can be from your keyboard. Sometimes I feel insane,

6 "Knowing Someone Gay/Lesbian Affects Views of Gay Issues," http://news.gallup.com/poll/118931/knowing-someone-gay-lesbian-affects-views-gay-issues.aspx

7 "Vast Majority of Americans Know Someone Who Is Gay, Fewer Know Someone Who Is Transgender," http://www.pewforum.org/2016/09/28/5-vast-majority-of-americans-know-someone-who-is-gay-fewer-know-someone-who-is-transgender/

8 "Fans Applaud Jennifer Lopez for Using Gender-Inclusive Pronouns," https://www.nbcnews.com/feature/nbc-out/fans-applaud-jennifer-lopez-using-gender-inclusive-pronouns-n785391

like a queer lady Nostradamus, as I witness the contrast between what my colleagues in the press seem to care about and what I now know to be the future of LGBT America.

One example: the coastal LGBT media these days continually mourn the closure of big-city gay and lesbian bars, with a new digital eulogy for them emerging seemingly every other week.[9, 10] Although it's true that gay clubs are still lifelines in places like Jackson, Mississippi, we shouldn't see their closure in a city like New York as a categorical step backward: the trend speaks, in part, to the fact that LGBT people are more comfortable going to places not specifically designed for us — or as *The Economist* put it, we no longer "feel the need to congregate in one spot" because it's now safe for us to spread out to different places.[11]

Forty-one percent of LGBT respondents to a 2013 Pew survey, for example, said that LGBT neighborhoods and bars "will become less important over time as LGBT people are more accepted into society."[12] Even more — 72

---

9 "More Than Half of London's Gay Pubs, Clubs Have Closed in Last Decade," https://www.nbcnews.com/feature/nbc-out/more-half-london-s-gay-pubs-clubs-have-closed-last-n780601

10 "Why Are So Many Gay Bars Closing?," https://www.queerty.com/many-gay-bars-closing-20161223

11 "Gay Bars Are Under Threat but Not from the Obvious Attackers," https://www.economist.com/news/christmas-specials/21712031-disappearance-gay-bars-and-clubs-unhappy-side-effect-far-more

12 "5 Key Findings About LGBT Americans," http://www.pewresearch.org/fact-tank/2017/06/13/5-key-findings-about-lgbt-americans/

percent—said they had never lived in an LGBT neighborhood. It's hard for me to shed a tear for the big-city gay
bar when the entire country is getting queer enough to
make some fraction of them obsolete.

The future of LGBT history in this country will not
be about just nightclubs and urban migration or even
protests in the street. It will also be about churches and
schools and families and, eventually, an entire country
that leans slowly and steadily toward love.

Already two of the struggles I have written about in
this book have been won—or are rapidly on their way
to being overcome: the Texas bathroom bill died and the
transgender troop ban was blocked by a federal judge
who cited Trump's erratic tweets in her favorable decision.[13] More injunctions against the transgender military
ban quickly followed.

Change is coming—and probably faster than I want to
admit, lest I get my hopes too high. When I hear people
like Chris Paulson—the lesbian executive director of Indiana Youth Group—report that five years ago there were
only five Gay-Straight Alliances in schools throughout the
state whereas now there are ninety-two, I start to think
that maybe I will live to see full LGBT equality after all.

On November 9, 2016, I was scared—and for good

---

13 "Trump's Transgender Military Ban Just Died in Court. He Helped Kill
    It.," https://www.thedailybeast.com/trumps-transgender-military-
    ban-just-died-in-court-he-helped-kill-it

reason. The Trump administration, up to this point, has rescinded Department of Education guidance protecting transgender students, removed federal discrimination protections for transgender workers, and supported a Christian baker who refused to make a wedding cake for a same-sex couple. It has been—and will continue to be—a threat to the LGBT community as long as it is in power. But whatever the political fate of the Trump administration, LGBT people will win. We don't need an ally in the White House to bring change to our own homes.

In Tampa, after six weeks on the road, I lay down on an air mattress at my sister's house and slept the sleep of the dead. The next day, she and my brother-in-law asked me a question I have fielded dozens of times since: "How was your trip?"

I struggled to answer them. I opened my mouth but didn't know where to begin: Playing cards with queer kids at Encircle? Looking at the stars in Arkansas with Teri Dawn Wright? Hugging Rachael on the porch of Bloomingfoods? How could I ever communicate the range of emotions I had experienced and the diversity of people I had met except, of course, by getting this book out of my head and onto paper—or, in this case, onto an iPad that I have stashed in my purse on the dozen plane rides and road trips I have taken since?

Corey arrived in Tampa later that weekend to pick me up and we held each other with the desperation of people who need to reassure one another that they are still tangible beings. But before we went back to our apartment in South Florida, we took my sister, brother-in-law, and our four-year-old nephew to our favorite spot in the entire state: the Weeki Wachee River, a turquoise stream fed by a spring that plays host to an iconic underwater mermaid show.

From rented kayaks that morning we were lucky enough to spot a baby manatee floating in an eddy, almost invisible in the crystal-clear water because its gray skin blended with the silty river bottom.

In the afternoon we sat inside an underground theater and watched the "mermaids" perform their routines through angled panes of glass that allowed us to peer into the depths of the spring. The dancers twirled and spun and flipped their tails at us, taking deep breaths from a long oxygen tube between maneuvers. In lieu of a curtain going up between songs, air jets covered the glass with bubbles to obscure our view long enough for the dancers to reset positions.

My nephew, a rambunctious little boy with dusty blond hair not unlike my own when I was younger, pushed his glasses closer to his eyes to better take in the surreal sight.

It occurred to me, sitting together as a family, that he has two aunties married to each other. He will grow up knowing how perfectly normal that is, in a changing country that will increasingly accept families like his.

Everyone I met writing this book has made that possible in some way, just by living. *Red state* and *blue state* could mean very different things by the time he is old enough to read this book. Maybe by then they will all be rainbow.

The penultimate song in the mermaid show ended and then we heard the opening bars of Lee Greenwood's "God Bless the U.S.A." start to play over the speakers—a patriotic tune that has played at several inaugurations, including Donald Trump's.[14] The jets obscured our view for a moment, but when they stopped we spied a giant American flag emerging from the deep. The mermaids had swapped out their tails for red, white, and blue marching regalia.

As the final notes of the song rang out—and Greenwood sang in a slow-tempo drawl, "There ain't no doubt I love this land / God bless the U.S.A."—a single turtle swam up stage left toward the sunlight penetrating the spring from above, looking triumphant and aspirational all at once. Just then the jets came back on for the final time, sweeping the turtle away in the bubbles, and we all broke out laughing at the strangeness of it all.

*This is such a beautifully weird country,* I thought.

I would even call it a queer one.

---

14 "'God Bless the U.S.A.': The (Apparently) Apolitical Origins of a GOP Inauguration Favorite," http://www.chicagotribune.com/entertainment/music/ct-lee-greenwood-anthem-gop-inauguration-20170119-story.html

# ACKNOWLEDGMENTS

In the summer of 1994 my parents piled all four kids into a Dodge Ram Van that had been kitted out with bucket seats, a high-top fiberglass ceiling, and a TV/VCR. We set out from Long Beach to drive up the entire Pacific Coast Highway—and then back down again. But my siblings and I had brought along only two movies on VHS, both starring Harrison Ford: *Return of the Jedi* and *The Fugitive*. By the end of the trip we must have watched them each seven times. To this day I can still hear faint echoes of Dr. Richard Kimble shouting, "I didn't kill my wife!"

We called that trip "The Nightmare." But it is now one of our fondest memories as a family. I would not be anything, let alone an author, without the love of my incredible parents, my two brothers, my sister, and my brother-in-law.

A book, I have learned, is a lot like a long road trip: both—ideally—are cohesive experiences in hindsight, but when you're in the process of completing them the sheer number of variables and moving parts can be almost overwhelming. To that end, I am lucky that I had so much support while writing *Real Queer America*.

Leila Campoli, my goddess of an agent at Stonesong, messaged me out of the blue in early 2017 and told me I had a tale worth sharing. Then, at a time when the idea of a reported LGBT travel memoir seemed difficult to distill into a pitch, my peerless editor Jean Garnett at Little, Brown saw the vision and took a chance; I couldn't have asked for better eyes on my words than hers.

I am indebted also to amazing mentors and friends who helped me get to this point: Tessa Miller kickstarted my writing career. Danielle Friedman clarified and nurtured my autobiographical prose. My brother-in-law, Ryan McIlvain, author of the excellent novels *Elders* and *The Radicals*, demystified the publishing world and patiently talked shop with me. And from the beginning, Nico Lang has believed in me more than I believe in myself.

Which brings me to the trip. Compared with what Billy did for *Real Queer America*, I feel like I had an easy job. He heroically transcribed dozens of hours of interviews and spent six weeks by my side 24/7. I just drove the car and talked to people. (You know, the fun part.) Billy was a constant source of support and encouragement, all while doing more actual work than I did.

This book is full of stories that were entrusted to me—and I don't take that trust lightly. All of my interviewees were so generous with their time and with details about their lives. I hope I have done some justice to these friends, old and new. They broadened my world by letting me into theirs. I will always cherish the summer of 2017, not because it resulted in a book, but because of the beautiful moments I shared with such a remarkable and diverse group of people.

And I would have to write a second book composed solely of acknowledgments to fully thank my wife, Corey, for everything she has done for me. She may be my toughest critic, but because she has such high standards for my work, her compassion and praise are the most meaningful of all. Corey is my Big Boo, my one true love, and the brains behind this whole operation. The hardest part of writing this book was being away from her. I can't wait until we can pack up a kid-filled van of our own one day and hit the road. That would be a "Nightmare" come true.

# ABOUT THE AUTHOR

Samantha Allen is a GLAAD Award–winning journalist and the author of *Love & Estrogen* (Amazon Original Stories). She is a senior reporter for the *Daily Beast* covering LGBT issues and a former Sex + Life reporter for *Fusion*. She received her PhD in Women's, Gender, and Sexuality Studies from Emory University in 2015 and was the 2013 recipient of the Kinsey Institute's John Money Fellowship for Scholars of Sexology. Her scholarly writing has been published in *Feminist Theory,* and her freelance work has appeared in *Paste, Rolling Stone, Salon,* and many other publications. She has appeared on MSNBC, CNN, and NPR's *On the Media.* She met her wife in a Kinsey Institute elevator—a true queer love story.